This is a book about the nature of film: about the nature of moving images, about the viewer's relation to film and about the kinds of narrative that film is capable of presenting. It represents a decisive break with the semiotic and psychoanalytic theories of film which have dominated discussion over the past twenty years.

The central thesis is that film is essentially a pictorial medium and that the movement of film images is real rather than illusory. A general theory of pictorial representation is presented which insists on the realism of pictures and the impossibility of assimilating them to language. It criticizes attempts to explain the psychology of film viewing in terms of the viewer's imaginary occupation of a position within the world of film. On the contrary, film viewing is nearly always impersonal.

Gregory Currie provides a general theory of narration and its interpretation in both pictorial and linguistic media, and concludes with an analysis of some ways in which film narrative and literary narrative differ.

Image and mind

Image and mind

Film, philosophy and cognitive science

GREGORY CURRIE

CAMBRIDGE
UNIVERSITY PRESS

PUBLISHED BY THE PRESS SYNDICATE OF THE UNIVERSITY OF CAMBRIDGE
The Pitt Building, Trumpington Street, Cambridge CB2 1RP, United Kingdom

CAMBRIDGE UNIVERSITY PRESS
The Edinburgh Building, Cambridge CB2 2RU, United Kingdom
40 West 20th Street, New York, NY 10011-4211, USA
10 Stamford Road, Oakleigh, Melbourne 3166, Australia

First published 1995
Reprinted 1997

Printed in the United States of America

Typeset in Palatino

A catalogue record for this book is available from the British Library

Library of Congress Cataloguing-in-Publication Data is available

ISBN 0-521-45356-9 hardback

For Gabriel Christopher, future film watcher

Doctrine and life, colours and light, in one
When they combine and mingle, bring
A strong regard and awe; but speech alone
Doth vanish like a flaring thing,
And in the ear, not conscience, ring
George Herbert, *The Windows*

Contents

Preface   *page* xi
Acknowledgements   xxi
Film, 1895–1995   xxiii

Introduction: the essence of cinema   1
I.1   Film as representation   2
I.2   Film and the visible   3
I.3   Degrees of inessentialness   6
I.4   The visible and the pictorial   7
I.5   Fictional pictures   9
I.6   Documentary and fiction   12

Part I   Representation in film

Chapter 1   The myth of illusion   19
1.1   Transparency, likeness and illusionism   19
1.2   Cognitive illusions   22
1.3   Film and dreaming   27
1.4   Perceptual illusionism   28
1.5   The reality of cinematic images   30
1.6   On the motion of images   34
1.7   Two ways or three?   42

Chapter 2   The imprint of nature   48
2.1   Representational media and representational
      arts   49

vii

Contents

2.2   Presenting and representing   49
2.3   Photographs as evidence   52
2.4   Counterfactual dependence   53
2.5   Inconclusive arguments   56
2.6   The conditions for perception   61
2.7   Putting movement in the picture   69
2.8   The significance of similarity   70
2.9   The aesthetics of photography   72
2.10 Photography, painting and the real   75

Chapter 3   Realism   79
3.1   Depictions   80
3.2   Natural generativity   88
3.3   Nondepictive representation in film and other
      media   90
3.4   Three kinds of temporality   92
3.5   Representing time by means of time   96
3.6   Spatial representation   103
3.7   Realist film style   106
3.8   The relativity of likeness   108

Chapter 4   Languages of art and languages of film   113
4.1   Finding the thesis   114
4.2   Cinema language and natural language   117
4.3   The shape of natural language   120
4.4   Objections rejected   124
4.5   Interpretation and utterance meaning   126
4.6   Confusions about convention   128
4.7   Relations between images   134
4.8   A language of vision?   136

Part II   Imagination

Chapter 5   Imagination, the general theory   141
5.1   Perspective shifts   142
5.2   Simulation   144
5.3   Fiction and two kinds of simulation   152

viii

Contents

5.4	Consequences	155
5.5	The dangers of imagining	162

Chapter 6   Imagination, personal and impersonal — 164
6.1	The classical theory	165
6.2	Cinema, theatre and other visual fictions	168
6.3	Against imagining seeing	170
6.4	Impersonal imagining and film	179
6.5	Perceptual imagining	181
6.6	Clarifications and rebuttals	185
6.7	The myth of total cinema	191
6.8	Psychologism	193
6.9	Iconic signs	196

Chapter 7   Travels in narrative time — 198
7.1	Tense in film	198
7.2	The proper treatment of anachrony	206
7.3	Is this revisionism?	216
	Appendix: anachrony and ellipsis	219

Part III   Interpretation

Chapter 8   The interpretive problem — 225
8.1	Intersubjective agreement and interpretive principles	226
8.2	Terms and conditions	231
8.3	Interpreting behaviour and interpreting works	235
8.4	Interpreting works as interpreting behaviour	239
8.5	Real authors, implied authors	243
8.6	Why we still need intention	247
8.7	Interpretive deadlock and truth	249
8.8	The evidence for a cinematic interpretation	251
8.9	Implied author and auteur	258
8.10	Structure and function	259

Chapter 9   Narrative and narrators — 260
9.1	Implied authors and narrators	261
9.2	The asymmetry between literature and film	265

Contents

9.3   Kinds of unreliability   270
9.4   Ambiguous and unreliable narratives   272

In conclusion   281

Named propositions   283
Bibliography   285
Index   297

Preface

Hard is his lot, that here by fortune placed,
Must watch the wild vicissitudes of taste,
With every meteor of caprice must play,
And chase the new-blown bubbles of the day.

Dr Johnson

This book aims to place film in relation to other things: to other arts of the same and of different kinds; to modes of representation like pictures and language; to time and the representation of time; to narrative and the comprehension of narrative; to imagination and belief; to the real world. To all these things, film stands in interesting and controversial relation. Getting that relation right will mean we are on the way to understanding the medium of film.

This is a philosophical book about film, a claim that I had better expand on, lest it be written off as a vague gesture in the direction of depth and subtlety. I mean, quite specifically, that the method of this book is generalizing, systematizing, argumentative and conceptual. It aims at conclusions of maximum generality rather than a concentration on particular works, schools or genres; it aims to integrate what can be said about film with (what I take to be) our best theory of the rest of the world; it proceeds in steps, laying out premises and conclusions, indicating how we get from one to the other; it tries to provide analyses of opaque, complex and contested notions like language, image, representation and belief.

The book continues the project of an earlier work, *The Nature of Fiction*, in which I presented a basic framework for the analysis of fictions of all kinds, though I had little to say there about film. At various points in this study I draw on the theory presented earlier, but I try to enable the reader to follow my argument without having to turn to the earlier work for help. Also, at various points in this volume I deviate from the theory of fiction in the earlier book. I have not in general attempted to explain or justify the deviations, or even to indicate that this is what they are. I have assumed that the reader will be less interested in the development of my ideas than in getting a relatively coherent theory. There are references to the previous book in the footnotes to this one for those who want to follow up certain issues in more detail.

One aspect of the relations between that book and this one deserves mention here. At the end of *The Nature of Fiction* I noted that almost everything in my analysis of fiction depended on the concept of make-believe or imagination, a notion which was itself left unexplained. The present work attempts to fill the gap. It does not offer a conceptual analysis of imagination; rather, it postulates a mechanism by which imagining can be understood to work as part of the ordinary, evolutionarily adaptive functioning of the mind. That mechanism is mental simulation. Chapter 5 explains the idea in outline, an idea I hope to develop in more detail in a further work.

While nothing is discussed here unless it is put to use in understanding film, I provide answers to a number of questions of general artistic concern: What is a pictorial medium, and what kinds of pictures can we call realistic? What, if anything, is special about the photographic method of producing pictures? Do pictures represent by convention, or by resemblance? What is the relation between picturing and language? Can there be a pictorial language, or a linguistic picture? By what means do we interpret works of fiction? Is there an account of interpretation that covers both cinematic and other media? How does imagination work, and what role does it play in our response to fictions? Is there a distinctively pictorial mode of imagining?

It may be inferred from this budget of questions that the central concepts I use are representation and imagination. Both are general categories with special application to film; by taking them in a connected way as my leading notions I aim to place film within a broader framework of theorizing about the fictional. One question I don't ask: what makes a film good or valuable? I have nothing to say here about the value of films, aesthetic or otherwise, either individually and in comparison with one another, or collectively in comparison with other kinds of arts. This neglect is not the result of indifference. With film as with other arts, questions about value are the most important ones. But they are also the hardest, partly because answering them depends on answering a lot of other questions first. Some of those prior questions are answered here.

My decision to approach film by way of a number of other, more general issues may raise the suspicion that I fail to take film seriously, or that I use it simply as a convenient peg on which to hang other concerns. This is not so, as I think I can briefly indicate.

Film certainly has not been taken seriously by most philosophers of the kind in which I place myself. With philosophers of the broadly analytical stripe, film is generally assumed to be a marginal phenomenon within that almost terminally marginalized subdiscipline, aesthetics. As a consequence, film has become almost exclusively the theoretical province of those who take their inspiration from other schools: semiotics, psychoanalysis and Marxism. Much has been said about the relation of cinematic "signs" to the signs of language, about the relations between film, dreaming and illusion, about the role of film in creating and promoting a false consciousness of self. The result has been disappointing. But there are indications – few in number but significant in content – of a growing dissatisfaction with these sorts of models for the theoretical analysis of film.[1] My aim is to develop an alternative, and to connect the analysis of film with the best work in contemporary metaphysics, philosophy of mind, philosophy of language and cognitive science.

It is primarily because I reject the old framework and seek a

---

[1] See Noël Carroll, *Mystifying Movies*. See also George Wilson's *Narration in Light*, for fascinating studies of particular films in which Wilson rejects the tired categories of realism and illusionism usually trotted out to analyse "the Hollywood Film". Some deficiencies in the methodology of contemporary film theory are explored in depth, especially as they apply to the production of particular film interpretations, in David Bordwell, *Making Meaning*.

new one that I have emphasized the connections between film and other things; a framework for film that bore no interesting relations to other arts and representational forms, and could not claim explanatory success in other areas, would have little to recommend it. But a framework of any merit must also help in understanding film itself. The framework I offer does so. It enables us to answer a number of specifically filmic questions: What are cinematic images? What is the nature of our imaginative involvement with film? What is the truth in the claims of so-called cinema-realism? How is time represented in film, and what are the limits of this representation? What strategies does the viewer use to interpret a film, and how do they relate to the strategies we employ to understand verbal fiction?

For those familiar with contemporary film theory, some of the answers I give will have an air of wilful implausibility. But our judgements of plausibility are determined largely by our framework of background assumptions; implausible theories can be cogent, highly explanatory, even true, and background assumptions hopelessly false. I'll say something about how my assumptions differ from those of film theory as recently practised.

The first assumption I reject is a conjunction: that psychoanalysis, or some version of it, is correct, and that it is capable of illuminating our experience of film. I happen not to believe this, since I believe that psychoanalysis is false, not just in the sense of getting a few things wrong, as relativity theory probably does, but in the sense of being wildly, deeply and unrescuably false, as Aristotle's physics is. And even if I believed psychoanalysis or some version of it to be true, I would be sceptical of recent applications of it to our experience of the cinema. Of course the experience of cinema, like that of anything else, is a matter for psychological investigation, and cannot be understood in a priori philosophical terms. But the psychology we need is not psychoanalysis – particularly not in the version of Lacan, about which I shall say a little in a moment. Contemporary empirical psychologists and philosophers of language and mind have found a way to pool their resources in the project called cognitive science. The aim is to build plausible models of the mind and its functions more detailed and specific than philosophers on their own could devise, and more flexible and abstract than neuropsychology alone could deliver. In contrast with the psychoanalytic program, cognitive science combines rigorous and clear argument with a commitment to the most demanding standards of empirical testability we can devise.[2]

Cognitive science is not a doctrine. While its practitioners share broad assumptions, there is no one theory of mind which all or a majority of cognitive scientists accept. The view of the mind which I adopt here as a working hypothesis has certain features I can lay out very briefly: it treats the mind as a hierarchically organized structure with levels of more or less intelligent decision making going on in it; it regards some of the systems of the mind – visual perception, for example – as operating in relative isolation from other systems and consequently unable to benefit from certain information sources; it regards the mind's knowledge of other minds as resulting not (or not only) from the possession and deployment of a theory of mind, but from the ability to make empathetic contact, an ability I shall explain in terms of mental simulation. The components of this view will receive appropriate elaboration as the steps in the argument require.

One particularly damaging consequence of the psychoanalytic paradigm has been the tendency to think of film as an essentially illusory medium, capable of causing the viewer temporarily to think of the film world as real, and of himself as occupying a place of observation within that world. Thus film theorists have expended a great deal of effort in trying to show that the point of view of the camera is usually understood to represent that of a perceiving agent – that of a character, a supposed narrator or the spectator, who is assumed to occupy the camera's position through a process of identification.[3] I shall argue in Part I that

---

[2] The contrast I see here between Freudian theory and cognitive science is not accepted by everyone. See, e.g., Clark Glymore, "Freud's Androids".

[3] See, e.g., Kaja Silverman, *The Subject of Semiotics*, p. 202: "The gaze which directs our look seems to belong to a fictional character rather than to the camera." See also Jacques Aumont, "The Point of View", p. 2: "The frame in narrative cinema is always more or less the representation of a gaze, the auteur's or the character's."

films are not standardly illusionistic, and in Part II that it is simply false that the spectator identifies with the camera.

The second assumption of traditional theorizing about film is the semiotic assumption: that there is a fundamental commonality between pictures and language. This is a belief that goes along with the rejection of the hopelessly old-fashioned view that, while words operate by convention, pictures operate by similarity. On the semiotic view, all representation is conventional, and the idea that pictures might in some sense be like the things they picture is part of a benighted ideology of realism. This assumption, unlike the psychoanalytic assumption, has broad support across the intellectual community. A version of it has been argued for by Nelson Goodman, and there are hints of it in the work of the art historian Ernst Gombrich and the perceptual psychologist Richard Gregory, whose views are connected to Karl Popper's idea that perceptions are "hypotheses".[4]

The semiotic assumption has seen hard times, as people have come up against awkward dissimilarities between the structure of language and the structure of visual images.[5] Yet it has shown a remarkable tendency to persist, particularly in film studies. Christian Metz, for example, recognized fairly early on that there is nothing in the cinema corresponding to "a language-system's characteristics and internal organization".[6] But he has continued to apply the categories, or at least the terminology, of linguistic analysis to film; he says, for example, that photographs lack the "syntactic components of discourse so numerous in cinema", and he describes optical effects as "clauses of speech".[7] And while the emphasis in film theory has moved

---

[4] Popper is a self-proclaimed realist, but his views on perception seem to me to undermine realism.

[5] Gombrich, for example, has recently distanced himself from the semiotic relativism of Nelson Goodman's *Languages of Art*. But Gombrich's view that pictures can be genuine likenesses sits uncomfortably with his insistence that pictures are conventional. See his "Image and Code: Scope and Limits of Conventionalism in Pictorial Representation", p. 12.

[6] Christian Metz, "On the Notion of Cinematographic Language".

[7] Christian Metz, "*Trucage* and the Film", pp. 158 and 165. See also Jacques Aumont et al., *Aesthetics of Film*, chapter 4.

away from the straightforwardly linguistic to the psychoanalytic, the impetus for this move seems to have come not from a rejection of the linguistic model, but from the thought that psychoanalytic models are themselves language-like. Thus one of the ideas that seems to put the psychoanalytic thinker Lacan in favour with the film theorists is his claim that the unconscious is "structured like a language".

I am of the contrary opinion: that pictures and language are fundamentally distinct, that there is a sense in which pictures are able to represent by means of likeness rather than convention. But it is important not to create a false dichotomy here between those who think that works in pictorial media are wholly understandable in terms of perceptual skills universal across humankind and those who think that pictures require an act of interpretation which by no means guarantees the same outcome for everyone.[8] If pictures appeal to basic perceptual skills which are widely shared across communities and, as I believe, to some extent across species, there is still a good deal of interpretive work left to be done once perceptual skills are deployed. I take up issues of interpretation in the final part of this book, where I argue for some fundamental commonalities between the interpretation of linguistically encoded works and the interpretation of film and other pictorial media, despite the existence of the nature/convention gulf which divides them.

So film theorists have misunderstood the relation between the symbolic and the pictorial orders, and they have failed to produce a plausible psychology of the experience of cinema.[9] But the failures of film theory are more than failures of doctrine.

---

[8] As do Norman Bryson et al., in their editorial introduction to *Visual Theory*.

[9] This failure and the ones I discuss later are not exemplified everywhere in theoretical writing on film, though the better kind of writing tends to be critical rather than constructive. See, e.g., Brian Henderson, "Two Types of Film Theory". There is also some spirited resistance to the Lacanian model, as with Raymond Durgnat: "Film watching is no more phallic, self- (mirror) centered, or voyeuristic than any other self forgetful activity, like reading or listening to music" ("Theory of Theory – and Buñuel the Joker", pp. 32–44). In a review of Metz's *Psychoanalysis and Cinema*, Durgnat notes that Metz "swallows Lacan bones, feathers, fur and all" (p. 60).

They are also failures of style and of method. The failures of doctrine cannot be fully understood in isolation from these other difficulties.

It is frequently and truly said that writing in film theory has a tendency to be obscure. There is also a great deal of unexplained jargon which is then used in so unsystematic a way that no clear meaning for it can be inferred from its use.[10] This failure of style connects with the failure of doctrine: the lack of clarity of much writing on film functions to protect bad theory from the light of criticism.

The failure of doctrine is even more closely connected with a failure of method. Film theorists have used intellectual strategies that were almost bound to lead to disaster. One of them is the casual employment of vague analogies. Profound connections have been claimed between the cinema and Plato's cave, between the screen and the breast, between the experience of movie watching and dreaming.[11] Here is an example of the film-is-like-something-else phenomenon, with Gilles Deleuze discovering some unlikely parallels between film and mathematical physics:

> Crystalline narration will fracture the complementarity of a lived hodological space and a represented Euclidean space. . . . It is in this sense that we can talk about Riemannian spaces in Bresson, in neo-realism, in the New Wave and in the New York School, of quantum spaces in Robbe-Grillet, of probabilistic spaces in Resnais, of crystallized spaces in Herzog and Tarkovsky.[12]

[10] Others see the issue of clarity differently: Vivian Sobchack speaks of the "sloppy liberal humanism that retrospectively characterized cinema studies before it was informed by the scientific methods and technically precise vocabularies of structuralism and semiotics"; Sobchack, *The Address of the Eye*, p. xiv.

[11] See also Anne Friedberg's exploration of the relations between cinema and shopping ("*Les Flâneurs du Mal(l)*: Cinema and the Postmodern Condition", pp. 419–431).

[12] Gilles Deleuze, *Cinema 2: The Time-Image*, p. 129. See also the discussion of a "gravity-free world" in Rick Altman, General introduction to *Sound Theory, Sound Practice*, pp. 3–4.

Out of context of course, and a translation too, but at least a prima facie example of wheels idly turning. Not that we should retreat to a narrow formalism, or insist that nothing useful can be gained by comparing cinema with other things. But we must pick our analogies with care and attend to the details of their justification. We can learn a great deal about cinema, I shall argue, by comparing the interpretation of cinema with that of language and of intentional behaviour. But these comparisons cannot be implemented at the level of vague likenesses that are really nothing more than metaphors. Metaphors are useful for certain purposes; they can also be extremely misleading. That is especially likely when it is forgotten that they are, after all, metaphors, or when the investigator has lost a sense of the distinction between the literal and the metaphorical.

Perhaps the most significant failure of method in film theory has been the habit of appealing uncritically to controversial, and sometimes poorly corroborated, theories from other disciplines. This is evident in the move to connect film with psychoanalysis. It is standard for film theorists to appeal casually to Lacan's idea of the "mirror stage" as support for some theory about the relation between film and the viewer, remarking simply that Lacan "has shown" that such and such is the case.[13] When someone appeals to a theory as if it were established fact it's natural to suppose that there is a substantial body of evidence in support of the theory in question, and that this evidence is so much a part of our common knowledge that it would be tedious to explain or even to refer to it. But there is no such well-known body of evidence in the case of Lacan's claims about the mirror stage. So far as I have been able to gather, there is no evidence for them at all.[14]

---

[13] See, e.g., Laura Mulvey: "Jacques Lacan has described how the moment when a child recognizes its own image in the mirror is crucial for the constitution of the ego" ("Visual Pleasure and Narrative Cinema", p. 807). See also Daniel Dayan, "The Tutor-Code of Classical Cinema", p. 441; and Christian Metz, *The Imaginary Signifier*, p. 6.

[14] Jacques Aumont put it mildly: "The metapsychological model elaborated by Metz, Baudry and others around 1975 is not easily supported by empirical evidence" ("The Point of View", p. 19).

I could go on. But extended polemic is a tedious thing; constructive theory is much more exciting. I suppose many pre-Copernican astronomers had moments of gloom when they stood back a little from the vast implausible shambles that was Ptolemaic astronomy. They probably found consolation in the idea that it was the only game in town. What is on offer in this book may not be of Copernican proportions, but it is, at least, another game.

Acknowledgements

The pleasures of writing this book have been many, and some of them have to do with people and places. A draft was written in 1991 during a year's sabbatical from the University of Otago. It began at the Research School of Social Sciences at the Australian National University in Canberra; I doubt if there is a better environment for philosophical research anywhere. The philosophers there who helped straighten out my early ideas on the subject I thank later. Here I thank Professor Tom Campbell, for the use of his delightful house and exciting car. The writing continued in Washington, D.C., and at the nearby College Park campus of the University of Maryland, where teaching the philosophy of film and talking to the excellent and friendly philosophers helped to give the idea of this book a workable shape. A first draft was completed in Cambridge, where the staff and fellows of Clare Hall made us welcome. My special thanks go to the president, Anthony Low, and to the bursar, John Garrod.

Through that year and on subsequent occasions I gave talks, based on draft chapters of the book, at institutions as far apart as Tromsø and Sydney, San Diego and Sussex. A great many people made important contributions to the discussions that followed, and I have tried to incorporate their suggestions and to shore up my position against their criticisms in this book. Among those whose contributions I recall are John Bigelow, Andrew Brennan, Neil Cooper, George Couvalis, Martin Davies, John Haldane, Jane Heal, David Hills, Robert Hopkins, Ian

Acknowledgements

Hunt, Frank Jackson, Philip Kitcher, David Lewis, Paisely Livingston, Gary Malinas, Hugh Mellor, Graham Nerlich, Philip Pettit, Charles Pigden, Anthony Price, Georges Rey, Gideon Rosen, Bob Sharp, Elliott Sober, Ivan Soll, Roger Squires, John Stokes, Scott Sturgeon, Kenneth Taylor, Michael Tooley, Aubrey Townsend, Kendall Walton, Peter Wetherall, Timothy Williamson, Jamie Wyte and Steven Yalowitz. To Jerrold Levinson I owe especial thanks for his careful reading of parts of various chapters and for the discussions we have had in Washington, Cambridge, London and Dunedin.

This book was completed during the first half of 1994 at Flinders University, Adelaide. My colleagues in the Philosophy Department deserve thanks for their warm welcome and their critical acumen. Marty Davies was especially helpful in reading the penultimate version, making important suggestions for changes and subediting the whole thing. Vladimir Popescu helped prepare the index. Three readers for Cambridge University Press made helpful suggestions that I have incorporated.

In writing this book I have tried to bring together certain aspects of my work in recent years from different areas – mainly from film and from philosophy of mind. I have therefore incorporated ideas, and sometimes text, from articles appearing in a variety of places: parts of Chapter 1 appeared in "Film, Realism and Illusion", in D. Bordwell and N. Carroll (eds.), *Post-Theory*, Madison, University of Wisconsin Press, 1995; parts of Chapter 2 in "Painting, Photography and Perception", *Journal of Aesthetics and Art Criticism*, 1991; parts of Chapter 4 in "The Long Goodbye", *British Journal of Aesthetics*, 1992; parts of Chapter 5 in "Imagination and Simulation: Aesthetics Meets Cognitive Science", in M. Davies and T. Stone (eds.), *Mental Simulation*, Oxford, Blackwell, 1995; parts of Chapter 6 in "Fictions in Visual Media", *Philosophical Quarterly*, 1991; parts of Chapter 7 in "McTaggart at the Movies", *Philosophy*, 1992; parts of Chapter 8 in "Interpretation and Objectivity", *Mind*, 1993; and parts of Chapter 9 in "Unreliability Refigured", *Journal of Aesthetics and Art Criticism*, 1994. I thank the editors of these books and journals for permission to republish.

Film, 1895–1995

Film is an art of recent invention. In fact it is just one hundred years old. We know more about its early history than about that of any other medium: the technical inventions and discoveries involved, the intentions of the early pioneers, the reactions of audiences, the transitions of style and genre, the social forces which affected film and the impact of film on society. Film's development is laid out before us with a completeness that historians and theorists of other cultural phenomena must envy. Yet I believe that the nature of film is less well understood than that of any other art. If my arguments are correct, current theory is based on a serious misunderstanding of the film medium and its effects on the viewer.

The roots of that misunderstanding go back to early writers like Münsterberg, who thought that cinema was preeminently a medium of subjectivity. That error is as strongly entrenched in film theory today as at any other time. It might have been otherwise; the work of Bazin contained within it the seeds of a better view. But Bazin's "realism" was overstated, and the reaction against it was inevitable.

There is too much in Bazin that is confused or simply wrong for his work to constitute the basis of a theoretical renewal. The intellectual roots of the present work would be as foreign to Bazin as they are to most contemporary film theorists. It owes much, in spirit at least, to the linguistics of Chomsky, and nothing to Saussure; much to contemporary philosophy of mind and cognitive science, and very little to Freud and his followers. But the strongest influence on this work is that almost obsessional concern with realism so distinctive of the best in Australian philosophy.

Image and mind

Introduction: the essence of cinema

Tired of the ponderous prescriptivism that dogged much film aesthetic (and, until recently, much aesthetics in general), film theorists frequently tell us they have put aside "essentialism". Why bring it back? My essentialism is not especially prescriptive: no more so than the claim that water is essentially H_2O. Films, like samples of water, have something in common that makes them films rather than something else. It's more than just being films, and it's more than just family resemblance. It's an essence, but knowing what that essence is doesn't help much in figuring out what films are good, typical or paradigmatic.[1] Since the subject of this book is film, I ought to say something about the essence of film. What I say has some bookkeeping significance for what follows, but not much intrinsic interest. This is the boring part; let's get it over with. Alternatively, you can skip it and come back if and when you need to.

[1] Claims about the aesthetics of film based on some supposed essence of the media are still made. Sometimes they are very strained. Thus Stanley Cavell: "The most significant films ... will be found to be those that most significantly discover and declare the nature of the medium of film ... a feature of the medium of film ... is film's power of metamorphosis or transfiguration. In remarriage comedy, this feature ... is expressed as the woman's suffering creation, which cinematically means the transfiguration of flesh-and-blood women into projections of themselves on the screen. Hence the obligation in those films to find some narrative occasion for revealing ... the woman's body" ("Ugly Duckling, Funny Butterfly", pp. 222–223).

Introduction

I.1 FILM AS REPRESENTATION

Representations come in a variety of kinds: words written and spoken, gestures established by convention or made up on the spur of the moment, pictures drawn and painted, carved or moulded shapes, smoke signals, flashed headlights, sound recordings, photographs, the projected images of film. Just about anything we do or use can be a representation, though some things are richer than others in their representational capacities; they are more apt to allow the communication of complex meanings, and what cannot be represented cannot be communicated.

Film is a representational medium; it is a means by which representations, themselves distinctively cinematic, are produced and displayed. What distinguishes cinematic representations from those of other kinds? One thing separating them from representations of *some* other kinds is their pictorial character. One of the peculiarities of recent film theorizing is that it has been concerned almost entirely with what the theorists regard as the supposedly hidden or "deep structural" features of film – the supposed codes by which films are "read" – and has had nothing of significance to say about the matter film so obviously does trade in – pictures. Perhaps the reason is that it is assumed by the theorists that the idea of a picture needs no independent explanation, because picturing is just one kind of linguistic or semiotic representation. I shall argue later that pictures and linguistic signs are different kinds of things. There is no language of pictures, and pictures have little of theoretical interest in common with linguistic items. Nor is their representational function significantly the product of, or mediated by, convention. That is as true of cinematic pictures as of any other kind.

Cinematic pictures are not like the static images of painting, nor are they made in the way that paintings and drawings are made. These are differences we need to take account of; in Part I we shall do so. But these differences must not obscure the fact that film is a pictorial medium; it gives us – exactly – moving pictures.

2

I.2 FILM AND THE VISIBLE

Films, like other kinds of pictures, are meant to be seen. The cinema, by which name I denote the medium to which particular movies belong,[2] is a visual medium. A work in the cinematic medium is an artefact with certain properties accessible to sight, and no one has made appropriate contact with the work unless she is visually acquainted with these properties. Movies often have other properties, accessible through senses other than sight, and appropriate contact with those movies requires acquaintance, through the right sense, with those properties. Auditory properties are the most obvious and widely used, but there are other less well explored, and perhaps less rewarding, possibilities: recall Smellorama and Sensurround. But all these, including sound, are incidental accretions so far as cinema itself is concerned, because there can be, and in fact there are, works in the medium which eschew all sensory engagement except the visual. Visual properties are what cinematic works *have* to have.

But the same is true of painting, still photography, sculpture, mime and musicless dance. What, then, distinguishes cinema from these other media? Typically, a cinematic work involves projection onto a surface of an image that is capable of giving the appearance of movement. (Later I will ask whether this appearance is illusory or not.) But it is unclear whether any of these standard conditions are essential to the medium.[3] Imagine

[2] I have no interest in distinguishing movies and films here, and I use those terms interchangeably, always to refer to particular works, specified or unspecified, within the medium of cinema. But a distinction can be made, and might be useful in other, more aesthetically conscious contexts. See, e.g., Gerald Mast, *Film/Cinema/Movie*.

[3] Attempts to identify the essential features of cinema have not been very successful. Gerald Mast's idea that projection is the essential feature of the cinematic medium is especially off the mark. Television's failure to achieve the clarity, luminosity and size of the cinema screen is, as Mast concedes (ibid., p. 267), likely to be a temporary restriction that future technology will overcome without resorting to projection. Nor is it true that projection ensures the pastness of the events we are watching (p. 266). And while projection may emphasize the artificiality of cinema (p. 270), so would many other salient pieces of technology devised to deliver an image; see text immediately following.

a device you load film into, then plug directly into your brain to give you visual sensations exactly like those you would get if you were watching a conventionally projected film. Isn't that cinema without the projection of an apparently moving image on a surface? If so, what is essential to cinema is the visual experience, irrespective of how it is delivered. Difficulties also arise when we try to specify the more distant causes of the experience – the existence of animated film shows that the cause need not be photographic.[4] What, anyway, constitutes a photographic method? Creation of a series of images by exposure to light? Expectant parents can testify to the cinematic, or at least televisual, quality of images produced by ultrasound. What is so special about light rays?[5]

But we need not get involved in a debate about what, exactly, constitutes allowable methods of production and delivery for the cinema in the ordinary sense of the term. Instead we can shape a concept of our own to suit our theoretical purpose. There is a group of artefacts, interesting and worthy of study because of the problems to which they give rise, which we may characterize in the following way. They are produced by photographic means and delivered onto a surface so as to produce, or be capable of producing, an apparently moving image. Things of that kind I am going to call movies, films or works of cinema. As long as it is remembered that the expressions "movie", "film" and "cinema" have here this quasi-stipulative use, we can concentrate on the class of entities they name when so used, and forget verbal issues. What I shall say about cinema in this sense will be applicable in some degree to the plug-in, sonic, and other nonstandard forms, as well as to real-life relatives of film like television; but I leave it to others or another occasion to work out precisely what degree that is.

Cinema as I define it is an essentially visual medium. Movies may or may not present audible speech and other sounds as well as visual representations, and such auditory accompaniments may or may not constitute part of the fictional content

---

[4] As Gerald Mast points out (ibid., p. 5).
[5] For more on light rays and seeing, see Chapter 2.

the movie presents (sound, where it occurs, may be "intra-" or "extradiegetic", in the favoured lingo). The auditory, as well as the olfactory and the rest, are optional. Where these things do accompany the visual component we have a work that is more than purely cinematic; it has the features a thing must have to be a cinematic work, and it has others besides.

The claim that the auditory is optional needs careful handling; it is not the claim that we could delete sound from films that possess it without loss to our understanding or appreciation of them: an obviously false proposition. Nor is it the claim that the sound possessed by a given film is inessential to it; we need to distinguish what is optional for the medium and what is optional for any particular work in the medium. Thus I take it to be an essential (that is, an obligatory) feature of a film with diegetic sound that it *has* diegetic sound; to run *Lawrence of Arabia* without the sound would be to fail, in some degree, to give access to that film. My claim concerns the medium itself, not any particular work that exemplifies it. That's just one example of the difference between what is essential to a thing which happens to belong to a kind, and what is essential for belonging to that kind of thing. On one view, a person's origin is essential to his or her identity; no one lacking the parents Albert had could be Albert. But having Albert's parents is not a condition for membership in the kind *human being*.

I am not claiming that we would make better films if sound were not available, or that films of the very best kind would not employ sound because "being of the very best kind" means being an example of pure cinema, which in turn means having no optional elements. Nor, finally, am I claiming that visual properties always or usually contribute more to the value of particular films than do auditory properties (a somewhat more plausible claim than the others, but still controversial). Those are all aesthetic claims, and mine is not of that kind; it is the claim that a work without visual properties would fail, for that reason, to count as a cinematic work of whatever value. Auditory properties are not like that; they are optional so far as the medium is concerned.

I.3 DEGREES OF INESSENTIALNESS

We can take our analysis a little further than a simple distinction between the optional and the obligatory. Consider three changes to cinema that have been controversial at one time or another: sound, considered as something synchronized with the action and as part of the diegesis, colour and the wide screen. These developments are not all on the same footing. Wide screen is optional in that the screen does not have to be – and once was not – wide, where "being wide" means having an aspect ratio of 1:2.35 or something like it. But the basic technical machinery of cinema requires that there be *some* ratio of screen dimensions. The determinable property, *having some ratio of width to height*, is an obligatory property of cinema in the sense that a cinematic work must have that property; but no determinate of that determinable (say a screen ratio of 1:1.33) is obligatory.[6] Diegetic sound is innovative in a quite different sense; *having this combination of diegetic sounds* is a determinate property optional for a cinematic work, but so is the determinable property, *having some combination of diegetic sounds*, since films don't have to have any combination of diegetic sounds. Wide screen is merely a weak option, while sound is a strong one. An option is weak if some option of that kind must be chosen, and strong if no option of that kind need be chosen. (Slightly more technically: an option is weak if it is an optional determinant of a determinable that is obligatory, strong if it is a determinant of a determinable that is not.)

This rather scholastic-sounding distinction gives us theoretical backing for the intuition that the introduction of sound was a more dramatic change to cinema than was the introduction of the wide screen – a more dramatic change because sound is a strong option and wide screen a weak one. Is colour a weak or a strong option? That depends on how we conceptualize the relation between colour and monochrome cinematography. If black and white and shades of grey are colours, then having

---

[6] The meaning of "determinate of a determinable" should be clear from the context. Another example: *red* is a determinate of the determinable *colour*.

colour is an obligatory determinable, while the precise choice of colour is optional, and so colour is weakly optional. If black and white are considered not to be colours, then colour is strongly optional. But the question whether black and white are colours in the sense relevant here seems to be dangerously verbal. So the issue of whether colour is a strong or a weak option also sounds dangerously verbal. The best we can say is that colour doesn't fall obviously into either of the categories occupied, respectively, by wide screen and sound. If we think of it as falling between the two, we again match theory with intuition, since colour seems less innovative than sound and more innovative than the wide screen.

I.4 THE VISIBLE AND THE PICTORIAL

It is one thing to say, as I have said, that the cinema is a visual medium; it is another to say, as I have also said, that it is a pictorial one, that it is a medium that trades essentially in pictorial representations. So far I have ignored this distinction, but it is theoretically crucial. All pictorial representation is visual, but not all visual representation is pictorial. Subtitles and those helpfully orienting dates and place names that used to appear on the screen (and occasionally still do) are visual representations and not pictorial ones. The subtitles are visual because they have to be seen, but they are not pictorial; the name "Vienna" is not a picture of Vienna – not, anyway, in the sense of picture I am going to explain more fully in Chapter 3. When the words "Paris 1939" appear on the screen over an image of the Eiffel Tower, they serve to inform us about what is fictional – they tell us that, fictionally, the scene is now Paris in 1939 – but they do not convey this information pictorially. The reason, briefly, is this. I have, let us assume, a visual capacity to recognize Vienna. That is, there are certain things which, if I see them from certain points of view, let me recognize that what I am seeing is Vienna, or parts thereof. A painting, a photograph, or a cinematic image is a picture of Vienna when it is possible to recognize what it represents by deploying my visual capacity to recognize Vienna when I see it. But the word "Vienna", though I may recognize it as referring to Vienna, does not represent Vienna pictorially. The visual capacity to recognize Vienna alone would not enable me to recognize that "Vienna" represents Vienna. I need, in addition, some knowledge of English. More on this in Chapter 3.

On the other hand, if the hero is shown reading a letter, and the camera closes in to show the letters and words on the page for us to read, there is a sense in which the visual image here functions pictorially. That is, it functions in one way pictorially, as well as in another way nonpictorially. The shapes and other visual properties of the letters on the page inform us pictorially about something that is part of the fiction, that the character who wrote the letter formed words with just those shapes and other visual properties (this might, or might not, be important to the development of the fiction, but even if it is unimportant it is still part of the story). The capacity I deploy to recognize the shapes displayed on the screen is exactly the capacity I would deploy to recognize the shapes on the page if I were looking at it. Here the visual image functions pictorially *and* nonpictorially; pictorially to inform us about what is fictional concerning the shapes and other visual properties of certain written characters, and nonpictorially to inform us about what the content of the letter was – what was actually said in it. For no purely visual recognitional capacity will enable me to know the meanings of words.

The conclusion is, then, that among the ways in which visual images can function to inform us about what is fictional, three broad categories can be distinguished. There are images or elements of images which function only pictorially (as an image of red wallpaper may function pictorially to tell us that it is fictional that events are taking place in a room wallpapered thus, while not telling us anything about what is fictional). There are also visual images which function nonpictorially, as with subtitles and scene setters. Finally, there are images that function in both ways, as with the camera-attracting letter, read by a character.

There is a corresponding distinction to be made for the way that sound represents in film. If the sound includes the audible speech of characters, that sound will function in two ways. It will represent sonic qualities of the fiction – the tone and volume of a character's voice, for example. The capacities I deploy in order to recognize the tones and volumes of sounds on the sound track are just the capacities I use to recognize the tones and volumes of speech directly heard. But sound here will also function to convey semantic properties of the fiction, the meanings of words and sentences uttered by the characters. In the first way it functions as the audible analogue of a picture; in the second way it is analogous to the visual but nonpictorial use of the image.

When image and sound function to represent visual and auditory features of the fiction itself, let us say that their function is a *sensory* one. Our sensory experience of those images and sounds is crucial to our understanding what is represented; if the shapes or colours onscreen were different, we would understand that the shapes and colours of objects represented were different. And if the sensed quality of the sounds were different, we would understand the characters to be speaking in a different tone of voice. Literary representation is not like that; it does not matter, for the purpose of conveying what is true in the story, what exact shapes or colours go to form the words on the page. Replacing the author's handwriting with print does not affect what is true in the story. Literary forms like the novel are not sensory; we may read by looking at the print, but exactly how it looks doesn't matter.

I.5 FICTIONAL PICTURES

Suppose we have a visual image that functions pictorially. The image I see onscreen is a pictorial representation of a man. That image represents a fictional character who appears in the story the film presents: Harry Lime. Seeing that image tells me all sorts of things about what is fictional in this story, for example, that the man called "Harry Lime" has a certain visual appearance. If the image I see onscreen were different in various ways, it would tell me different things about what is fictional in the story: that Harry is slimmer or shorter, or has a different facial expression. What we seem to have here is pictorial representation of a fictional character.

Introduction

There is a problem. Cinematic images certainly are representations of the people and objects of which they are photographs; the photograph (or the sequence of photographs that makes up the film) of Orson Welles represents Orson Welles. It also pictorially represents him; the capacity to recognize that this is a film image of Welles is the capacity to recognize Welles when and if I see him. But if our concern is with movies like *The Third Man* that present narrative fictions (rather than, say, documentaries about film stars) we are surely concerned with the representing relations that hold between the cinematic images and the fiction itself, its characters and events. So far as the fiction goes, we are concerned with Harry Lime rather than with Orson Welles. But the problem is that, at least in typical cases, there are no such things as those characters and events, and so there are no relations, representing or otherwise, between the movie and fictional things.[7] And so our image is not, after all, a picture – or any other sort of representation – of Harry Lime.[8]

One way to solve the problem would be to deny the obvious – to insist that Harry Lime does exist (or that he has some other, positive grade of being), and that the film images represent him pictorially. Another would be to say that images can pictorially represent the nonexistent as well as the existent. I shall not attempt a solution of either kind.[9] On the other hand, we should not give up too easily; the problem posed by the nonexistence of fictional characters looks like a technical hitch. If cinematic images are not, literally, pictorial depictions of (nonexistent) fictional things, then whatever representational function they do

---

[7] Sometimes the characters of fiction are real things, as Hitler is a character in *The Last Days of Hitler*. There the cinematic images represent (in fact misrepresent) him pictorially. But this is not the typical case. There are also cases hard to classify. Is Erich von Stroheim a character in *Sunset Boulevard*, played by himself, a character of whom it is fictional that (among other things) his name is Max von Mayerling?

[8] This problem is not peculiar to film. In any medium that represents pictorially, there are fictional representations: pictures and sculptures of imaginary beings, plays that tell us about people who never lived and events that never happened.

[9] For reasons, see my *Nature of Fiction*, chapter 4.

have seems, intuitively, to be pictorial. Let us examine this idea of functioning pictorially to present fiction.

The cinematic images in *The Third Man* pictorially represent Orson Welles. They do not pictorially, or in any other way, represent Harry Lime, since there is no such person for them to represent. But there is such a thing as *The Third Man*, a certain fiction of the cinema. Think of a particular sequence of cinematic images as giving information about that, rather than as representing the characters of the fiction. The manner in which the images convey that information is, I shall argue, a pictorial way.

What do we learn about a fiction from the images we see on screen? We learn what is *fictional* in that fiction.[10] In a given fiction, various things are fictional, and different fictions are distinguished, partly, by the different things that are fictional in them. One difference between *The Third Man* and, say, *Stagecoach* is that in the former but not in the latter, it is fictional that there is a man whose name is "Harry Lime" who is engaged in various criminal projects, who has a certain appearance, who moves in a certain way and who stands in a certain setting on a certain occasion. How he looks, moves and stands are among his visible features – or, more precisely, they are among the visible features concerning which it is fictional that someone has them in this film. How do we come to know that they are among these features? We know that by looking at the screen, and recognizing there an image of a man (Orson Welles) who looks, moves and stands in that way. And the recognitional capacity we exercise in order to do this is just the recognitional capacity we would exercise if we saw a man in front of us who looked, moved and stood that way. That, long-windedly, is the story about how our knowledge that certain things are fictional in the film depends upon the visual capacities we have to recognize the visible features of things when we see them. And that is what it is for the film's images to function pictorially in their representation of the story.[11]

[10] On being fictional (what is sometimes called "being true in fiction") see ibid., chapter 2.

[11] For a somewhat more precise account of picturing, see this volume, Chapter 3, Section 3.1.

This does not mean that the image is a pictorial representation; that would require it to be a pictorial representation of something, which it isn't.[12] It is not, in particular, a pictorial representation of fictional characters and things. And it is not a pictorial representation of the fiction itself. A fiction does not have the kinds of properties – shape, size, colour – that could be represented pictorially. Saying that cinematic and other images function pictorially to present fictions is as close as we can get to saying that they are pictorial representations without saying something false. That is close enough for our purposes. It will enable us to make all the distinctions we want to make – especially that between functioning pictorially to present fiction and functioning linguistically, which is how literature functions. This will turn out to be a very significant distinction, as I argue in Chapter 4.

Despite my scepticism about the idea that cinematic images are pictorial depictions of fictional things, it will be convenient to speak as if they are, and hence to blur the distinction between being a pictorial representation of fictional things and functioning pictorially to present fictions. From now on I shall simply speak as if an image represents Harry Lime, and represents him pictorially as well as visually. Instead of speaking like that, I could say that the image functions pictorially to present a fiction in which a man called "Harry Lime" does such and such. But that would be tedious.

I.6 DOCUMENTARY AND FICTION

I have said that cinematic images, at least the photographically made ones we are considering here, represent real people in real settings and situations. Should we say that a movie is always a documentary as well as being a piece of fiction – a (highly selective) documentary about the activities of actors and film makers as they go about making a fictional movie? I say no. There

[12] Goodman's suggestion that, while there are no representations of Mr Pickwick, there are "Pickwick representations" strikes me as a purely verbal solution to the difficulty posed by representation in fiction (see his *Languages of Art*, chapter 1).

are two representing functions that cinematic images can perform: the photographic and the fictional. Documentary films perform only the first, while fiction films perform both. A fiction film, like a documentary, is a record of what happened in front of the camera at the time the film was exposed. But with the fiction film and not with the documentary, that record is intended for the further purpose of presenting a fictional story. A rough way to indicate the distinction would be to say that a documentary has as its primary purpose the representation of the real, whereas the fiction film uses representations of the real to represent the unreal or the fictional. What the movie really represents is determined by the causal processes which result in the exposure of cinematic film, and not by intention.[13] A film may (really) represent something quite other than what its makers intended it to represent, as when we find evidence concerning crimes or unsuspected historical information in casual holiday footage. But however hard we look at a film, we shall not find unsuspected fictional stories represented there; it is fictional – presents a fictional story – only if it was intended to be fictional.

What intention might a film maker have in giving us representations of the unreal? The more or less traditional view is that we are intended to "suspend disbelief" in the presence of cinematic (and other) fictions. It has never been very clear what the suspension of disbelief is supposed to be, but one result of the use of this phrase has been that writers on cinema have been able to claim that, in various ways and to various degrees, the viewer comes to believe in the reality of these fictional events. In Chapter 5, I argue that this is wrong, and that what is distinctive of the experience of cinematic and other fictions is not belief but what I shall call *imagining*. In general, what is presented as fictional is what we are intended to imagine, and we engage in the appropriate way with the fiction when what is fictional and what we imagine coincide.[14]

[13] For more on the role of causation in photographic representation, see this volume, Chapter 2, Section 2.4.
[14] See Currie, *Nature of Fiction*, chapters 1 and 2; and Kendall Walton, *Mimesis as Make-Believe*, chapters 1 and 2.

It is easy to conflate the two representing functions of cine-matic images – the photographic and the fictional. The costs of doing so are high; grand theories can collapse when the confla-tion is recognized. The claim that the essence of cinema is the representation of "reality as such" cannot survive the recogni-tion that, with the fiction film, what is intended to be repre-sented isn't real at all; what is real is just the means towards that representation.

There are documentary films, just as there are literary docu-ments; and there are fictional films and fictional works of liter-ature.[15] *Gone with the Wind* is fictional cinema based on fictional literature; *Citizen Kane* is fictional cinema with no such antec-edents. It is fictional despite its (partial) basis in actuality. But there is an asymmetry between the cinematic and the literary case. There is a threefold categorization possible for film that is not possible for literature. Consider first the literary case. Someone wishes to inform us of certain events that have oc-curred, say the British poll-tax riots of 1990, and he sets down a written description of them to the best of his knowledge; that is what you do when you write nonfictional literature.[16] But what does the film maker do, if his aim is the same? He may do either of two things (unless one of them is excluded by the passage of time or the prohibitions of distance). He may first capture those very events on film and present them in the form of a documentary. Second, he may capture on film a contrived *representation* of those events by the artful manipulation of ac-tors, extras and settings. Perhaps the aim of informing is better realized, other things being equal, in the first way than in the second; but the second does seem to be a way of realizing that aim, however imperfect it may be. In both cases the film maker

[15] Sometimes people speak and write as if fiction and film were contraries. Thus the subtitle of a recent work announces its subject as "the rhetoric of narra-tive in fiction and film", thereby imposing, one must presume, a distinction between the two (Seymour Chatman, *Coming to Terms*). But I take it this is not so; fiction applies as much within film as it does within literature.

[16] Of course you can write deceptive nonfiction, but I exclude that case as not relevant here and as potentially distracting.

P.o.V

informs us about what he believes to be the case by giving us cinematic representations. In neither case do we have fiction as a result.[17] But the representations the film maker gives us in these two ways are otherwise very different. In the first, documentary, case, what is represented is a matter to be settled by facts about causation: it is causal connections between rioters rioting and the camera that makes it the case that the riots are represented on film. In the second case there are the same kinds of causal connections at work, but they do not get us to the representations we are looking for. They connect the film with actors and sets instead. In this second case the representational target – the riots – is arrived at by intention; the film represents those riots because the filming of actors and sets was intended to provide a representation of those riots.[18]

Is there a comparable distinction, within the class of works of written literature, between causal and intentional representations? No. The writer cannot choose between recording real events and merely producing verbal representations of them; the latter is the only option available. And written literature is, essentially, an intentional form of representation, for the process of writing is mediated by belief in a way that photographic representation need not be. Automatic writing, if there is such a thing, must be intentionally mediated – via the writer's subconscious intentions, or through the magical agency of another – or it would be the production of meaningless shapes rather than writing. An accidental photograph, on the other hand, can easily occur (there is more on photography and causation in Chapter 2).

So cinema presents us with a threefold distinction where lit-

---

[17] Assuming that, in the case in which the events are restaged with actors, the intention is to convey *only* that which is factual. Most "dramatic recreations" on film are not like this and contain much that is invented and which will be understood as such by the audience. Films of this kind are fictions; at least, they contain fictional elements.

[18] There might be more to it than intention; we might need a condition specifying that the intention has been carried through in a reasonably successful way. The point is that intention is relevant in this case but not in the documentary case; the documentary film maker might have been thoroughly confused about what he was filming.

erature allows only two possibilities. In cinema we may have events and characters presented not as fact but as the material for make-believe, we may have actors and sets artfully contrived to inform us of actual events or we may have straightforward documentary film. Within the realm of the literary, we have distinctions corresponding to only the first two of these three.

So far, we have seen some of the things that are essential to cinema, and some of the things which are, to varying degrees, inessential. We have made distinctions between the visual and the pictorial, between the pictorial and the linguistic, between documentary and fiction and between the kinds of nonfictional aspirations which can be realized in film and those which can be realized in literature. Distinctions are useful, but their usefulness is always relative to the theory they serve. What we have so far are distinctions in search of a theory, and it is time to begin to construct that theory.

Part I

Representation in film

FILM is said to be in various ways a realistic medium of representation. I distinguish three kinds of realism that might be attributed to film. Only one of them, I shall argue, is correctly attributable. I also examine, and find wanting, the idea that filmic representation is language-like in structure.

Chapter 1

The myth of illusion

Film gives simultaneously the effect of an actual happening and of a picture.

Rudolf Arnheim

Arnheim is just one of many, now as in his own day, who say that film creates illusion. Like others, he qualifies the claim, saying the illusion is partial. I say film does no such thing; it creates no illusion, partial or otherwise. Film has considerable powers to engage and to persuade, but these powers are not accounted for in terms of illusion. I'll argue in Part II that they are accounted for in terms of imagination. In this chapter we shall see that there are different kinds of illusions, and that claims that film engenders illusion can be more or less plausible depending on what kind of illusion is in question. I'll distinguish two kinds of illusions film might be said to engender, concluding that it engenders neither of them. Before I get to that, I need to distinguish claims about the illusory nature of film from other claims which are sometimes made.

1.1 TRANSPARENCY, LIKENESS AND ILLUSIONISM

Let us start by distinguishing three doctrines about cinema; all of them have been called ('realism'), and each is to some degree deserving of the name. They are, however, quite distinct, and to underline their distinctness I shall give each a different title.

There is first the claim that film, where it uses the photographic method, reproduces rather than merely represents the real world, because photographs capture objects themselves

19

rather than likenesses or representations of them. This view is associated most notably with André Bazin. Following Kendall Walton, I shall call this the doctrine of *Transparency*: film is transparent in that we see "through" it to the real world, as we see through a window or a lens.[1] Next is the idea that the experience of film watching approximates the normal experience of perceiving the real world. I shall call this *Likeness*; it says the experience of film is, or can be, like the experience of the real world.[2] This doctrine has been asserted, again by Bazin, in connection with long-take, deep-focus style. But as I shall argue, this kind of realism is a matter of degree, and long-take style is merely more realistic in this sense than is, say, montage style. Finally, there is the claim that film is realistic in its capacity to engender in the viewer an illusion of the reality and presentness of fictional characters and events portrayed. I shall call this view *Illusionism*. It is, as I said, widely believed. Studio publicity writers, Marxist critics of the Hollywood film, as well as more conventional figures like Arnheim, constantly assert it.

Much of the history of film and film theory can be reconstructed as a debate about the relations between these three doctrines. Some theorists – I am thinking of the early montagists – have argued that Transparency requires us to play down the likeness film makes possible; film's mechanistic commitment to reality has to be compensated for by visual styles that give us visual experiences unlike our visual experiences of the real world. Others, like Bazin, say that Transparency *requires* the film maker to exploit the possibilities for reproducing in film our visual experience of the world; film presents the real world, so it should do so in a way which approximates as closely as pos-

---

[1] See Kendall Walton, "Transparent Pictures". "Transparency" is used in other senses by other authors. It sometimes refers to a certain kind of supposedly invisible narration (see, e.g., Edward Branigan, *Narrative Comprehension and Film*, p. 84). The reader should be careful to distinguish my (Waltonian) sense from these others.

[2] So "Likeness", with an initial capital, is the name of a thesis, namely the thesis that the experience of film is, or can be, like that of the real world, while "likeness" is here used in its ordinary senses: (i) the quality of being like (something); and (ii) something which is like something (as in "a likeness").

sible our experience of that world. And many theorists have agreed that Likeness makes for Illusionism; the closer the experience of film watching approximates the experience of seeing the real world, the more effectively film engenders in the viewer the illusion that he or she is watching reality.] What is not agreed is whether this is a desirable goal. Other theorists have argued that the very notions of likeness, verisimilitude and realism in film are suspect or even incoherent.

Whatever disagreements there have been between particular theorists on these issues, there is general agreement about the close connection between the three doctrines: Transparency, Likeness and Illusionism. I, on the other hand, take the three doctrines to be independent from one another. Adopting any one of them, we are free to adopt or reject the others. In this first part of the book I tentatively reject Transparency, firmly reject Illusionism and accept Likeness.

Transparency and Likeness are doctrines I discuss later. About Illusionism, which is the subject of this chapter, I argue two things. First, I shall argue that it is a mistaken doctrine. Second, I want to distinguish between two versions of illusionism: the view that film creates an illusion of the presentness and reality of the fictional events it portrays and the view that the basic mechanism of film creates an illusion of movement. So there are, as I indicated at the beginning of this chapter, two doctrines of illusionism. Sorting them out will require a distinction between cognitive and perceptual illusions.

There is another kind of realism about film which has been historically important and which I shall not discuss: the view that films can be placed along a dimension of realism according to whether and to what extent they represent deeply significant social relations.[3] A fictional film might be said to be realistic in this sense because it portrays fictional characters as standing in social relations important for determining the outcomes of interpersonal interactions in real life, and portrays the outcomes of the characters' interactions as (largely) determined by their

---

[3] Here I am grateful to George Couvalis.

standing in those relations. This seems to me a perfectly intelligible sense of realism. The question of whether there are such relations and, if so, what they are, is an important – perhaps the most important – question of social theory. I leave that question to be settled by social theorists, whose skills and knowledge are quite different from those typical of film theorists and philosophers.

1.2 COGNITIVE ILLUSIONS

The claim that film causes cognitive illusions is this: film watching, in some systematic way, and as part of the normal process of the viewer's engagement, causes the viewer to have the false belief that the fictional characters and events represented are real.[4] Strictly speaking, there are weaker and stronger versions of the thesis. A weak version says merely that the film viewer comes to believe that what is represented onscreen is real. A stronger version also asserts that the viewer believes that he or she is watching real events. On the weak view, what is happening onscreen is taken for what it really is, namely a representation, and the illusion comes in when we say the viewer takes it to be a representation of real events. On this view, film functions in a way not essentially different from, say, the novel. Illusionism about the novel says that the reader takes the events described in the novel to be real, but no one would seriously assert that readers think that the words on the pages they read *are* those events. As far as I can see, most people who think film is illusionistic take the stronger view. They think film has the

---

[4] "In cinema it is perfectly possible to believe that a man can fly" (John Ellis, *Visible Fictions*, p. 40); "One knows that one is watching a film, but one believes, even so, that it is an imaginary [*sic*] reality" (Maureen Turim, *Flashbacks in Film*, p. 17); "Conditions of screening and narrative conventions give the spectator an illusion of looking in on a private world" (Laura Mulvey, "Visual Pleasure and Narrative Cinema", p. 806); "The camera becomes the mechanism for producing an illusion of Renaissance space" (ibid., p. 816). This view is by now more or less standard; see, e.g., Robert B. Ray, *A Certain Tendency of the Hollywood Cinema*, p. 38.

capacity to make the viewer think that he or she is actually watching real events.

Perhaps there is a sense in which the film viewer is watching real events. If the thesis of Transparency is correct, then when I watch a film which stars Cary Grant and Ingrid Bergman, I really see those people; I don't merely see representations of them as I would if I was looking at a painting or an animated cartoon which had Bergman and Grant as its subject. But Transparency is something I take up in the next chapter, since it stands to one side of my present concern. The strong version of Illusionism just characterized is not the claim that we see, and believe we see, real actors on sets and locations acting out parts. If Transparency is correct, there would be no illusion involved in having that belief, since the belief would be true. The strong version of Illusionism asserts, rather, that when I see the film starring Bergman and Grant, I believe I am watching the fictional events which the film presents: the activities of, say, U.S. counterespionage agents coming to grips with a postwar Nazi plot in South America.

Illusionism is rarely spelled out in the stark terms I have just employed. Various qualifications are sometimes made, some of which I shall consider. But the strong view sits comfortably with much else film theorists say, particularly concerning the role of the camera and the viewer's act of identification. The standard theory seems to be something like this: the illusion peculiar to film is that the viewer is present at the events of the story, watching from the position actually occupied by the camera, which the viewer thinks of as his or her position. Thus Béla Balázs: "In the cinema the camera carries the spectator into the film picture itself. We see everything from the inside as it were and are surrounded by the characters of the film."[5] And Erwin Panofsky: "Aesthetically [the spectator] is in permanent motion as his eye identifies itself with the lens of the camera."[6]

---

[5] Béla Balázs, *Theory of the Film*, p. 48.

[6] Erwin Panofsky, "Style and Medium in the Motion Pictures", p. 218. See also Paul Weiss: "A film is completed by the viewers before it; they are transformed by the film into occupants of a world part of which the film makes visible" (*Cinematics*, p. 5; quoted in Ian Jarvie, *Philosophy of the Film*, pp. 131–

I do not deny that it is possible for film to engender this sort of an illusion on the part of a viewer. On a liberal enough view of possibility, it is possible for anything to create an illusion of anything else. But this mere possibility is not at issue when people claim that film is illusionistic; rather, they claim that the standard mechanism by which film engages the audience is illusionistic, that the creation of an illusion of reality is a standard feature of the transaction between film and viewer. That is what I deny.

There are two serious objections to the idea that film induces the illusion that fictional events are real and that the viewer is directly witnessing them. The first is that film viewers simply do not react in the way that people would react who believed in the reality of the fictional events the film depicts.[7] You have only to reflect for a moment on how you would react if you saw, or thought you saw, a threatening monster, or if you thought yourself alone in a house with an axe murderer, or if you thought you were watching someone about to be attacked by an axe murderer, to see that your behaviour in the cinema is quite unlike that of someone who really did believe in the reality of the fiction presented.

There are celebrated cases of viewers reacting to a movie as if they were in the presence of the thing it depicts, though whether these cases belong to the history or merely to the folklore of cinema I do not know. It is said, for example, that in 1895 a Parisian audience fled in terror during the showing of a film by the Lumière brothers which depicted the arrival of a train.[8] If it really happened, this is to be explained in terms of the unfamiliarity of the medium to that audience; it sheds no light on our standard and intended response to cinematic fictions.

---

132). In Chapter 4 I shall examine a way of taking the statements of Balázs, Panofsky and others which does not commit them to illusionism.

[7] This is well argued in Walton, *Mimesis as Make-Believe*, chapter 5. Films may be intended to promote belief at a secondary level, as concerning, for example, the rightness of a cause, and they may in fact achieve this result. But it is not usually the case that they are intended to get the audience to believe in the reality of the fictional characters and events they depict.

[8] See, e.g., Metz, *Imaginary Signifier*, p. 73.

The case is also not an example of the audience reacting to fictional events as if they were real; the film really showed the arrival of a train. Examples of this kind cannot be used to support any general hypothesis about the deceptive powers of cinema, especially when it is fictional cinema at issue.

The reactions I have described as lacking on the part of the normal film viewer are reactions of behaviour; I said that people watching movies do not behave like people who believe in the reality of the fictions they are watching. This might be objected to on the grounds that this is behaviourism, a discredited doctrine; but in fact, the argument does not depend on behaviourism. Behaviourism is the view that mental states like belief are items of behaviour, or, in a more sophisticated version, that they are dispositions to behave. You do not have to accept this behaviourist identification to think that behaviour is relevant to the question of whether someone is in a certain mental state. When I make a claim about a person's mental state it is relevant to raise questions about behaviour, because behaviour is an important source of evidence for an hypothesis about a mental state. We are entitled to be sceptical of the claim that a person believes in God if the person never engages in any behaviour we think of as typical or exemplary of a belief in God. Similarly, there is very little evidence from behaviour that film viewers believe in the fictions they see. Explanations of our responses to cinematic fictions in terms of belief work only so long as we do not take the connection between belief and behaviour seriously. Of course we do need a psychological explanation of our sometimes very intense responses to film. In the absence of an explanation in other terms, an explanation that appeals to belief can seem attractive, for all its evident drawbacks. In Part II I shall give an explanation of our responses to fictions in terms of imagining.

So the first objection to Illusionism cites the evidence from behaviour. The second objection cites the evidence of introspection. Illusionism is at odds with much of the experience of film watching. Consider what would be involved in the film viewer believing that she was watching real events. The viewer would have to suppose that her perspective is that of the camera, that she is positioned within and moves through the film space as the camera is positioned and moved. There have been elaborate attempts to argue that the viewer does identify with the camera.[9] But identification with the camera would frequently require us to think of ourselves in peculiar or impossible locations, undertaking movements out of keeping with the natural limitations of our bodies, and peculiarly invisible to the characters. None of this seems to be part of the ordinary experience of film watching. In the attempt to associate the camera with some observer within the world of the action with whom the viewer can in turn identify, film theorists have exaggerated the extent to which shots within a film can be thought of as point-of-view shots, and have sometimes postulated, quite ad hoc, an invisible narrator from whose position the action is displayed and with whom the viewer may identify. It would be better to acknowledge that cinematic shots are only rarely from a psychological point of view, and to abandon the thesis that the viewer identifies with an intelligence whose point of view is the camera.[10]

I have already said that film theorists sometimes try to distance themselves from the strong version of Illusionism I have described by adding various qualifications. Sometimes the claim that the viewer believes the fiction to be real is qualified so as to suggest that the belief is partial or of lower intensity than those we get from real life.[11] This move solves nothing; the film viewer does not behave like one who merely suspects, or believes to some degree, that he or anyone else is in mortal danger, or like one within whom belief is in tension with simultaneous disbelief. If I even vaguely suspected there was a monster on the loose I would leave the theatre immediately and call the

[9] "[The viewer] certainly has to identify ... if he did not the film would become incomprehensible" (Metz, *Imaginary Signifier*, p. 46). See also Nick Browne, *The Rhetoric of Filmic Narration*, chapter 1.

[10] For more on this see Chapter 7, Section 7.2.

[11] Christian Metz, for example, discusses how film creates "a certain degree of *belief* in the reality of an imaginary world". He also says that "somewhere in oneself one believes that [the events of the fiction] are genuinely true" (*Imaginary Signifier*, pp. 118 and 72, emphasis in the original). Jean Comolli says that "we want ... to be both fooled and not fooled [by cinema]" ("Machines of the Visible", p. 759).

police. Nor is there in the experience of film watching any evidence that we suspect, or partially believe, or are prone to believe, that we are flying through space or suspended from a ceiling.

1.3 FILM AND DREAMING

There is a version of Illusionism which might seem to avoid the problems I have just now raised. It is the view that the mental state induced by film is like the state of dreaming. Dreams involve fantastical occurrences which we accept uncritically while we dream, and which don't provoke much reactive behaviour; moreover, dreaming seems to have a visual quality in the way that watching cinema does – though the relation between dreaming and mental images is in fact more controversial than many writers on film seem to appreciate. We frequently encounter confident statements to the effect that, in watching films, the viewer approximates the condition of the dreamer, and that it is in fact the aim of cinema to induce this condition.[12] In that case the camera would correspond to a supposed "inner eye" by means of which we perceive the images of dreams.

The analogy with dreaming has been a powerful stimulus to the development of psychoanalytic theories of film and film experience. In fact, as Noël Carroll has shown, the analogy proceeds by systematically failing to compare like with like. If film experience is to be like dreaming, it is what happens *in* the dream that matters, and in our dreams we are certainly motivated to avoid danger, though, notoriously, the dream usually makes this frighteningly difficult. Few of us feel the same desperate urge to act when watching film, unless it be simply to

[12] Thus Sally Flitterman: "The look . . . is an integral part of filmic structure. The cinematic apparatus is designed to produce the look and to create in the spectator the sensation that it is she/he who is producing the look, dreaming these images which appear on the screen" ("Woman, Desire, and the Look: Feminism and the Enunciative Apparatus in Cinema", p. 243). Christian Metz emphasizes a number of differences between film and dream, but concludes that "among the different regimes of waking, the filmic state is one of those least unlike sleep and dreaming, dreamful sleep" (*Imaginary Signifier*, p. 128).

leave the theatre. Another disanalogy: in dreams the central character is typically the self, whose acts and sufferings are of central concern. But film watching is notable for its capacity to *suppress* consciousness of the self in favour of the fiction, and even those who claim that film "puts us in the space of the action" would not, I suppose, claim that we imagine ourselves to be active participants in the events portrayed. That both dreaming and film watching frequently take place in the dark is another irrelevant consideration; darkness is not typically part of the experience of dreaming, though it does typically accompany the experience of film watching. Besides, if people were reduced to the condition of dreamers by film, they would not be the noisy conversationalists I often find so irritating.

Perhaps in some way film watching is like dreaming; perhaps everything is in some way like everything else. There does not seem to be any substantial, systematic likeness between film experience and dreaming that holds out promise of serious explanatory gains.

1.4 PERCEPTUAL ILLUSIONISM

The version of Illusionism I have been considering so far is very strong; it commits the Illusionist to saying that film viewers are systematically caused to have false beliefs. It is interesting to argue that a strong view is true, but less interesting to argue that it is false, as I have done. By definition, strong views are more likely to be false than weak ones. Might there be some weaker, apparently more plausible, version of Illusionism? If there is, and if I can show that this weaker version is also wrong, that would be a result of some interest. I believe there is a weaker, more plausible version of Illusionism, and I shall argue against it.

I called the view that film induces false beliefs *Cognitive Illusionism*. There certainly are cognitive illusions of various kinds. When you see two lines of equal length, but provided with "arrowheads" pointing in different directions so that the lines seem to be of different lengths (as in the so-called Müller–Lyre illusion), you might believe the lines to be of different lengths. You are then suffering a cognitive illusion. But not all illusions are cognitive. You may know the two lines are of equal length and still be subject to the Müller–Lyre illusion: the lines just *look* as if they are of different lengths. It is a common feature of the many kinds of visual illusions that they are, in Zenon Pylyshyn's phrase, "cognitively impenetrable": belief doesn't make any difference to the way the illusory phenomenon looks.[13]

An illusion of this kind, which is what I am going to call a *perceptual illusion*, occurs when experience represents the world as being a certain way, when in fact it is not that way and the subject does not believe it to be that way. My experience of the two lines may represent the two lines as being of unequal length, even though I know this experience misrepresents the relation between the lines.[14]

Someone might claim that cinema is illusionistic in this perceptual sense and not in the cognitive sense I have been considering up until now. My arguments so far presented against Illusionism are ineffective against Perceptual Illusionism because they are designed to show we lack the beliefs necessary to underwrite the claim of Cognitive Illusionism. I need different arguments if I am going to oppose Perceptual Illusionism. I shall

[13] See Zenon Pylyshyn, "Computation and Cognition: Issues in the Foundations of Cognitive Science", pp. 111–132. See also Jerry Fodor, "Observation Reconsidered". This way of setting up the debate over illusion in film – in terms of a distinction between cognitive and perceptual illusions – will do for our purposes. Some writers are sceptical about the distinction, claiming that our perceptual systems are cognitively penetrable all the way down to the sensory periphery (see, e.g., Paul M. Churchland, "Perceptual Plasticity and Theoretical Neutrality: A Reply to Jerry Fodor", especially pp. 183–185). The most such arguments show, I believe, is that there is a continuum between highly cognitive mental systems within which beliefs are formed on the basis of other beliefs, and only marginally cognitive systems over which beliefs can exert some slight influence. What I am here calling the cognitive and perceptual illusions supposedly created by film would then correspond to opposite extremes of this spectrum. The arguments I am considering here are robust under shifts of framework from the dichotomy model to the continuum model. The continuum model is well argued in W. M. Davies, *Experience and Content: Consequences of a Continuum Theory*.

[14] See Christopher Peacocke, *Sense and Content*, pp. 5–6.

provide some. But bear in mind a point already made: Perceptual Illusionism is a distinctly weaker thesis about cinema than Cognitive Illusionism, and one with quite different consequences. There has been a tendency to assume that the (alleged) truth of Perceptual Illusionism somehow supports the claim of Cognitive Illusionism. Perhaps Perceptual Illusionism is the Trojan horse by means of which advocates of Cognitive Illusionism about film hope to gain their victory.[15] It needs to be said, therefore, that Perceptual Illusionism, even if true, does not in itself provide an argument for Cognitive Illusionism, though it might do so in conjunction with other premises. It is not essential to my opposition to Cognitive Illusionism that I oppose Perceptual Illusionism as well. Nonetheless, I do oppose Perceptual Illusionism. I do not claim to be able to refute it; at most I shall sow the seeds of doubt about it.

The most common version of the claim that cinema induces a perceptual illusion says that cinema induces a perceptual illusion of movement – that we seem to see movement on the screen, but really do not. I shall come to this. Before I do, I want to consider a worry some might have, not just about the reality of movement within a cinematic image, but about the reality of the cinematic image itself.

1.5 THE REALITY OF CINEMATIC IMAGES

I said in the Introduction that film is a pictorial medium. Someone might question whether the pictures which film employs are themselves real. There does seem to be a difference between the *substantial* pictures we make contact with when we look at a painting or a photographic print, and the insubstantial pictures of film – the images on a screen. With painting, the picture we see is an enduring physical object. The medium of painting is paint on surface, and when we look at a painting what we look at is, exactly, paint on a surface. With film, there

---

[15] See, e.g., Jean-Louis Baudry, "Ideological Effects of the Basic Cinematographic Apparatus".

is a disparity between qualities of the physical material – the strip of celluloid that passes through the projector – and the qualities we perceive when watching the movie. In cinema we watch images. But these images are not the strips of celluloid themselves. Someone might say, "The celluloid and all the rest of the apparatus is real, but the image is not; it is a product of the mind." I want to argue that this dichotomy is false. There is a sense in which the image we see on the screen is a product of the mind, but that is not a sense which would justify our saying that the image is unreal. What we see when we view a film is a pattern of colour on a surface, usually a screen. That pattern of colour is, I claim, really there. (For present purposes, I consider black, white and shades of grey to be colours.)

Some philosophers think generally that colours are "not really there" on a surface, and that when our experience represents an object or surface as having a certain colour we are thereby subject to an illusion, because there are no colours to be there.[16] It would be a distraction to get deeply involved in this dispute here; we are after all trying to see whether there are *special* problems associated with the idea of cinematic images. We could proceed simply by ignoring ontological issues about colour altogether and simply assume that colours, whatever they are, are real things. However, it will be useful to say something general about the nature of colour, for what I say about that will be helpful when we consider the nature of cinematic movement. I shall argue that cinematic images are real in just the sense colours are real, so we had better establish what this sense is.

I take colours to be properties of surfaces, but properties those surfaces have in virtue of their being a standard or normal pattern of response to those surfaces on the part of sentient observers. Colours are, in Mark Johnston's phrase, *response-dependent* properties, and in this they differ from properties like being square, being tall, and being ten miles from Cambridge.[17] These

---

[16] See Paul A. Boghossian and J. David Velleman, "Colour as a Secondary Quality". See also C. L. Hardin, "Color Subjectivism".

[17] See Mark Johnston, "Dispositional Theories of Value". See also Philip Pettit, "Realism and Response-Dependence". I am especially indebted to Pettit's discussion.

last three properties are not response dependent because they are not possessed by an object in virtue of that object's capacity to elicit a certain psychological response. Of these three properties, the first is an *intrinsic* property: to tell whether something is square you need look no further than at the thing itself. The last two are extrinsic: whether you are tall depends on the height of things other than yourself, and how far you are from Cambridge cannot be discerned without taking Cambridge into account. All response-dependent properties are extrinsic but the converse is not true, since being tall and being ten miles from Cambridge are not response-dependent properties, though they are extrinsic. Being funny is a response-dependent concept and it is, consequently, extrinsic; things are funny according to how people react to them, though it is not easy to say exactly what reactions count as grounds for saying the thing reacted to is funny.

We can now see how colour properties are different from many other kinds of properties, while admitting them as real properties of things. There is some tendency to express the peculiarity of colours by saying they are less real than other properties, but I find it difficult to make sense of the idea that reality admits of degrees. Better to put it in terms of a difference between that which is intrinsic and that which is in various ways extrinsic. If people grow I shall no longer be tall, though my height does not change; and if a comet affects our organs of sight so that things look differently coloured to all of us, they will be differently coloured though they do not change internally. Being tall and being red are extrinsic properties of things, whereas being six feet tall, and having such and such a constitution of molecules on your surface, are intrinsic properties; changing those properties would involve a change in you. But extrinsic properties can be as real as intrinsic ones.

In order to establish the reality of cinematic images, it is not sufficient to establish the reality of colours in general, for cinematic images might constitute a special case where there appear to be colours but really are not. And there does seem to be a difference between the image on the cinema screen and that on the painting. The conditions for the presence of colours in the two cases are rather different, and significantly more precarious in the case of the screen. The colours of the picture are those it has for any normally sighted person in conditions roughly approximating daylight. In our environment, those conditions frequently hold. But what is required for the screen to have that pattern of colours we identify as a cinematic image is for the film strip, projector and light source to stand in the right, rather complex relation to the screen, and that is the case only when we go to considerable trouble to make it so. These requirements make the colours of the screen more extrinsic than the colours of the painting, for they depend not just on our capacity as observers to respond to them in a certain way, but on the presence and activation of all the relevant cinematic technology. The colours on the screen are, we may say, extrinsically sustained, while those of the painting are intrinsically sustained – what sustains them is the condition of the canvas itself. Once again, we should not treat this as grounds for denying that the colours we see are colours on the screen. All colour is extrinsic to the extent of being response dependent. There is no such thing as absolutely intrinsic colour. It is just that the colours on the screen are extrinsic to a greater degree than are the colours on the canvas.

Cinematic images are pictures of a peculiarly transitory and precarious kind. Their precariousness makes for a further distinction between them and what we conventionally call pictures. For a painting or a drawing, we can make a distinction between the work itself and the intended, standard or ideal viewing conditions for the work. The painting may best be viewed from about four feet, at eye level, in good diffused light; but the same picture, with the same colours in the same pattern on its surface, is still there when viewed from twenty yards in poor light or in a darkened vault. But screening conditions for a film are to some extent essential to it. If they are unfavourable to a considerable degree – as when there is strong ambient light or a very poorly reflecting surface as a screen – the cinematic image simply is not there at all, though there is no sharp boundary between acceptable and nonacceptable conditions. My claim is just that, when those peculiar conditions necessary to display the film hold, the film image is really there.

1.6 ON THE MOTION OF IMAGES

Let us now introduce the idea of movement, which is so crucial to understanding the nature and reality of cinematic images. There is a widely held belief that this movement is illusory. Speaking of the appearance of movement in film, Hugo Münsterberg said, "We do not see the objective reality, but a product of our own mind which binds the pictures together."[18] And Francis Sparshott writes that "a film is a series of motionless images projected onto a screen so fast as to create in the mind of anyone watching the screen an impression of continuous motion" – an impression Sparshott goes on to call "the basic illusion of motion".[19] I believe this plausible view to be false. There is no illusion of movement in cinema; there is real movement, really perceived.[20]

Before I argue for this, I want to note that an apparently attractive position here is really not available. We cannot say, "There really are cinematic images, but there is not really any movement involved when such an image is projected on the screen." If you reject the reality of movement, you must reject the reality of the image as well. Consider an image which lasts for a few seconds and where there is, apparently, a good deal

[18] Hugo Münsterberg, "The Means of the Photoplay", p. 332.

[19] Francis Sparshott, "Basic Film Aesthetics", p. 284. See also Haig Khatchadourian, "Remarks on the 'Cinematic/Uncinematic Distinction in Film Art'", p. 134: "a film ... is *necessarily* a sequence of visual images that create the illusion of movement" (emphasis in the original). Jacques Aumont and his coauthors speak of "the simple illusion of movement", concluding that "psychologically speaking, a film does not exist on film stock or on the screen, but only within the mind" (*Aesthetics of Film*, p. 184).

[20] My argument here is presented in terms of the case of cinematic representation of movement, but could easily be altered to apply against those who deny that there is real motion observed on a television screen or video display, where the technical mechanism productive of the appearance of movement is different from that in the cinematic case.

of movement, perhaps that of a crowd of people running about. Take away the movement and what is left that could constitute a real image? If there isn't any motion, the real image must be static. But what then is it an image of? Nothing, we will assume, was stationary in the photographed scene. The image can hardly be of people *not* moving. Is the image an undifferentiated blank, with no representational features? Then it is not an image. You might claim that, when there isn't even any apparent movement in the image (a fixed closeup of a static object, for example), then the image is real. But it is hardly credible that when I look at a static cinematic image I am not subject to an illusion, but become subject to one as soon as movement appears. Also, since as a matter of fact few cinematic images are static, there would be little comfort for the realist in the claim that static cinematic images are real. To be a realist about cinematic images, you have to be a realist about cinematic movement.

I am taking the view that cinematic motion is illusory to be a version of the view that cinema involves a perceptual rather than a cognitive illusion. Someone might argue that this supposed illusion of cinematic motion is a cognitive, and not merely a perceptual illusion, because most people who watch films actually believe they are watching moving images; it is only when you reflect on the technical mechanisms of cinema that you realize this is not the case. That may be true, but the fact is that the appearance of cinematic motion does not go away for those people who convince themselves that it is, indeed, an illusion. If cinematic motion is illusory, then it is essentially a perceptual illusion and only incidentally a cognitive one. That is why I shall treat it simply as a (putative) perceptual illusion.

Before I consider the arguments about the reality of movement in cinematic images, I had better clarify exactly what I mean when I speak of "moving images". Strictly speaking, the cinematic image is the whole area of illumination on the screen during projection. We all agree, I take it, that this does not move, unless, due to some mechanical failure, the projection equipment starts to shift around. What moves when there is movement of an image is a part or parts of this image; if we are watching a shot of a man walking along a street, the part of the image which represents the man will move from one side of the screen to the other. Movement of this kind, which is what I am concerned with here, needs to be distinguished from the movement which occurs as a result of a continuous change in the position of the camera during a single shot; the man might be stationary relative to the background while the camera moves with respect to him. This latter kind of movement introduces somewhat complex considerations which I shall not attempt to deal with here. Also, the movement with which I am concerned here is not the radically discontinuous movement which might be said to occur across shots, for example, when we see the image of the man in one place on the screen in one shot, and in another place on the screen in the next shot. All I am claiming here is that there really is movement within a single shot taken from a fixed perspective. That, obviously, is enough to contradict the claim that movement in film is an illusion produced by the juxtaposition of static images.

I had also better say a word on metaphysical background. Arguments about motion, and about change generally, sometimes raise deep questions about what motion and change actually are. There are two basic and mutually incompatible views about this. One, which I shall call three dimensionalism, says that change takes place when a thing has a property at one time which it, that very same thing, lacks at another. The other view, four dimensionalism, says that change occurs when a certain temporal stage possesses a property and another temporal stage lacks it, where those stages constitute temporal stages of the same object. I don't believe there is anything in our common belief about change which decides one way or the other between these two theories, and nothing I shall say about cinematic movement here is intended to prejudge which view is correct.[21] So while I shall speak of our cinematic experience as representing to us that an image moves from one place to the other, this is to be taken as neutral between the view that there is one thing which is in one place at one time and in another place at another

---

[21] See Frank Jackson, "Metaphysics by Possible Cases".

time, and the view that there are distinct but suitably related temporal parts in different places. Both constructs I take to be inconsistent with the view that there is, literally, no movement of an image on the screen.

One way to argue that there is real movement of cinematic images would be to adopt very liberal criteria of reality. In particular, if we could persuade ourselves that there is no clear distinction between what it is useful to say and what it is true to say, it would be easy to establish the reality of cinematic movement. There is, after all, utility in describing a film by reference to the movement of the images it presents us with. Daniel Dennett has recently advocated a kinder, gentler realism that allows us to say that all sorts of things are real on account of their usefulness.[22] In Dennett's example, Smith and Jones claim to detect different patterns in the same visual array, the differences between them being accounted for in the different signal-to-noise ratios they claim to detect; both do fairly well in predicting extensions of the array, chalking up their different patterns of failure to their respective assumptions about noise. Who is right? Both, says Dennett, and so is anyone else who can do comparably well by detecting yet another pattern in the array. It's no good saying, "Yes, I know they are all making money out of their systems, but who is right?" That, for Dennett, is symptomatic of the outmoded, inflexible and unforgiving realism he wants to supersede – we might call it "first-strike realism". While Dennett's argument is complex and fascinating, at the end of it I still wanted to retain a distinction between usefulness and truth in areas where it seemed to me Dennett blurs the distinction. I shall not, therefore, be arguing for the reality of the movement of cinematic images simply on the grounds that it is useful for us to think and speak as if there really were such movement, though the usefulness of this way of thinking and speaking is certainly why we are interested in whether this

[22] Daniel Dennett, "Real Patterns", pp. 27–51. I am grateful to Jerrold Levinson for drawing my attention to this work, and for valuable discussion of the topic of this chapter.

kind of movement is real. So I remain a first-strike realist. As we shall see, even we hawks are capable of ontological generosity.

In fact, I shall not be looking for a positive argument in favour of the reality of cinematic motion. In debates over whether some type of experience is illusory, the burden of proof, or perhaps merely of argument, lies with the party which asserts that the experience in question is illusory, just as it does with someone who asserts that a certain belief is false. In both cases – belief and perception – we have grounds for treating veridical and nonveridical states asymmetrically, since states of belief and perception are states we have *because* they tend to be veridical. In that case, we should hold that cinematic experience of movement is veridical unless there is a significant weight of evidence and argument against the idea.

However, it is worth pointing out that, from the perspective of someone who adopts what I have called Transparency, it is difficult to deny the reality of the cinematic motion we seem to see.[23] The thesis of Transparency – which I shall assess in some detail in the next chapter – has it that when I see a cinematic image of Cary Grant, I really and literally see Cary Grant. Someone who holds this view would find it hard to deny that the movement we seem to see on the screen is real movement. If Grant was filmed while moving from one place to another, and the film represents him as moving, and if I really do see Grant when I see the film, then surely I really see him moving. In that case, the appearance of movement cannot be an illusion of movement. But of course this argument weighs only with someone who accepts Transparency and not with anyone else, so I shall not put much weight on it here.

What is the argument for saying the experience of cinema involves a perceptual illusion of movement? Clear statements of the argument are hard to come by. I have the impression the argument sometimes appeals to the fact that there is no movement on the cinematic film roll itself, but rather a sequence of static images. This is true, but it does nothing to establish the

[23] This point emerged during discussion with Graham Nerlich.

unreality of cinematic movement. After all, when we listen to a tape recording, there is no sound on the tape itself, but just a pattern of selective magnetization. We would not conclude from this that when we listen to a tape recording of music we are subject to an auditory illusion. The claim of Perceptual Illusionism is that there is no movement *on the screen*; for this, after all, is where we seem to see movement.

An argument which might seem to favour Perceptual Illusionism is the following: the supposed movement on the screen is the product of our perceptual system, and cannot be thought to exist independently of it. Suppose you described the events on the screen from the kind of objective viewpoint we try to occupy in physical science: you exhaustively describe the impact of particles or waves of light on the screen, and you thereby describe all the relevant physical events at that surface. But you do not describe any movement of the kind we claim to observe there; you do not describe any object as moving from one place on the screen to another. So there simply isn't any movement, since the objective description comprehends all the relevant physical facts but describes no movement. It is only when you take a subjective point of view and include in the description the viewer's subjective experience of the screen that movement enters your story.

This is a poor argument. It is parallel to a class of other arguments that would establish the illusory nature of all our experience of what are called secondary qualities. Consider again the case of colour; we describe the object from a physical point of view exhaustively, including everything about the spectral-reflectance profile of its surface, but we say nothing about the way it looks; colour enters our vocabulary only when we include the observer's subjective point of view in the story. So there are not really any colours. There are those who welcome this conclusion, and say the experience of colour is indeed illusory; experience represents things as having colour properties when in fact they do not have them.[24] But on the whole philosophers resist such starkly revisionist conclusions, and I go along with

[24] Boghossian and Velleman, "Colour as a Secondary Quality".

them. What a realist about colour should say is what I have already said: colours and other secondary properties are real, response-dependent properties of things. And so it is, I claim, with the "apparent motion" of projected film; this is real, response-dependent motion.

Perhaps the greatest source of resistance to the idea that cinematic images are real is the idea that the apparent motion of the image is not "tracked" by any comparable motion of a physical object. As I have said, no particle or wave, or any physical thing, moves across the screen as the image of Cary Grant (seems to) move across it. But normally, when we say that something moves, we can identify a correlated moving physical object – or at least we have good reason to believe there is one. If a person moves, then his body does also; if a car moves, there is a mass of molecules out of which the car is constructed which moves. Moreover, the movement of the person or the car supervenes on the movement of the underlying physical object; a person's movement logically requires the movement of his body – similarly with the car and its constituent molecules. The movement I have claimed for cinematic images is not like that. But this is explained in terms of the basic difference between persons and cars, on the one hand, and cinematic images on the other. Cars and persons have relatively stable physical constituents, while images do not. The movement of the image supervenes on the pattern of light particles striking the screen. But the image has qualities not possessed by any of the physical things and events to which we appeal in explaining it: in particular, it has movement. In just the same way, the colours on a surface are explainable in terms of the physical properties of those surfaces, and ultimately in terms of their subatomic constituents. But the colour has qualities not possessed by any such constituent; the greenness of the colour is not to be found in any greenness of its subatomic parts.

So I say that part of the content of cinematic experience is that there is movement of images, and there really is such movement. We see the cinematic image of a man, and we see that it is in one place on the screen, and we later see that it is in another; indeed, we see that image move from one place to another

on the screen. That image is not to be identified with some particular physical object. It is not like the image in a painting,
which consists of a certain conglomeration of physical pigments,
at least relatively stable over time. It is an image sustained by
the continuous impact of light on the surface of the screen, and
no particular light wave or particle is more than minutely constitutive of it. Nonetheless, that image is a particular thing, and
a thing which moves.

To say there is a movement is to say that a certain thing is in
one place at one time and in another place at another time (or,
on the four-dimensionalist view, that a temporal part of the object is in one place and a different temporal part is in another).
Motion requires reidentification over time of that which moves.
But what allows us to say that the image in one place on the
screen at one time is the same as the image at some other place
on the screen at another time?[25] One initially plausible answer
is that images get their identity conditions from their causal antecedents: this image now and that one then are both cinematic
images of the same man, so they are the same image. But this
answer is unsatisfactory. First of all, I would make the same
claim for the identity of the image over time in an animated
cartoon. That is, I would claim that we see the real movement
of the image of Mickey Mouse from one side of the screen to
the other. But in this case the argument from sameness of causal
antecedents will not allow us to reidentify images over time,
because there is no Mickey Mouse to be the common causal
ancestor of the image I see in one place and the image I see in
another. We might say that sameness of causal antecedent is a
sufficient but not a necessary condition for identity among images. The better criterion for the identity of cinematic images
across time is given by their relation to the mental states of the
viewer. This image now is the same as that one then because
both are identified by normal viewers in normal conditions as
being images of the same individual. And that is as true of the
image of Mickey Mouse as of the image of Cary Grant. Here

---

[25] Remember that this question is to be taken as neutral between three and four
dimensionalism.

again, as with colour, the concept we appeal to is response dependent. Identity between images is itself a response-dependent concept, because questions about how to reidentify images across time are answered by appeal to facts about the psychological responses of the viewer to those images. But just as with colours, this response dependence is compatible with the reality of the images concerned.

1.7 TWO WAYS OR THREE?

In arguing against Perceptual Illusionism I have been insisting that cinematic motion is real, using that term to contrast, naturally enough, with "illusory". You may think this taxonomy is insufficiently refined. After all, we commonly contrast reality with appearance. My dichotomy will then have us identify that which belongs to the realm of mere appearances with that which is illusory. That seems hard on appearances. There ought to be room for a position which says colours and other secondary properties belong to the realm of appearances, but which denies that the experience of colour is illusory.[26] (Perhaps in the end this position will turn out to be incoherent; I just don't want to rule it out at this stage.) On that view, the real contrasts with the illusory and with the apparent. Equivalently, we could say there are two senses of "real": a weak sense which has as the complement of its extension the illusory, and a stronger sense which has as the complement of its extension the illusory and the apparent, which we can then lump together as the unreal. If we adopt that taxonomy, my view is simply that cinematic motion is real in the weak sense. I can then agree that in a strong, metaphysical sense we ought to be antirealists about cinematic motion (thinking of it as unreal), and perhaps about colour as well. But we shall need to make a distinction between, on the one hand, antirealist concepts applicable in the realm of mere appearances and, on the other, antirealist concepts applicable in the realm of illusion. Whatever your view on colour, there is surely a difference, for example, between ascribing blue-

---

[26] Conversation with Brian Medlin suggested this position to me.

ness to a U.S. mailbox, and ascribing greenness to the (actually white) stripes displayed in a McCullough aftereffect experiment.[27] The difference, I submit, is that in the second case but not in the first, you are subject to an illusion. So, if my parallel between cinematic motion and colour does not persuade you to be a strong realist about cinematic motion, it may still be enough to undermine illusionism about it.

To underline this last point, notice a feature of response-dependent concepts sometimes thought to be grounds for being an *antirealist* about such concepts. Realists sometimes emphasize the radical fallibility of our beliefs about any domain to which they claim realism applies; if it's possible, even under epistemically ideal circumstances, for us to be mistaken in our beliefs about that domain, that is a sign we are in the realm of reality. But with certain kinds of response-dependent concepts, radical fallibility is ruled out.[28] If a normal observer in normal circumstances judges that something is red, it is red; similarly, if a normally sighted person, sitting in a darkened cinema at the appropriate distance and attending to the screen as the projector rolls, judges that the cinematic image is moving, then it is. That, as I say, might be grounds for rejecting metaphysical realism about colour, and about cinematic motion. But it cannot be grounds for thinking cinematic movement is an illusion. Where there is no possibility of error, there can be no illusion.

If calling cinematic motion "apparent" in a sense which contrasts with illusory is to have any significance, we ought to be able to point to phenomena which are illusory rather than apparent; the appearance–illusion distinction won't be worth much if the extension of the illusory is empty. Indeed, one common and natural thought in response to my assertion that cinematic motion is not illusory is that the assertion can be

---

[27] The McCullough effect produces an illusion of green or red stripes where there actually are white stripes. Which colour it seems to produce depends on the orientation of the bars (horizontal or vertical) on the cards presented prior to the induction of the illusion. It is therefore called "an orientation-specific color aftereffect".

[28] See Richard Holton, "Intentions, Response-Dependence and Immunity from Error".

sustained only at the cost of reducing, almost to nothing, the class of phenomena that count as illusory. It is worth seeing that this is not so.

Someone might claim that, by an argument parallel to the one I have given for the reality of cinematic motion, we can establish that the experience induced by the Müller–Lyre phenomenon is veridical. In those cases of experience singled out as exemplifying the Müller–Lyre illusion, we are to say that what experience represents is the holding, between two lines, of the relation *being longer* than*, where length* is not the metrical property of objects we measure with rigid rods, but rather a response-dependent length: a length which stands to metrical length as the response-dependent movement I have been advocating for cinematic images stands to the movement we measure by tracking physical objects across space. In that case there is no illusion involved in the Müller–Lyre phenomenon, but merely the veridical experience of one line being "longer* than" another.

This objection fails. Our experience of the Müller–Lyre illusion represents the lines as standing in the relation "longer than", not the relation "longer* than". The visible appearance of the lines suggests that, were one to measure them in the conventional way, the result would be that one was measurably longer than the other. That is why this is genuinely a case of an illusion, rather than a veridical experience of a response-dependent property. With the experience of screen watching, however, it is doubtful whether the movement our experience represents as taking place is of a kind that would be undermined by independent checks analogous to the measuring check we can carry out in the case of the Müller–Lyre illusion. Our experience of screen watching does not have this as its representational content: "there are reidentifiable physical objects moving in front of our eyes" (a content the falsity of which could be established by independent checks). Rather, its content is: "there are *images* of reidentifiable physical objects moving in front of our eyes." In this respect the experience of cinematic motion seems not to be undercut by information from other sources, and therefore to be crucially different from that induced by the Müller–Lyre setup.

44

Someone might also object that my appeal to response dependence in the filmic case has the false consequence that there is no illusion involved in our perception of the movement of a wave. Our perception of wave phenomena suggests there is something, namely a wave, which moves outwards from the centre of disturbance. But if we examine the matter closely we discover there is no physical object – no single, reidentifiable body of water – which spreads outwards when wave motion occurs. There is only the transfer of energy from one molecule to the next, as can be established by placing a free-floating object on the wave surface and seeing it remain stationary with respect to the horizontal axis. But it would seem that my argument for the reality of the movement of the cinematic image applies equally to the movement of the wave, in which case we should have to say that there is, after all, no illusion of movement in the case of the wave, and that seems wrong.

But again there is a difference between the cinematic image and the wave. In the case of the wave, but not in that of the cinematic image, there is a physical object, namely a body of water, which perception represents to us as moving outward as the wave "spreads". But our perception of the motion of cinematic images does not suggest that there is some particular physical object which moves when a cinematic image does. That is why there is a perceptual illusion, or at least a perceptual error, in the perception of wave motion but not in that of cinematic images.

There are a number of other apparent motions which are normally classed as merely illusory and which retain their status as illusions on my account. For example, psychologists speak of *induced* motion, a phenomenon noticeable when we see clouds drifting across the face of the moon; if the clouds drift slowly to the left, the moon appears to be drifting to the right. Similarly, tall buildings viewed from below against a background of moving clouds seem to be falling.[29] In these and like cases we have a perceptual illusion of movement; experience represents something moving which is not moving, as independent checks

---

[29] See Stuart Anstis, "Motion Perception in the Frontal Plane: Sensory Aspects".

would establish. But these cases are unlike that of cinematic motion. There are even kinds of motion which cinema sometimes gives us and which are, or can be, illusory rather than real. For example, films in 3-D display an illusion of depth; our experience of watching 3-D is such that objects are perceived as moving towards or away from the viewer when this is not the case. The cinematic motion I claim to be real is not of that kind; it belongs to the kind which psychologists call "motion in the frontal plane".

But even within this restricted class of motion phenomena I can make distinctions, for not all motion in the frontal plane will count as real by my lights. It is well known, for example, that if one looks at a point of light in an otherwise darkened environment, the point will seem to shift around when in fact it remains steady. The explanation seems to be that the appearance of movement is produced by random eye movements which are uncompensated for because the viewer has no visible frame of reference other than the light source itself.[30] Now suppose that, instead of looking directly at the light source, the viewer looks at the image of it projected on a screen. Then the projected image will seem to move around, just as the light source itself would. And this, I claim, is a case of illusory rather than of real motion on the screen. For the following is a necessary condition for there to be genuine movement of an image: that at each place on the screen occupied by the image as it moves, there should be illumination at that place (and at the relevant time) on the screen. But in the case we are considering, there will be only one fixed and unchanging place on the screen illuminated, and at many places on the screen where the image seems to be, there will be no illumination. So here we seem to see movement of an image where no movement exists. But in the case of what is conventionally called the moving image of film, at the places to

[30] I am grateful here to Sue Feagin and Dan Gilman for helping me to see the significance of this phenomenon to my theory, and to Michael White, who explained the details to me. The illusion described is called "autokinetic movement". See E. L. Brown and K. Deffenbacher, *Perception and the Senses*, pp. 412–415.

which the image seems to move, there really is illumination on the screen.

Cinematic images are unlike those of, say, painting; they are temporary, response dependent and extrinsic in ways the images of painting are not. Still, cinematic images are real objects, reidentifiable across time and occupying different positions at different times during the viewing of the shot. Or, for those who insist on a tripartite distinction between the real, the apparent and the illusory, they are apparent, nonillusory objects. The basic mechanism of cinema is not, after all, based on illusion. Nor do I believe there is any other substantial, interesting sense in which cinema is a medium which creates illusions. Certainly, it does not typically function to produce the cognitive illusion that what is represented onscreen is real and present to the viewer. Realism is a notion film theorists have been uncomfortable with for a while. I shall argue in Chapter 3 that it has been misunderstood, and that it is an indispensable tool for understanding the nature of film. Illusion, on the other hand, is something we can well do without.

The conclusions of this chapter go beyond film theory to embrace general metaphysics. It is traditional to regard motion as a paradigmatically primary quality, to be contrasted with those secondary qualities which are in some sense observer dependent, like colour. If what I have said here about cinematic motion is correct, we shall have to acknowledge a kind of motion which takes its place among the secondary qualities.

Chapter 2

The imprint of nature

A painting is a world; a photograph is of the world.

Stanley Cavell

There are people who say that the photographic method gives the cinema the power not merely to represent the world, but to present it. Exactly what this means may not be clear; I shall try to make it clear. But note that this claim (I'll call it the *Presentation Thesis*) and the argument it has engendered predates the cinema, having arisen first in connection with still photography. I'll begin by considering the claim just for the case of still photography. Later, I shall ask whether the claim is more plausible when applied to the moving images of cinema. Most people who argue for the Presentation Thesis restrict their claim to photographic images which have not been subject to substantial manipulation after exposure. I shall follow them in this.

One source of confusion has to be cleared up right away. In the Introduction I pointed to the representational duality of film. When we ask what is represented onscreen, there are two possible kinds of answers: "Ingrid Bergman and Cary Grant acting on a set" or "two spies trying to foil a Nazi plot". The claim that cinematography presents rather than represents the world must be understood as the claim that it presents the real world of actors, props, sets and locations, not the unreal world of fictional characters. If the thesis is right, film presents us with Ingrid Bergman and Cary Grant, not with the characters they play in the movie, for these characters do not exist. Photography may have special powers, but it does not have the power to turn nonbeing into being.

48

2.1 REPRESENTATIONAL MEDIA AND REPRESENTATIONAL ARTS

Painting is a representational medium; one thing – an object, scene or event – is represented by another thing, a pattern of paint. And painting is a representational art in the sense that the artistic or aesthetic values of a painting can derive, at least in part, from its representational features.

No one doubts that painting is a representational medium, and few these days deny that it is a representational art. But there are those who doubt one or both of the corresponding theses concerning photography, though which one is sometimes not clear. I shall argue that photography is representational, both as medium and as art.

Painting is a representational medium in that works within that medium can be – though they need not be – representational. We should not automatically assume, however, that all representational media allow the creation of works which are representational works of *art*; perhaps there are conditions on a medium in addition to its being representational which have to be satisfied before it will allow for the creation of works of art. What those extra conditions are is unclear, partly because the notion of art is itself unclear. I shall simply assume that there are two distinct questions to be answered: Is photography a representational medium, and is photography a representational art? I shall argue first that photography is a representational medium, and second that it is a representational art. That will leave us with the task of explaining the difference between photography and painting, which I hope to make clear by the end of this chapter.

2.2 PRESENTING AND REPRESENTING

Representations extend our epistemic access to things in the world; if they are reliable, representations give us information about things when those things are not directly accessible to us. And for some purposes a description, a detailed picture or some other kind of representation can be more informative than a direct perceptual examination of the thing itself; compare the difficulty of closely examining a furious and hungry tiger with closely examining a suitably detailed picture of one.

Other devices enhance our perceptual access to things themselves. Lenses help us see detail inaccessible to the naked eye. No one will say, I suppose, that lenses give us representations of things. They are, rather, aids to vision; they help us to see things themselves. They present the world to us rather than representing it; they just present the world in more detail than the naked eye can.

Do photographs present or represent? A certain tradition says they present. But this tradition has not, on the whole, been well served by its defenders. They have said things which must either be taken as so obscurely metaphorical as to be unhelpful, or as literal statements of what is obviously false. André Bazin, for example, said that "it is false to say that the screen is incapable of putting us 'in the presence of' the actor. It does so in the same way as a mirror ... but it is a mirror with a delayed reflection".[1] But the screen is not literally a mirror, and its action is not even very much like that of a mirror; nor are we really in the presence of the actor when we watch the screen.

The Presentation Thesis gets its clearest statement, and its most careful defence, in the hands of Kendall Walton, whose version is pleasingly straightforward: To see a photograph of X is to see X.[2] But to see a painting of X is not to see X. For one thing, paintings can be "of" things that do not and never did

---

[1] André Bazin, *What Is Cinema?* vol. 1, p. 97. See also Stanley Cavell, *The World Viewed*. For remarks critical of the tradition see Joel Snyder, "Photography and Ontology".

[2] "With the assistance of the camera, we can see not only around corners and what is distant or small; we can also see into the past. We see long-deceased ancestors when we look at dusty snapshots of them" (Walton, "Transparent Pictures", p. 251). For similar arguments, see Roger Scruton, "Photography and Representation". But Scruton, whose concern is mostly with the aesthetics of photography, does not offer so precise an account of the difference between photography and painting. See later in this chapter for an analysis of some of Scruton's arguments. For an examination of the history of this problem, see Patrick Maynard, "Drawing and Shooting: Causality in Depiction".

exist. You can see a painting of a dragon, but you cannot see a dragon. Nor can you see a photograph of a dragon.

While Walton's thesis is straightforward, his argument for it is subtle and depends on some technical notions in philosophy. Accordingly, I shall spend some time in laying out the argument and explaining the technical notions. The effort will be worth it; the argument is a good and an instructive one, even if, as I believe, it fails to establish its conclusion.

Walton's thesis is not Bazin's, if we take Bazin at his literal word. Walton's thesis is not that a photograph of *X* is, or is part of, *X*. It is not that, when we are in the presence of a photograph of *X*, we are in the presence of *X*. It is just that when we see a photograph of *X* we see *X*. Photographs are, Walton says, "Transparent"; we see through them to the things they are of (I'll call this the *Transparency Thesis* and sometimes just "Transparency"). I shall argue that the Transparency Thesis is not susceptible to many of the criticisms levelled against other versions of the Presentation Thesis. But I shall also argue that Walton has failed to establish a case for Transparency, and that what is correct in his argument can be accommodated by the view that photographs are representational, that seeing a photograph of *X* is a matter of seeing a representation of *X* rather than of seeing *X* itself. The representations photographs give us are certainly very different in kind from those we get by drawing and painting, and these differences are the product of differences between the ways photographs and hand-made images are produced. But a photographic image is a representation.

A remark on terminology: to avoid lengthy formulations I shall use certain expressions in a special way. I shall contrast "ordinary seeing" with "seeing photographs", and sometimes with "seeing paintings". In literal fact there is no contrast here, because we see photographs and paintings in just the same way we see other things – by looking at them. The intended contrast is between seeing an object or scene in the ordinary way, when the object is before your eyes, and seeing a photograph or painting *of* the object or scene.

2.3 PHOTOGRAPHS AS EVIDENCE

In the central and enthralling sequence of his otherwise somewhat pretentious *Blow Up*, Antonioni shows a photographer discovering, by the successive isolation and enlargement of ever-smaller sections of a photograph, the evidence that a murder has been committed. His photograph had recorded something of which he was unaware at the time he took it. Suppose we came to suspect that there was a dead body lying under a hedge on the day and in the place where Constable had painted *The Haywain*. It would be absurd to examine the canvas in minute detail in order to find evidence of the body there; at least, it would be absurd if we thought that Constable was unaware of the body's presence. Constable could have known about the body, and painted it in such a way that it would be very hard to spot unless you knew what you were looking for. But if he did not know about the body we shall not find evidence of it in the canvas, however hard we look. We cannot, it seems, discover things in paintings in the same way we can discover them in photographs.

In Hitchcock's *Rear Window*, a photographer confined by injury to his apartment discovers evidence that a murder has been committed in the building opposite. He discovers this, not by looking at photographs he or anyone else has taken of the events in that apartment, but by looking in through the window. The photographer might have taken photographs and found the evidence later by examining enlargements, but that was a twist to the tale Hitchcock chose to ignore or did not think of. What he could not have done was discover the evidence by looking at paintings of the apartment next door unless the painter intended to place the evidence in his picture.

Blow Up and *Rear Window*, between which there are obvious connections of influence, depend on strikingly similar ideas. One photographer looks at photographs of a scene and discovers evidence of a crime; the other looks at the scene itself and discovers the same thing. They do things by way of photography and sight that they could not do by way of painting or other handmade images.

Perhaps there is here the beginning of an argument that photographs are transparent. It is an argument which needs some underpinning.

2.4 COUNTERFACTUAL DEPENDENCE

There are rich patterns of *counterfactual dependence* between a photograph and the object photographed. Under certain conditions – "normal conditions" as I shall call them[3] – we can expect a photograph of X to display the visible properties of X in such a way that if X's visible properties were different, the photographic image would be correspondingly different. Had the building photographed been differently shaped, the image of the building on the photograph would have been correspondingly differently shaped. That is a case of counterfactual dependence between the appearance of X and the appearance of the photograph of X. In the same way, my visual experience when seeing the photograph is counterfactually dependent on the object photographed: if X's visible properties were different, my visual experience when seeing the photograph would be correspondingly different.

Ordinary seeing is like that too. When I see the building under normal conditions I have a visual experience which matches the scene before my eyes, and I do so in virtue of connections between the scene and the visual experience which are such that, if the scene were different in various ways, my visual experience would be correspondingly different.[4]

Counterfactual dependence alone will not distinguish photography from painting. Under certain conditions, a painting of

[3] "Normal" does not mean "average". Conceivably, a majority of all the photographs ever taken were so over- or underexposed as to put the relevant counterfactual connections in doubt. I take "normal conditions" in something like Ruth Garrett Millikan's sense: a normal condition for photography is a condition for its proper functioning. (See Millikan, *Language, Thought, and Other Biological Categories*.)

[4] See David Lewis, "Veridical Hallucination and Prosthetic Vision". The condition of counterfactual dependence may not be sufficient for seeing; see Martin Davies, "Function in Perception".

X will display the visible properties of X in such a way that, if those visible properties were different, the painted image would be correspondingly different. If the building were differently shaped the painter would paint a correspondingly different shape on the canvas. But in the case of the painting, and not in that of the photograph, counterfactual dependence is mediated by the beliefs of the artist. The appearance of the painting depends counterfactually on the appearance of the object because the beliefs of the painter are similarly dependent. If the painter were having an hallucination, thinking there was a pink elephant in front of him, his painting would display a pink elephant, not the actual scene before his eyes. With the photograph things are different. Because of the "mechanical" way photographs are made, it does not matter what the photographer thinks the object in front of the lens looks like; once the camera is set up and the film exposed, the camera records the scene before it. Imagine the same scene successively photographed and sketched. Now imagine that the scene had looked different in some way; in that case the photograph and the sketch would both look different. Now imagine that the scene had looked different *and the artist's beliefs about the scene's appearance remained the same.* In that case only the photograph would be different. Both the photograph and the sketch depend for their appearances on the appearance of the scene, but in the sketch and not in the photograph, that dependence is mediated by the artist's beliefs and other mental states.

We can extend this counterfactual dependence between scene and photograph/sketch to a similar dependence between the scene and my visual experience of the photograph/sketch. Had the scene been different my visual experience on looking at the photograph/sketch would have been different. But if the scene had been different and the artist's mental states the same, my experience of looking at the photograph would have been different, while my experience of seeing the sketch would have been the same. In the case of the photograph, the counterfactual dependence between the scene and the observer's visual experience is, we may say, independent of belief, but in the case of the sketch it is not. That is why we might find, in the photograph, evidence for something the photographer didn't suspect was there, while we could not find any such thing in a painting.

Suppose we consider a simpler case: I just look at the scene. Now there is counterfactual dependence between the scene and my visual experience. Is this counterfactual dependence like the photograph case, or like the sketch case? It is like the photograph case. Imagine that the scene I am looking at were different; my visual experience on seeing the scene would be different also, whether or not people's beliefs remain the same. My visual experience doesn't depend on anyone's belief.[5]

Call the counterfactual dependence exhibited by ordinary seeing and seeing photographs "natural counterfactual dependence", or simply "natural dependence".[6] Call the dependence exhibited by seeing paintings "intentional counterfactual dependence", or simply "intentional dependence". The argument for the transparency of photographs is this: what makes ordinary seeing a way of perceiving objects is its natural dependence. Since seeing photographs exhibits natural dependence also, it too is a way of perceiving objects. But seeing paintings exhibits intentional dependence, and so is not a way of perceiving objects.[7] Thus photography is transparent and painting is not.

[5] There are some technical difficulties connected with backtracking arguments here. Interested readers are invited to consult David Lewis, "Counterfactual Dependence and Time's Arrow".

[6] Note that my definition of "natural dependence" is partly stipulative. To say that a process exhibits natural dependence carries no implication that the process is naturally occurring, and many of the examples following in the text are of processes that are not naturally occurring, as with the working of thermometers, ammeters and mechanically generated descriptions.

[7] I take this to be Walton's central argument for the "sharp break" between painting and photography. There are occasional hints of other arguments in his paper. Thus, he emphasizes the "slippery slope" we are on, down from unaided vision, through seeing with the aid of telescopes and mirrors to seeing photographs (see Walton, "Transparent Pictures", p. 252, and idem, "Looking Again Through Photographs: A Response to Edwin Martin", especially pp. 805–806). But, as other critics have noted, we can ask what is to stop us going further down the slope, to seeing paintings. Presumably the answer is that we should stop at the point where natural dependence gives way to intentional dependence. In that case, the slippery-slope argument re-

I shall look at this argument in some detail. Before that, I shall briefly note one other argument for Transparency – and some arguments against it. These latter arguments are prevalent, but not persuasive.

2.5 INCONCLUSIVE ARGUMENTS

Certain of our intuitions about and reactions to photographs seem to be explained by Transparency. We have the sense, when looking at a photograph, of being in a particularly intimate relation to its subject – more intimate than when we look at a painting of the same subject. At least, that is so where photograph and painting are of comparable accuracy and definition. Photographs of atrocities affect us more than paintings of them do. And one who finds explicit sexuality offensive is more likely to be offended by a photograph with explicit sexual content than by a painting with such content (other things being equal). This is all explained by the Transparency Thesis: when we see photographs of atrocities or of sexual acts, we see atrocities, we see sexual acts. This is not the case when we see paintings with comparable subjects.[8]

But this argument cuts both ways. While it is true that a photograph of something distressing or offensive has greater impact than a comparable painting does, it is also true that seeing that thing directly (without the aid of a photograph) is more distressing or offending than seeing a photograph of it. The argument just given fails to put seeing directly and seeing photographs in one class and seeing pictorial representations in another. At best, it suggests a continuous scale of psychical effect, with photographs in the middle, between hand-made images and ordinary, unmediated seeing. Later, I shall explain this ordering in terms of the nature of photographic representation.

So one supplementary argument for Transparency fails. But some arguments against Transparency go wrong also.

lies for its force on the argument from natural dependence, and any weakness in the latter will be inherited by the former. So I ignore the slippery-slope argument.
[8] See Walton, "Transparent Pictures", pp. 247 and 255.

There seem to be clear cases of seeing photographs of things that are not cases of seeing the things they are photographs of. When I see a grossly over- or underexposed or ill-focused photograph of X, I surely do not see X.[9] The same can be said for unaided sight, when my visual equipment is impaired. Seeing an object is a matter of there being rich patterns of counterfactual dependence between my visual sensations and the object seen. For me properly to see X, my visual experiences must reflect a good number of the observable properties of the object, and be such that, if the object's observable properties had been different, my visual sensations would have been different. (There is vagueness in all this, but the concept of seeing is vague, so we can expect a realistic analysis of the concept to be vague to the same degree.) One whose eyes receive too much or too little light, or for whom the light is not focused by a lens, does not see objects in his surroundings. So too with seeing through photographs. If the photograph is uniformly black, its appearance fails to have the right kinds of counterfactual dependence on the appearance of the object, and so I do not see the object when I look at the photograph. But this does nothing to raise doubts about the transparency of "ordinary", well-focused and well-lit photos.[10]

Another objection to Transparency is that it entails that we can now see long-dead people because we can see photographs of them; but how can we now see people who do not now exist? This objection is countered by noting that with the naked eye we see stars so far away that the light from them has taken millions of years to get here – during which many of them will have ceased to exist.

A further objection to Transparency is that photographs do, in various ways, depend on mental states.[11] Usually, a photo-

[9] See, e.g., Edwin Martin, "On Seeing Walton's Great-Grandfather".

[10] See Walton, "Looking Again Through Photographs", p. 804.

[11] Thus Arnheim: "People who contemptuously refer to the camera as an automatic recording machine must be made to realize that even in the simplest photographic reproduction of a perfectly simple object, a feeling for its nature is required which is quite beyond any mechanical operation" (*Film as Art*, p. 19).

graph is the result of a deliberate exposure at a scene chosen, framed and focused on in a certain way, perhaps with the arrangement of objects and the lighting organized for the occasion. If the scene had not looked the way it did to the photographer, she would not have chosen to take the shot. Again, this is no objection to Transparency. For in *this* sense, ordinary seeing depends as much on intention. That I organize the furnishing and lighting in my study, together with the fact that I am so aesthetically sensitive that I refuse to look at anything disorganized or badly lit, does not show that I do not really see my study and its contents when I choose to look at it. Once I focus my eyes in a given direction it is not, from this point on, up to me what I see. The same holds for the photograph; once the shutter is opened and the film exposed, it is not up to me what appears on the negative.

We can see from this that the argument for Transparency is not that photography is an entirely mechanical activity. So it is irrelevant to point out against Transparency that most artistic human activities are mechanical after a certain point, as with piano playing: once you have hit the key, everything else in the sound-making process is done mechanically.[12] The advocate of Transparency need not be saying that photography is uncreative.

People who dispute the similarity between seeing photographs and ordinary seeing sometimes emphasize the relation between seeing and the path of an uninterrupted light ray. When we see in the ordinary way, even with the aid of lenses and mirrors, light emitted by or reflected from the object seen passes into our eyes. The lens or the mirror merely collects or deflects the light rays. And when we see those stars that no longer exist, the light from the stars enters our eyes. But with a photograph, things are different. The light reflected from the surface of the photograph into my eye is not the light that travelled from the object to the photographic plate. Should we give this as a reason for saying that seeing photographs and ordinary

[12] See Ted Cohen, "What's Special About Photography?" See also Jarvie, *Philosophy of the Film*, p. 109.

seeing are not much alike? No. First of all, light is not essential to seeing. It is true that, for our organs of sight to function unaided, light rays must be reflected from an object into our eyes. But there *could* be seeing in which light rays play no part. Richard Dawkins raises the possibility that bats might have visual experiences qualitatively similar to our own, but caused by their very different perceptual systems, which depend on bouncing sound waves off solid objects.[13] I understand this is not likely to be true of real bats,[14] but we can imagine batlike creatures complex enough for this to be a plausible story. Their visual sensations, if they exist, are caused by sound waves instead of by light – an odd idea, but not a confused one. Sonar is capable of giving information about objects in a creature's local environment which is sufficiently detailed and up-to-the-minute for the creature to build up a complex mental representation of its environment. This representation is informative in the way our visual representation of the environment is. Super bat sonar is not functionally dissimilar from our organs of sight; whether the representations it gives are qualitatively like our visual ones we cannot know, but there is no reason in principle why they could not be. Perhaps we shall invent a device which emits high-frequency sound waves, which can be fitted to humans as a prosthesis and which gives us visual sensations as a result. Then the blind would have their sight restored; they would "see" by means of sound waves.[15]

You may respond that, while seeing need not involve light rays, it must involve the uninterrupted transmission of something functionally equivalent (modulo the purposes of seeing) to a light wave, and sound waves might do the job. It is

[13] Richard Dawkins, *The Blind Watchmaker*.
[14] See Kathleen A. Akins, "What Is It Like to Be Boring and Myopic?"
[15] It is worth noting also that there are auditory microscopes – but I admit that there may be other problems connected with the claim that we see through such devices. See Ian Hacking, "Do We See Through a Microscope?" Hacking's answer to his question is yes. Also relevant here, as Marty Davies pointed out to me, is the phenomenon of "tactile vision". See, e.g., G. Guarniero, "Experience of Tactile Vision", and P. Bach-y-Rita et al., "Vision Substitution by Tactile Image Projection".

the idea of *uninterrupted transmission* that is important, not the particular thing that does the transmitting. That normal seeing and seeing through lenses and mirrors involves an uninterrupted light wave seems important because it is responsible for some of the informational features of seeing I have described in connection with bats and to which I shall return: the features of seeing which enable us to place ourselves in spatiotemporal relations to the things seen. That kind of information is obtained from sight because the light ray is uninterrupted (though there are other factors that contribute to this as well). And it is the maintenance of uninterrupted light transmission which enables us to track objects over time.

But what is responsible for an essential or quasi-essential property of X need not itself be an essential property of X: recall the functionalist's point that neural activity is not essential for a sentient creature; it is merely what realizes, in us, those functions required for sentience, functions which might be realized in other ways. So perhaps something other than uninterrupted transmission could give us the kind of information we normally get from sight – a simple transducer for instance. Suppose there is a screen which registers a pattern of light on one side and emits a qualitatively identical pattern of light from the other – all this done more or less instantaneously. Looking at the screen would be just like looking through a window at an object beyond. The screen interrupts the light ray, but I think we would say that when we look at it we see the object on the other side (assuming the mechanism preserves counterfactual dependence between our visual sensations and the appearance of the object beyond). That our way of seeing involves the passage of uninterrupted light does not imply that all ways of seeing must. What is important is that some mechanism make the required connections. Light propagation (uninterrupted or otherwise) is one such mechanism; there may be others.

So the fact that there is interruption of the light ray between the object and my eye when I see a photograph of the object is not itself an argument against the claim that I see the object when I see the photograph. However, interruption raises complex issues which will be dealt with later.

2.6 THE CONDITIONS FOR PERCEPTION

The primary argument for the transparency of photographs has been this: seeing photographs and seeing real things are both processes that display what I have called natural dependency, while painting does not display this feature. Seeing real things is, obviously, transparent: seeing a man, I see a *man*, not a representation of one. Seeing paintings isn't transparent: seeing a painting of a man, I do not see a man. So it looks as if natural dependency is the test of transparency. Seeing photographs passes the test, so seeing photographs is transparent.

But natural dependency is not the test of transparency, because natural dependence is neither necessary nor sufficient for transparency.

As things are, or as we presume they are, seeing real things is a process which displays natural dependence. But that is no necessary fact about seeing. Consider a case imagined by Kendall Walton: Blind Helen is provided with a prosthesis which gives her visual experiences matching the scene before her eyes. But the match is intentionally dependent: her brain is hooked up to a computer, which is operated by a neurosurgeon. By operating the computer, the surgeon gives Helen visual experiences which are just those she would have if she saw in the normal way. Because the dependence here is intentional, Walton claims this as a case in which Helen merely seems to see; the surgeon is seeing for her.[16] I disagree. The case involves an odd kind of seeing on Helen's part, but still a kind of seeing – as long as the surgeon's vigilance ensures counterfactual dependence between Helen's visual experience and the scene before her eyes.[17]

---

[16] Walton, "Transparent Pictures", p. 265.

[17] Perhaps it makes a difference to your intuitions about this case whether you assume the surgeon gives Helen visual experiences corresponding to what he (the surgeon) sees, or whether you assume he gives her visual experiences corresponding to what she would see if her eyes were functioning normally. As Walton describes the case, the surgeon gives Helen visual experiences "corresponding to what he [the surgeon] sees" ("Transparent Pictures", p. 265), and I admit at least some doubt about whether Helen could properly

If you say Helen is not really seeing in this situation, that may be because it is difficult to imagine how the surgeon could control the process to ensure the appropriate degree of counterfactual dependence. Another case, designed to screen out that factor, will make my point more clearly. Suppose Malebranche was right and there are no genuine causal powers in natural objects. God mediates between the scene and our visual experiences, acting, in his benevolence, to maintain counterfactual dependence. Under this supposition, we would, as Malebranche put it, "see all things in God" – but we would still see. We would see by a process which exhibits intentional dependence. (If God's omnipotence seems to you a barrier to ascribing to him actions and intentions in the way we ascribe them to mortals, think of God as just *very* powerful, but not as omnipotent.) So natural dependence is not necessary for perception.

Is natural dependence sufficient for perception? Walton points out that it is not.[18] A machine which mechanically generates descriptions of objects does not enable me to perceive those objects, even though there is natural dependence between features of the object and the descriptions generated.[19] So what makes seeing photographs a way of perceiving objects but reading mechanically generated descriptions not a way of doing so? Perhaps it is a matter of similarities between investigating things by examining pictures of them (either photographs or drawings) and investigating them by looking at them directly.[20] As Walton notes, the discriminations we find it difficult to make in cases of ordinary seeing and seeing photographs are quite different from those we find difficult in examining a written description. A house can easily be mistaken for a barn, and a photograph of

---

be said to see in that case. But if Helen is given visual experiences corresponding to what she would see if her eyes were functioning, it is much clearer that she does genuinely see, and under conditions of intentional dependence.

[18] Walton, "Transparent Pictures", p. 271: "A process of discrimination counts as perceptual *only if* its structure is thus analogous to the structure of the world" (my italics).

[19] Ibid., p. 270.

[20] Ibid.

a house can easily be mistaken for a photograph of a barn. But it is easier to mistake "house" for "hearse" than for "barn". The errors of ordinary seeing and seeing photographs are explainable by real similarities between things, but the errors of reading are not: a house is really more like a barn than like a hearse.[21] It is these differences between pictures and descriptions which allow photographs, but not mechanically generated descriptions, to give us perceptual access to things.[22]

We can now summarize the argument for Transparency. A mode of access to information about things counts as perceptual if and only if it (i) exhibits natural dependence and (ii) preserves real similarity relations. Painting fails to satisfy (i), and the mechanically generated description fails to satisfy (ii), so neither is a perceptual mode of access. Photography satisfies both, so it is a perceptual mode of access. Seeing photographs enables us to see the things the photographs are of. So photography is transparent.

I have already argued that (i) is no necessary condition for perceptual access (recall Malebranchean seeing). Nor are (i) and (ii) jointly sufficient for it. The length of the mercury column in a thermometer depends naturally on the amount of ambient heat. And because small variations in the level of heat correspond to small variations in the length of the column, the discriminatory errors we make when looking at a thermometer are similar to those we make when we perceive how hot something is by feeling it on the skin; it is hard to make very small temperature discriminations either by feel or by sight. So thermometers don't "scramble the real similarity relations" between temperatures.[23] If feeling (a degree of) warmth is a way of per-

---

[21] "Descriptions scramble the real similarity relations" between things, while visual experience, either direct or by means of photographs, preserves them (ibid., p. 271).

[22] Ibid., p. 273.

[23] Most thermometers are gradated, and we judge temperature by matching the length of the column with a numerical mark. In such cases, reading a thermometer is much like reading a description. But if the gradations on my thermometer have worn away and I have to judge temperature by height estimation, we would hardly say that I perceive heat when I see the mercury column.

ceiving heat, then, by the argument for Transparency, seeing the length of the column should be a way of perceiving heat also, which it is not. What I perceive is the length of the column, from which I infer the level of ambient heat.[24]

It might be argued in reply that there is a difference between seeing photographs and seeing thermometers that explains why photographs enable us to see people but thermometers do not enable us to see heat. There is, after all, only a patchy and unsystematic overlap between the errors involved in length estimation and those involved in heat perception. As light fades I will be prone to more errors in length estimation, but this will not affect my perception of heat. My perception of heat will be subject to significant error if I have a fever, but my estimation of column length will not (not, at least, in the same way). Comparing the perception of column length with the perception of heat, we find the overlap in discriminatory error insufficient to say that perception of the one is perception of the other. But in the case of seeing photographs and ordinary seeing, the overlap is sufficient for us to say that we perceive an object when we see a photograph of it, just as we do when we see it in the ordinary way.

There are two reasons why we ought not to accept this argument. First, no degree of discriminatory overlap, however great, could force us to the conclusion that seeing a photograph is a case of perceiving the object itself. There are pairs of objects *A* and *B* for which the following holds: (i) *B* exhibits natural dependence on *A*; (ii) the characteristic pattern of discriminatory error involved in examining *B* is exactly as for *A*; and (iii) perceiving *B* is not a case of perceiving *A*. By way of an example,

---

[24] I don't say we *could not* perceive heat in any way other than via the heat receptors at the skin. If our eyes were so constructed that we had monochromatic vision, and things looked darker the hotter they were, then perhaps we would *see* heat (see Paul M. Churchland, *Scientific Realism and the Plasticity of Mind*). Snakes, apparently, see heat (as Marty Davies pointed out to me; see Peacocke, *Sense and Content*, p. 90n; and E. Newman and P. Hartline, "The Infrared 'Vision' of Snakes"). I say only that we *do* perceive heat through our skin, and not by looking at thermometers.

consider another Malebranche-inspired case.[25] A and B are two clocks. The orientation of the hands of A governs that of the hands of B by means, let us suppose, of radio signals.[26] I am looking at clock B; clock A is out of sight. There is natural dependence between my visual experience of clock B and the appearance of clock A. If clock A's hands had been in a different orientation at the moment of my seeing clock B, the orientation of clock B's hands would have been correspondingly different, and so would my visual experience. But there is no plausibility in the claim that I see, or perceive in any way, clock A when I see clock B.[27] Degree of discriminatory overlap cannot be decisive for whether a naturally dependent mode of access to information about an object is a way of perceiving it. So even if the errors of discrimination characteristic of seeing photographs were the same as those for ordinary seeing, it would not follow that seeing a photograph of an object was a way of perceiving the object itself.

The second reason we should not accept the argument is this. Part of the argument we are considering is that, from the point of view of discriminatory error, looking at thermometers is not sufficiently like sensing heat through the skin for us to say that looking at thermometers is a way of perceiving heat. But a parallel argument will establish that looking at photographs of things is not a way of perceiving those things. From the point of view of discriminatory error, how much overlap is there between ordinary seeing and seeing photographs? Not much; not

[25] Malebranche inspired, but really not much like his occasionalism, or the pre-established harmony to which that doctrine gave rise. Here the one clock governs the other, rather than both being governed by a common cause. I adjust the example so as to bring it closer to the case of photography. Object and photograph are linked not just by a common cause; the object is one of the causes of the photograph.

[26] Assume all this is done by a mechanical process and involves no intentional states.

[27] Other examples meeting the same conditions come readily to mind. The replication of DNA molecules (by a process that displays natural dependence) gives rise to two "daughter" molecules qualitatively identical to the original one. In examining one of the daughters we are not perceiving the parent.

enough for us to agree that seeing photographs is strikingly analogous to ordinary seeing. There are kinds of judgements we make in cases of ordinary seeing – judgements subject to various failures of discrimination – which have no counterparts in the case of seeing photographs.[28]

With ordinary seeing, we get information about the spatial and temporal relations between the object seen and ourselves. We learn not merely that some possible state of affairs is actual, but that it is actual here and now. Call this kind of information "egocentric information". That seeing provides us with egocentric information is connected to the fact that seeing is perspectival. I could not place myself in the world if I saw the world from no particular perspective. And from what perspective I see things depends on the location of my body – or at least of my eyes – relative to the things I see.

In seeing, we often make errors about egocentric information. It's easy to be mistaken about the distance of a star (think of Ptolemy's estimates), and small mistakes about the distances and directions of much closer objects are common. Mistakes concerning temporal egocentric information are harder to make; it is hard to be mistaken about whether some directly visible condition holds *now*. But for astronomical distances we are prone to think, mistakenly, that what we see tells us how the seen object is now.[29] Photographs, on the other hand, do not convey egocentric information; seeing a photograph does not tell me anything much about where the object photographed is in relation to me. Since photographs convey no egocentric information, there is no question of my failing to discriminate properly concerning the egocentric information conveyed by one.[30]

[28] These and other differences are discussed by Nigel Warburton in "Seeing Through 'Seeing Through Photographs' ".
[29] Unless, as David Lewis suggests, "the stars, as I now see them, are not straightforwardly past; for lightlike connection has as good a claim as simultaneity-in-my-rest-frame to be the legitimate heir to our defunct concept of absolute simultaneity" ("Veridical Hallucination", p. 277n).
[30] Photographs can serve, along with information from other sources, in an inference to egocentric information. If I know where and when the shot was taken, and where I am now (and what the time is now), I may infer that the scene depicted stands in a certain spatiotemporal relation to my current time

Ordinary seeing also enables us to track objects and processes across time. As long as I am seeing the object, changes in its position and visible appearance will be reflected in changes in my visual experience of it. There are discriminatory errors we are liable to make in processing this kind of information. We may think it took the egg three minutes to boil when in fact it took three minutes and four seconds. We can be mistaken about exactly what happened during a time interval, thinking the object changed its shape, colour or position in one way when in fact it changed in a slightly different way. None of this has any counterpart in photography, since photographs do not give us temporally extended information.[31]

When we achieve a proper perspective on the range of discriminatory errors characteristic of vision, we find only a narrow overlap between ordinary seeing and seeing photographs. The overlap is no greater than that between the discriminatory errors characteristic of perceiving heat and seeing thermometers.[32] There are no grounds here for saying perception of a photograph is perception of the object photographed.

In that case photographs really are not like lenses and mirrors. We get a sense of the difference between lenses and mirrors on the one hand and photographs on the other if we compare the situation of a creature that has, by gift of nature, lenses or mirrors as aids to sight, with the situation of a creature which

slice. But the egocentric information available in ordinary seeing is not obtained by inference from the visual experience together with other information. Clearly, there are all sorts of inferential paths to egocentric information which do not count as perceptual paths.

[31] Photographs – particularly a series of photographs – can serve to inform us about temporal change, when we combine them with information from other sources. But as with egocentric information, the inferential paths are not perceptual paths. `

[32] It is instructive to compare the case of prosthetic vision via the surgeon (Section 2.6) with the following case. The surgeon gives me visual experiences, but he does not ensure a match between my visual experiences and the scene before my eyes. Rather, he gives me visual experiences corresponding to a collection of photographs he has taken at various times and places, quite unrelated to the time and place I now occupy. I have no inclination to say that in this case my sight has been restored.

has visual experiences approximating the condition of one who sees photographs. Suppose there are creatures which have evolved little telescopes in front of (or perhaps as part of) their eyes, or that live in a permanently dark environment but which have evolved periscopes which reach up to a level where there is usable light. We would hardly doubt that these creatures could see. Nor would we doubt that they do, in fact, see under conditions normal for their proper functioning; we would not say they had the capacity to see but were prevented from doing so by the presence of their biologically made lenses and mirrors. Suppose, on the other hand, there are creatures who have evolved cameras instead of eyes. Instead of receiving a continuous flow of visual information from their surroundings, they have a device which takes a snapshot of the local environment, "prints" it on the photographic analogue of the retina, and sends the visual information to the brain, which then – by a process as mysterious in them as seeing is in us – produces a visual experience, that of a static image which may last, say, five minutes before it fades. (To make these creatures' organs more closely analogous with our experience of photographs we would have to assume that there is no direct correlation between when and where the snapshot is taken and when it comes to the creature's consciousness: suppose the photographic images are jumbled so that the creature's visual experience now might equally be the result of a shot taken five minutes ago or five years ago, and that there is nothing in the visual experience itself to tell the creature which it is. And we must also suppose that a shot could be a shot of something that is not now in the creature's local environment but of something in a distant part of the world.)

Does this second creature see things in the external world? I think not. It has visual impressions. But the visual impressions it has do not relate the creature to the world in a way that would justify our saying that the creature sees the world. It is like a person who sees only photographs of things and not the things themselves. Photographic images, for all their sharing of counterfactual dependence with ordinary seeing, belong to a medium very different from lenses and mirrors; so we have good reason to say lenses and mirrors are transparent, while photographs are not.

2.7 PUTTING MOVEMENT IN THE PICTURE

How would the argument I have given against Transparency be affected if we considered cinematic images instead of still photographs? The significant difference is that with cinematic images we do, or can, get transtemporal information; watching a cinematic image, we are in a position to judge, just by watching, that a certain process took so long to occur, and that one process or event occurred before or after another. That is one way in which seeing cinematic images is like – and seeing still photographs unlike – ordinary seeing. Nevertheless, cinematic images are like photographs in failing to give us egocentric information. Watching cinematic images, we do not get information about the relation of what is there depicted to our own spatiotemporal position.

Does the presence, in a cinematic image, of transtemporal information make such images transparent? I'm not sure. Perhaps we are now in an area where the concept of perception is vague, and there simply is no answer to whether we perceive things when we see cinematic images of them. All the same, I'm inclined to say this: the absence of egocentric information in the cinematic case is a significant factor that dominates the presence of transtemporal information. The function of seeing is to give us egocentric information.[33] If it did not do that it would not contribute to our survival and thence to its own flourishing. Seeing cinematic images does not retain that crucial ecological connection with the environment; that justifies us in saying that cinematic images are not transparent.

What then of mirrors? We are happy to say we see things in

---

[33] David Marr wrote: "What does it mean to see? The plain man's answer (and Aristotle's too) would be, to know what is where by looking" (*Vision*, p. 3). It is clear, I think, that "what is where" means in this case "what is where in relation to the one who sees".

mirrors, but if the mirrors are confusingly iterated, with each reflection reflected yet again, we can be in a position where we get little or no idea about the present spatial position of the object relative to our own position. So mirrors are transparent, even though, on occasion, they do not convey egocentric information. So my case against the transparency of cinematic images collapses. But do we *always* see in mirrors? I think not. The reason we are happy to say we see things in mirrors is that we think of mirrors as functioning "normally" so that they *do* retain egocentric spatial information; this is especially the case since the thing we most often see in a mirror is ourselves! If our normal experience of mirrors was of confusing iterations that denied us that information, we would be less inclined to say they were transparent and more inclined to say that what we see in them are representations.

Earlier I mentioned a widely held view which I said was incorrect: that seeing requires the existence of an uninterrupted light ray. We can now see why it is both plausible and incorrect. Interruption to the light ray normally results in there being an unpredictable spatiotemporal gap between one ray transmission and the next, thereby destroying egocentric information. The transducer I described is an exception exactly because it allows no such gap and hence preserves egocentric information. That's why it is transparent; by means of it we see things beyond the screen. Interrupted transmission will typically result in loss of egocentric information, but not always.

2.8 THE SIGNIFICANCE OF SIMILARITY

The friends of Transparency might agree with my arguments, and protest that they do nothing to undermine the substance of their thesis. For I have agreed that seeing photographs and ordinary seeing are alike in sharing natural dependence, and that both of these are, in this respect, unlike seeing paintings. Isn't that enough to establish a fundamental commonality between seeing photographs and ordinary seeing, and a sharp break between seeing photographs and seeing paintings? It is not. Not every similarity is fundamental, nor every difference a sharp break. I have argued that, while photography is naturally dependent and painting is not, this difference does not make painting and photography radically different, the one a form of representation and the other not.

This is not to say that the natural–intentional dependence distinction is unimportant, but merely that it does not mark the divide between perceiving things and perceiving mere representations of things. Instead, it marks the distinction between two kinds of representations. Thermometers give us signs, or representations, of heat, not perceptual access to heat itself. They, and other "mechanical" measuring devices like barometers, ammeters and mechanically generated descriptions, provide us with what we might call *natural* representations, since they display natural dependence.[34] Paintings, intentional uses of language, dumb shows and the like also give us signs or representations – *intentional* representations, since they display intentional dependence. Representations, both natural and intentional, give us information about things without giving us perceptual access to them. The two kinds of representations differ from one another in how that information is generated.

Now we see where the argument from natural dependence to Transparency goes wrong. That photographs are not intentional representations does not mean that they fail to be representations altogether. Once we make a distinction within the class of representations between the natural and the intentional, we can do justice to our intuition that photographs and paintings are different without having to go to the extreme of saying photographs give us perceptual contact with the things they are photographs of. We may say instead that photographs are natural representations and paintings intentional ones.

---

[34] They are *natural* representations because the processes by which they function exhibit natural dependence. They are *representations* because they are used as such by us. I am not suggesting that something can be regarded as a representation (natural or otherwise) without reference to human intention.

2.9 THE AESTHETICS OF PHOTOGRAPHY

If we do conclude from all this that directly seeing a building and seeing a photograph or cinematic image of one are significantly different activities, rather than just different ways of seeing the building, certain other arguments concerning photography and film collapse. Roger Scruton argues that "representation can never be achieved by photography alone". He asks us to compare the photographer with someone who artfully places a frame in a street so as to give an aesthetically pleasing view of certain of its buildings and their interrelations. And he asks, "How could it be argued that what I see in the frame is not the street itself but a representation of it?"[35] I agree that the scene inside the frame is not a representation of the street. It does not follow that a *photograph* of the street is not a representation of the street. For that to follow we would need a convincing argument that photography is transparent, and I do not believe there is one.

Another claim Scruton makes is that the "brute" dependence of photographs on what is photographed means they are incapable of expressing thoughts about their subjects. A picture expresses a thought when we can see that thought as having guided the production of the picture; but the kind of guiding that is relevant here is absent in photography, because of brute dependence.[36]

The only plausible sense in which photographs are brute dependent on their subjects is the one I have examined in connection with Walton's argument: photographs are naturally dependent on their subjects. And that kind of dependence is consistent with there being, and our recognizing, all kinds of intentions that have played a role in the production of the photograph. For example, the photographer exerts intentional control in her choice of angle, lighting and subject. Scruton is aware that photography is in various ways under the agent's control,

[35] Roger Scruton, "Photography and Representation", p. 120.
[36] "With an ideal photograph it is neither necessary nor even possible that the photographer's intention should enter as a serious factor in determining how the picture is seen" (ibid., p. 111).

and that the outcome of the photographing process is dependent on various decisions the photographer makes, but he finds these facts insignificant when weighed against the (supposed) transparency of photographs. We could, he says, introduce an art of mirrors, which by their cunning placement, reveal what they mirror in aesthetically interesting ways. But this would not be a representational art, nor would photography be one. The answer to this is the same as that to the analogy of the framed building: the mirror art would not be a representational art because a mirror is not a representation. Mirrors are genuinely transparent (so long as they retain egocentric information) whereas, I have argued, photographs are not. So nothing follows for the case of photography from that of mirrors.

Scruton also claims that the emotional or aesthetic qualities of a photograph derive directly from the qualities of what it represents; a photograph is sad because its subject is sad, touching because its subject is touching.[37] Not always, and certainly not always in film. A photograph of people obviously happy can be sad, if the photograph suggests that these people have little reason to be happy, or because we know that their happiness is a prelude to sorrow. Scruton might argue that in that case the subject itself is sad, because the subject is, say, happy people who will or should be unhappy.[38] But if, as Scruton supposes, the sadness of the photograph has to be derivative on the sadness of its subject, the photograph can be sad, or express sadness, only if, as a matter of fact, those people will or should be unhappy. And a photograph of smiling people can be composed in such a way as to look sad, or to express the photographer's sadness or the sadness she intends to convey, irrespective of whether the photographer is *right* in thinking these people will or should be happy.

It might be hard, in any particular case of a photograph or cinematic image, to assign the effect of sadness as between subject and composition; perhaps there will always be some grounds for saying that the sadness derives exclusively from the

---

[37] Ibid., p. 115.
[38] "Should" in the sense of "having reason to be".

subject. But if, as I think we should, we reject the Transparency Thesis, we undercut the motivation for this move. Someone who holds Scruton's view ought to ask: apart from the claim that photography is transparent, is there any reason to insist that the expressive quality of a photographic image is dependent on its subject in a way that the expressive quality of a painting is not? One answer might be that the photographer/cinematographer lacks control over her medium by comparison with the painter, and that this lack of control is a barrier to expression. Indeed, Scruton says that a photographer who aims for aesthetically significant representation must also aim to control detail; but detail is hard to control in a photograph, and if it is controlled there are "few ways in which such intentions can be revealed in the photograph".[39] The point seems to be that an audience cannot tell, in looking at a photograph, which elements of detail were determined by intention, which by accident. Again, this simply is not true of all photographs and certainly not of all cinematic images. A photographer can, under certain circumstances, control detail very finely, and can make it clear that the detail was controlled. All that can be said is that detail is easier to control in painting, where each brush stroke is, ideally, the product of intention, and that, in painting, the intention to control is easier to signal. But such an argument cannot establish that photography is not a representational art: at most it establishes that it is less rich in its representational possibilities than painting is.

Perhaps it doesn't even establish that. There are aesthetically relevant features of works of art that depend for their effect partly upon our recognition that they are difficult to achieve. In examples of Chinese calligraphy, we admire the elegance and smoothness of the brushwork, and we do so partly because we realize how difficult it is to achieve elegance and smoothness in a medium that requires the artist to work very fast – any hesitation will result in a blotch of ink. It would be a misunderstanding of aesthetic value to suggest that calligraphy would be a better art if it employed a medium in which a greater degree of control could be exercised in the production of a character; it

[39] Scruton, "Photography and Representation", p. 117.

would equally be an error to suggest that a synthesizer is a better musical instrument than a violin because it is capable of producing a sequence of notes faster than any violinist could. An improvement in the degree of control possible for an artistic medium does not automatically mean an improvement in that medium's expressive power.

2.10 PHOTOGRAPHY, PAINTING AND THE REAL

A significant fact about photography and cinematography – one that distinguishes both rather strongly from painting – is said to be this: just as one can see only that which exists, there can be photographs only of things that exist.[40] There can be a painting of a unicorn, but no photograph or cinematic image of one, since there are no unicorns.

How significant is this difference? Allow me to stipulate that the phrase "the painting P is of M" is to mean the same as "M was the model for the painter of P". This stipulation will bring our use of "the painting is of M" into line with our use of the phrase "the photograph is of M", in the sense that the truth of each will require (i) that M's presence is a significant causal factor in the production of the photographic or painted image, and consequently (ii) that M exists. In this sense, no photograph, and no painting, can be of a nonexistent.

I grant this is not how we normally use the expression "the painting is of M", since we allow that a painting can be of something which does not exist, or of something other than the model, as with biblical subjects. But my point is that there is a relation in painting, call it what you will, between painting and model, that is as existentially committed as the relation between a photograph and what it is of; I have chosen to call it the "of" relation.

---

[40] Seeing through photographs "is like the ordinary variety [of seeing] in that only what exists can be seen"; Walton, "Transparent Pictures", p. 254. See also Scruton, "Photography and Representation", p. 112: "If a photograph is a photograph of a man, there is some particular man of whom it is a photograph."

My opponent might grant this, and still insist there is an asymmetry here: as I use the expression "of", *being of*, and *representing* are relations that come apart in painting, but not in photography. A painting can represent something other than what it is of in my sense; and a painting can represent something without being of (in my sense) anything. But a photograph must be of something and what it is of is what it represents. A photograph cannot represent a unicorn, and if I dress someone up to look like Saint Anne and photograph her, I do not end up with a representation of Saint Anne, but a representation of (in other words a photograph of) the model so dressed up; I end up with a representation of a representation.

Consider the photograph of the model dressed as Saint Anne. I think it is merely prejudice to say this cannot be a representation of Saint Anne. An exactly similar prejudice might have been evident at the time people started using models to paint pictures of biblical characters; a prejudice that would have showed itself in the insistence that the painting represents the model and not Saint Anne. We've now lost that prejudice (if we ever had it) in painting, through habituation to the conventions of the medium. The only argument I can think of in the case of photography is that the relation of natural dependence between model and photograph somehow precludes the photograph representing anything other than the model. But consider an analogous case: the craft of hand shadows. By setting my hands in a certain way and having their shadow appear on a wall, I produce a representation of Abraham Lincoln.[41] Here there is natural dependence, just as in photography, between the disposition of my hands and the shape of the shadow on the wall.[42] Following the logic of the argument just given, we should say that it is merely my hands that are represented, and not Lincoln at all. That is not very plausible. Nor is it plausible to deny that in cinema we have representations of the story's characters. Natural dependence ought not to preclude a photograph

[41] I take the example of shadow play from Maynard, "Drawing and Shooting".
[42] That is, if we keep fixed the beliefs of the shadow maker, the appearance of the shadow will depend counterfactually on the disposition of my hands.

or a cinematic image representing something other than what it is of.

One difference we must allow between photography and cinematography on the one hand, and painting on the other: while every photograph is of something, not every painting is. But this is no argument for the transparency of photography, for the same holds of any natural sign. In the sense in which every photograph is of something, every pattern of rings on the cross-section of a tree is also of something: it is of the age of the tree. But for all that, the rings are still *representations* of the age. And when we say a photograph is always of something we mean a photograph produced in the standard way – it is possible to draw or scratch on the negative, or to manipulate light so that it functions much as a paintbrush would, in which case you have a photograph that represents without being of anything. So the fact that photographs, as standardly produced, are always of something cannot be a reason for denying them the status of representations, unless we are prepared also to say, implausibly, that the cross-section of the tree does not represent the tree's age.

So is there nothing special about the photographic method, nothing distinctive about it as a medium of representation? There is something special about photography and cinematography: natural dependence. Because a photograph is naturally dependent on its subject, we may feel that its subject is more intimately connected with the photograph than it would be with a painting, and more intimately connected with us when we look at the photograph. But the natural dependence of photographs and of cinematic images does not take them outside the realm of representation. Photographs are natural representations, or natural signs of things, as footprints are natural signs of the people who make them, and the pattern of rings on the cross-section of a tree is a natural sign of the age of the tree. Paintings are nonnatural, intentionally mediated, signs.

In further ways, painting and photography might be representationally asymmetric; there might be representational features paintings can have but photographs cannot, or vice versa, and there might be representationally dependent values paintings can have but photographs cannot, or vice versa. Painting and photography may both be representational media, and representational arts, even while there are considerable differences between them from the points of view of representation and of art. But none of these differences between them entail that photographic and cinematographic images are transparent.

I haven't *established* that photographs or cinematic images are merely representations of things. To prove that we don't see people when we see photographs of them would require me to provide necessary and sufficient conditions for perception and to show that seeing photographs of things doesn't satisfy those conditions. But all the available candidates for such necessary and sufficient conditions are too controversial to carry much weight in the present dispute. My strategy has been defensive. I start from the position of one who believes photographs and cinematic images, like paintings, are representations, that we perceive representations of things when we see photographs, and not the things themselves. The arguments for Transparency reviewed here do nothing to undermine this view. In so far as the arguments point to a difference between photography and painting, I accommodate the difference by saying that photographs are natural representations while paintings are intentional ones. And this is no ad hoc move. We commonly recognize a distinction within the class of representations between the natural and the intentional. Paintings, gestures and acts of speech are all intentional representations; thermometers, barometers and the ringed cross-section of a tree are all natural representations – of temperature, weather and the tree's age, respectively.[43]

---

[43] The tree rings and the thermometer are favoured examples in the development of causal theories of representation. See, e.g., Dennis Stampe, "Toward a Causal Theory of Linguistic Representation"; and Robert Stalnaker, *Inquiry*, p. 12.

Chapter 3
Realism

The guiding myth, then, inspiring the invention of cinema, is ... a re-creation of the world in its own image.

André Bazin

In Chapter 1, I distinguished three theses about cinema: Illusionism, Transparency and Likeness. I have been hard on the first two. In this chapter I want to defend the thesis of Likeness, which has been under attack for a while now from those who reject the notion of likeness or resemblance between images and the things they are images of, and who stress the artifice, the conventionality, the "codedness" of cinema. This is one aspect of their rejection of film realism. I, on the other hand, hold that Likeness is a defensible version of film realism. I also want to defend the claim that there are styles of film making which are especially realistic in the sense explicated by Likeness; long-take, deep-focus style is a notable example. But I want to avoid a misunderstanding. My defence of Likeness is metaphysical, not aesthetic. I am not advocating that film makers adopt styles which, like long-take, deep-focus style, attempt to exploit the possibilities for realism in film. I am arguing that Likeness is a coherent thesis, and that it is possible to achieve a considerable degree of this kind of realism in film. Whether you think that is a worthwhile project is another matter.

First I shall offer a general theory of pictorial representation, or depiction, according to which depictions are like the things they depict. In this sense depictions are, to various degrees, realistic. The characterization of depiction I shall give will allow us to say that film depicts space and time; film does, or can, represent space and time realistically.

3.1 DEPICTIONS

Though philosophers have denied it, certain pictures do seem to be like their subjects; not so like them as to be indistinguishable, except under very peculiar circumstances, but like them nonetheless. Indeed, the denials of philosophers in this regard have an air of paradox. The likeness we think there is between some pictures and the things they are of is, of course, a matter of likeness of appearance; no one is (or should be) claiming that people and pictures of people belong to the same natural kind, or have the same essence. So what is claimed is that certain pictures and their subjects *appear* alike; that the experience of looking at the picture is in certain respects like that of looking at the subject. But how could philosophers be better placed than ordinary folk when it comes to judging what experiences are like others? Denying that pictures and their subjects can be alike in this sense seems well beyond the competence of a philosopher.

The sense in which pictures (or, as I shall sometimes say, depictions) can be like their subjects is not merely a matter of being "true to" the subjects. A description of a man can be accurate, without the experience of reading the description being anything like the experience of looking at the man. There can be accuracy without likeness, as a description can be accurate without being like its subject. When we read a description, we may recognize what is being described, and when we look at a depiction we may recognize what it depicts, but we do these things in fundamentally different ways. To comprehend the description I deploy my linguistic capacities, my understanding of the semantics and syntax of the language. To see that the picture is a picture of a horse, I deploy my horse-recognition capacities. That is, I use the same capacity to recognize the picture of a horse that I use to recognize a horse.[1]

We recognize objects when we see them by recognizing cer-

---

[1] I think Noël Carroll was the first person to give this characterization of realism; see his "Power of Movies". See also Flint Schier, *Deeper into Pictures*. I follow Schier's talk of "triggering recognitional capacities".

tain of their spatial features. I count shape, aspects of shape, colour, size and position as spatial features, and I count a conjunction of spatial features as itself a spatial feature. Among spatial features I also count higher-order features – spatial relations between spatial features, for instance. In this very general sense of spatial feature, our capacity to recognize an object when we see it must be a capacity to recognize some of its spatial features.[2] It might be a disjunctive capacity: being able to recognize an F might consist in associating a certain list of features $a_1, \ldots, a_n$ with the concept of an F in such a way that detection of the presence of any one of the a_i's in an object is sufficient to enable you to recognize that object as an F.

So my visual capacity to recognize a horse is the capacity to associate some visual feature of what I see with the concept *horse,* thereby enabling me to bring what I see under that concept. In that case, when I see that the picture depicts a horse I must associate some visual feature of what I see, namely a picture, with the concept *horse.* What the picture of the horse has in common with the horse is some spatial feature which triggers my horse-recognition capacity. It is in that sense that the picture and the horse are alike. And their being alike in this respect is consistent with them being very different in other respects. Some people never tire of telling us, for example, that pictures are flat and horses are not. So what? The likeness between picture and horse need not be likeness in any respect that is important for the horse. It need not be a matter of overall likeness explicable, say, in terms of sharing a preponderance of features picked from some favoured class. The likeness might be quite insignificant or artificial when judged from any perspective other than that of someone who wants to recognize horses and pictures of them by looking. But for such a person, the likeness is a significant one.

I said that the likeness between picture and horse is one of appearance, and I have said that this likeness of appearance is a matter of their sharing properties significant for our recognition of horses. Someone might object that two objects which

---

[2] See Jerry Fodor, ''Meaning and the World Order''.

share a property that triggers our horse-recognition capacities could appear quite different from one another. After all, plenty of things share certain spatial features without appearing similar. If that is the case, the likeness between horse and picture could not be explained entirely in terms of sharing recognitionally significant properties, and there would be some missing ingredient in my account of depiction.

In fact, no ingredient is missing. When we say that horse and picture look alike, we acknowledge also that they look quite different. We don't, for example, mistake the one for the other. Indeed, it can sometimes be very hard for us to identify explicitly the respect in which they look the same. There *is* a sense in which, while horse and picture trigger the same recognitional capacity, they look different. Their also looking (in some way) alike is, I suggest, *just* a matter of their triggering the same recognitional capacity. In the language of Australian materialism: saying that horse and picture are alike means just this: "something is going on in me when I look at the picture like what goes on in me when I look at a horse." What is going on, although most of us do not know it, is that our horse-recognition capacity is being triggered. Sometimes, when we recognize that the picture is of a horse, we can point to some spatial feature that horse and picture have in common, and that feature may indeed be the one which triggers the relevant capacity. But identifying such a feature is not necessary for us to judge that horse and picture are alike. Also, recall that the capacity to recognize an object of a given kind might be sensitive to a disjunction of properties. So the spatial property of the picture which is responsible for triggering my horse-recognition capacity need not be the same feature which would, if I were looking at the horse itself, trigger that same capacity. All that is required is that both spatial properties belong to the same favoured disjunction; both will, in the right circumstances, trigger my capacity to recognize a horse.

If pictures of horses trigger horse-recognition capacities, doesn't that mean that pictures of horses fool us into thinking that we are seeing horses when we see them? Is this not the discredited view that depictions of things are, by their very natures, devices which create in us the illusion that we are seeing the things themselves? In reply I say that having your horse-recognition capacity triggered and judging that there is a horse in front of you are different things. They differ as to the level at which these operations are conducted in the mind. Judging that there is a horse in front of me is something that I do; it is an operation conducted at the personal level. Having my horse-recognition capacity triggered happens at a lower, subpersonal, level of functioning; it is something that happens within me. I shall explain.[3]

The view of the mind prominent in Western philosophy since Descartes has been something like this: the mind is a unified and indivisible organ, transparent to itself, and identical with the person whose mind it is. I am my mind, and my relation to my bodily states and to other "external" features of the environment is incidental. I do not know anything with certainty about the external world – not even that I have a body – but I can have certain knowledge of the contents and workings of my own mind. Contemporary philosophy, at least within the broadly analytical, Anglo-American tradition, has largely rejected this picture. Most contemporary philosophers reject the idea that the mind is separate and distinct from the body, and they reject the idea that the subject has infallible access to at least a large class of his or her own mental states. They think that what we are learning about the brain tells us important things about the mind, in particular that the mind is not especially unified. Different mental processes and functions are localized at different places in the brain, and the appearance that the mind is a smoothly operating seamless web quickly breaks down when we look at cases where there is selective damage at particular sites of the brain. We know, for example, that the capacity to recognize objects can continue when the subject has, through injury or disease, lost the ability to locate objects in space, that the capacity to recognize certain kinds of objects can persist when the capacity to recognize others, for example faces,

---

[3] I am indebted here, as elsewhere in this chapter, to the work of Flint Schier. See his *Deeper into Pictures*, especially section 9.3.

has gone. We know that severing important connections between the two halves of the brain can lead to strange situations in which one half "knows" something which the other half does not. More and more, philosophers and cognitive scientists are coming to the view that the mind is a complex system of hierarchically organized subsystems, where information may regularly fail to pass from one subsystem to the other. Crucially, the subject herself may know very little about the overall architecture of the mind or about what is going on in it. Indeed, we can think of the person as constituted by a hierarchy (or complex of hierarchies) of intelligent creatures or homunculi. The farther down the hierarchy you go, the less intelligent is the homunculus carrying out the operations at that level, until we reach the ground floor, where intelligence bottoms out into straightforward causal interactions where notions of information, reason, evidence and inference play no role, and where everything that happens is driven by brute causal powers in accordance with natural law. The person or agent himself occupies the top level of the hierarchy and is more intelligent than any of the homunculi that operate at subpersonal levels. Many operations of the mind are conducted by the person himself; judging that there is a horse in front of me, or that there is a picture of a horse in front of me, is something that I do. But a great deal of mental processing can be thought of as conducted at a level below that of the person or agent. The primary insight of the homuncular or hierarchical view is that, when an operation is conducted below the personal level, we are not driven to describe that operation in purely causal, nomological terms. We can describe it as a task carried out for a certain purpose, employing information of certain kinds, and conducted within certain constraints of efficiency, reliability and so forth. That way, we describe it as a task performed by a subpersonal homunculus.[4]

Back to horses, and to pictures of horses. When I judge that there is a horse in front of me, I take into account a great deal

---

[4] See, e.g., Daniel Dennett, *Brainstorms*; John Haugeland, "The Nature and Plausibility of Cognitivism"; and W. G. Lycan, "Form, Function, and Feel".

of evidence from various sources, primarily perception, of course, but also from memory and from the sorts of general principles I have developed over the years concerning what sorts of things are likely to be located in what sorts of places (art galleries are more likely to contain horse paintings than horses). The bit of judging I do in this case is, as people say, a *top-down* process: the sort of thing Jerry Fodor describes as "slow, deep, global rather than local, . . . characterized by computations in which information flows every which way . . . the higher the cognitive process, the more it turns on the integration of information across superficially dissimilar domains".[5] But nature has endowed me with other, more automatic, less flexible, less rational capacities as well, among them a horse-recognition capacity – a quick-and-dirty mechanism which, somewhere deep in my visual-processing system, identifies a certain input as a horse. It does so, not on the basis of a detailed, comprehensive examination of the visual input in the light of background belief and all the rest, but on the basis of just a few clues extracted from the visual input itself. Fodor has described these perceptual processes as "input driven, very fast, mandatory, superficial, encapsulated from much of the organism's background knowledge, largely organized around bottom-to-top information flow". My horse-recognition mechanism is pretty good at detecting horses successfully, and might, in a more natural environment than our own, get it right almost all the time. But because it is quick and dirty, and responds to a few key horse-identifying features, it is prone to be fooled by donkeys at dusk, stuffed horses and, in particular, pictures of horses. And that is how it should be; in the environment in which we have evolved we have had – and sometimes still do have – a need for mechanisms of object detection that work very quickly, especially where those objects might be predators or prey. The price of speed is a proneness to false positives, as with the visual system's identification of a horse picture as a horse. No matter; there were few horse pictures around at the time we

---

[5] Jerry Fodor, "Précis of *The Modularity of Mind*", p. 4. For modularity in perception, see also Marr, *Vision*.

were evolving our present perceptual mechanisms, and we often could not afford to wait for the slow, deliberative processes which issue in such judgements as "There's a horse (lion, etc.) around here".

Perhaps this view of picture recognition constitutes a sort of illusionism about pictures. Taking seriously the homuncular model of the mind, it suggests that there is a not-very-intelligent homunculus in my visual system who is charged with the task of matching the visual input with a series of stored models of known objects and who is fairly easy to fool into thinking that the visual input derives from a horse, or whatever object is the best match he can find for the input.[6] But this is an illusionism we can live with. It allows, exactly, that the person seeing can recognize a picture as representing a horse without him supposing he is actually looking at one. That way, we can be realists about cinematic and other images, seeing recognition of the contents of images and recognition of the objects they are images of as fundamentally similar, without being illusionists about such images.[7]

In basing my account of depiction on the idea of capacities for object recognition, I do not mean to suggest that recognition of depictions depends on having a prior visual experience of the things depicted. Sometimes it is the other way about; if I have the capacity visually to recognize echidnas, that's because of my exposure to depictions of them, since I have never seen an echidna in the flesh. My claim is not that the capacity to recognize depictions of Fs is a capacity developed in response to visually presented Fs. It is the claim that my capacity to recognize depictions of Fs and my capacity to recognize Fs are one and the same capacity, however acquired. But note that this claim (call it the claim of capacity identity) is compatible with a

---

[6] For more on this process of object recognition, see Chapter 4, Section 4.8.

[7] As Daniel Gilman puts it, "If our perception of form, space and pattern is largely fixed by these fast, automatic early neurological processes, there is . . . no need for illusion here; we typically have a variety of submechanisms at play and the organism need not be fooled about what it is seeing just because some of its mechanisms respond alike to picture and subject" ("Pictures in Cognition").

weak version of the idea that really seeing things has what we might call "recognitional primacy" over seeing depictions of them. The weak thesis is this: that it is not possible to acquire the capacity to see something in a picture unless you already have the capacity to see something else in the picture, and exercise that latter capacity in coming to acquire the former one. Let us say that when an *F*-recognitional capacity is acquired by looking at pictures of *F*s, it is acquired pictorially. Then, combining the capacity-identity claim and the weak thesis, we say: For every *F*, it is possible that the *F*-recognitional capacity is acquired pictorially, but it is not possible for every *F*-recognitional capacity to be acquired pictorially.

It is also a consequence of my explanation of depiction that you cannot tell for certain whether something is a depiction just by looking at it; something is a picture if it functions in a certain way, and not otherwise, whatever its appearance. Thus we might devise a hieroglyphic version of English in which little icons replace names, thus: "⚲ is tall," where the icon ⚲ replaces the name "Fred". The icon may look like Fred, or as much like Fred as any picture looks like its subject. It may trigger your Fred-recognition capacity in virtue of its likeness to Fred. But the icon is not, in this context, a picture; it serves merely to refer to Fred, and not to make any claim about him – the claim is made by the sentence in which the icon occurs. And what is claimed in this sentence about Fred depends not at all on the spatial properties of the icon, but merely on its being a referring device.[8]

By explaining depiction in terms of visual capacities to recognize objects, I have confined the notion of depiction to visual media. That is certainly in line with our common understanding of the idea of depiction. But having explained depiction that way, there is a natural generalization of the notion to other media. Thus, to consider a somewhat artificial example, we can conceive an art of olfactory representation in which smells are represented. How are they to be represented?

---

[8] See Jerry Fodor, *The Language of Thought*, chapter 2. See also Zenon Pylyshyn, "Imagery and Artificial Intelligence", p. 179.

All sorts of ways are possible, of course, but one natural way would be simply to rely on the odour-recognition capacities of the audience; when the artist wants us to recognize that odour X is represented, he or she gives us a representation with odour properties which trigger our odour-X recognitional capacities. That, roughly, is the function of the scratch cards handed out to members of the audience at some showings of John Waters's *Pink Flamingos*. Such a device is of questionable usefulness or aesthetic merit. But film commonly and profitably uses depictive representation, in my now-generalized sense, along another dimension of perception: diegetic sound. When the film represents, by means of diegetic sound, the character speaking, we recognize what the character is depicted as saying by using our capacity to understand the speech of others when we hear it. So film is realistic along (at least) two dimensions: visual images and diegetic sound. By contrast, the use of subtitles is not, in my sense, a realistic mode of representation, a point I made briefly in the Introduction. When the film represents a character as speaking by means of subtitles we recognize what is said not by our capacity to understand speech but by our capacity to read.

3.2 NATURAL GENERATIVITY

My explanation of depiction can now be used to explain something that would otherwise be puzzling. Flint Schier and Richard Wollheim have noted that systems of depiction display a certain feature: that our understanding of them is *naturally generative*.[9] With classical Western depictions, for example, you can recognize that the picture is of, say, a cow, if you can recognize a cow; and generally you can recognize that the picture depicts a Φ if you can recognize a Φ. You might need to overcome your general unfamiliarity with the system by being shown a few examples of depictions within the system and

---

[9] The term is due to Flint Schier. For a detailed and illuminating discussion see his *Deeper into Pictures*. See also Richard Wollheim, *Painting as an Art*, p. 77; and Crispin Sartwell, "Natural Generativity and Imitation".

having it pointed out to you what is depicted – imagine yourself
familiar only with classical portraiture and suddenly presented
with impressionist or cubist works. But very soon you become
familiar with the style, and can "go on" on your own, recognizing that this impressionist work depicts a lily, so long as you
know a lily when you see one. Learning a language, by contrast,
is not naturally generative; it's no good being exposed to a few
German colour words correlated with colour chips, expecting
then to be able to guess what colour is named by *other* German
colour words. You do not have to learn a "vocabulary" of depiction in the way that you have to learn the vocabulary of a
language – a significant point I shall take up in the next chapter.

Natural generativity is just what we would expect on the assumption that we use our capacity visually to recognize objects
in the real world in order to understand the depictive content
of pictures. If we recognize that the picture depicts a horse by
having our horse-recognition capacities triggered, we will expect
that anyone with that capacity will be able see that a horse is
depicted, which is just the condition of natural generativity. Indeed, it is hard to see how we could explain natural generativity
except by appeal to object-recognition capacities. Suppose, contrary to what I have been saying, that the capacity to recognize
that a horse is depicted is distinct from the capacity visually to
recognize horses. To explain natural generativity on that supposition, we would have to say that acquiring the visual capacity to recognize an object mysteriously brings with it the distinct
capacity to recognize depictions of that object: a more complicated and less plausible theory than the economical proposal
that these capacities are the same. And if words and sentences
are not depictive, as I have claimed they are not, and do not
draw on our natural capacities for object recognition, we have
an explanation of why our understanding of language is not
naturally generative.[10]

Where representation is naturally generative it is realistic in

---

[10] For psychological results concerning the distinctness of pictorial and linguistic recognitional capacities, see Glyn W. Humphreys and Jane M. Riddoch,
"Picture Naming", in their *Visual Object Processing: A Cognitive Neuropsychological Approach*, and the references therein.

my sense. For naturally generative systems of representation work by exploiting our visual capacities to recognize the objects represented, and so the experience of recognizing a picture of a horse is in an important respect like the experience of recognizing a horse when you see one. This kind of realism we might call *Perceptual Realism*. Conversely, where representation is not naturally generative, but works by convention, we should expect little or no perceptual realism. Where convention prevails, we can represent a given thing by means of anything which convenience suggests, and there is no a priori reason it would be convenient to represent an X by means of a thing which triggers our capacity visually to recognize Xs, given the other constraints that have to be satisfied by a system of conventional signs. And that is what we find with language. The experience of reading descriptions of objects is quite unlike the experience of seeing the objects themselves.

Describing our capacity to recognize what is depicted in a picture, Richard Wollheim has spoken of *seeing-in*.[11] We see the Duke of Wellington in the picture just as we see the face in the clouds or the figure in the frosted window pane. Seeing-in is a psychological phenomenon, a mental capacity we contingently possess. By what mental mechanism, then, does seeing-in operate? Wollheim does not say. I believe the answer is that it depends on the architecture of our visual object-recognition capacity. Because that capacity is quick and dirty, apt to be triggered by a few relevant cues and therefore subject to false positives, the mechanism which recognizes horses can be triggered by a picture of a horse. To see a horse in the picture is to have your horse-recognition capacity triggered by the picture and thereby to judge that you are looking at a picture of a horse.

3.3 NONDEPICTIVE REPRESENTATION IN FILM AND OTHER MEDIA

Realism of the kind I'm proposing is a matter of degree. Suppose we have a representation, R, of an object, A, and R represents A as

[11] Richard Wollheim, *Art and Its Objects*.

having properties F and G. R might represent F realistically, and G in some other way. R is such that you can recognize it as representing the F-ness of A in virtue of your visual capacity to recognize the F-ness of an A when you see one. But you can recognize R as representing the G-ness of A only in virtue of your knowledge of some convention of language, or perhaps of someone's intention. When we say that this representation or mode of representation is realistic, and that one not, we probably mean that this one is *more* realistic than that one: it represents more features realistically than the other does. It will be important to bear this in mind.

Since a depiction can, in my sense, be a depiction accessible to sensory modalities other than sight, depictions, including film, may cross sensory boundaries without ceasing to be purely depictive. So a sound film can be depictive in all its visual and auditory aspects. However, it would be rare for any film to be wholly depictive in its representation. Films, like works in other media, represent more than they depict. Films often represent things which could not be depicted, because what is represented is not a matter of the spatial properties of things, or of properties accessible through other senses. A cinematic image may represent the man it depicts as sad or as angry. These qualities are not depicted, because sadness and anger are not qualities that could be depicted; they are mental qualities not accessible to vision or the other senses. But often this nondepictive representation is strongly tied to what the work does depict. Usually, the representation of the nonperceptual quality of sadness occurs in virtue of the depiction of visible qualities; the man is represented as sad in virtue of being depicted as having a sad expression.

Sadness is the sort of thing which cannot be represented depictively and which, if it is to be represented at all, must be represented in some other way. Interesting cases arise when the medium allows a choice; a certain feature can be depicted, and it can be represented in another way, and the choice between the ways can have artistic and narrative significance. Nothing better illustrates this than film's capacity to represent space and time. Film can depict space and time, but this is not the only way it can represent them. Let us look at the ways an art can represent space and time. That will lead eventually to a discussion of realistic film style.

3.4 THREE KINDS OF TEMPORALITY

Everything that happens happens in time, and everything is temporally related to everything else. It takes time to watch a film, but so also does it to watch a play, read a novel, listen to a symphony and look at a painting. In this sense every art is a time art. But in some way, the cinema is very distinctively an art of time; to see what is distinctively temporal about it will require some careful handling of distinctions. Understanding the temporality of cinema will raise a question I shall answer only in Chapter 6: What role does tense play in cinema?

A word about terminology. Talk of space and time in this context really refers just to the placing of people and objects in spatial and temporal relations with one another, or making it be fictional that characters and fictional objects stand in such relations. Architectural writers speak portentously of so-and-so's creation and manipulation of space. In fact architecture is not a kind of metaphysics, and all the architect can do, irrelevant questions about relativity theory aside, is to place things *in* spatial relations. The same is true of the film maker. A substantive theory of space and time, according to which space and time are more than just relations between things, might be true. But film makers are not in the business of representing space and time themselves, supposing there are such things; their concern is with spatial and temporal relations between objects and events. If occasionally I take a verbal shortcut and speak as if the film maker's business is with space and time themselves, please do not take this seriously.

There are three basic ways to treat temporality in art: we can focus on temporal properties of the work, on temporal properties of the observer's experiences of the work or on temporal properties of what the work represents.[12] (Recall my earlier de-

---

[12] See the excellent discussion in Jerrold Levinson and Philip Alperson, *What Is a Temporal Art?*

cision to speak as if works can represent fictional things.) Later, we shall see how these basic ways combine to give something more complex and more interesting. Concentrating for the moment on temporal properties of the works themselves, we can say this: while all works have temporal properties, some have them more distinctively, more intrinsically and more interestingly than others. In particular, works which involve change over time seem more distinctively temporal than those that do not. But it is change of a special kind that is relevant here: not the change in a painting as dirt accumulates and pigments fade, but what we might call the *unfolding* of a play, movie or symphony over time. How do we distinguish temporal unfolding from mere aging?

Characteristic of unfolding is the presence of temporal relations between constitutive elements of the work. With cinema, image succeeds image in a temporal order that must be specified if one is to say what counts as constitutive of that film; when you watch the film it matters, from the point of view of understanding and appreciating it, in what order you see its images. For plays, considered as performances rather than as scripts, the same applies. With the painting that ages (rather than unfolds) over time, there are temporal relations between constitutive features – the pattern of colours we somehow identify as canonical – and other features – the later altered, and possibly degraded, pattern. But there are no temporal relations, except, trivially, the relation of co-occurrence, between constitutive elements themselves. Nor are there significant temporal relations between textual elements of the novel; the words and sentences of the novel are ordered, but not temporally ordered.[13] In this sense cinema, theatre and music are temporal arts, while literature, painting and static sculpture are not. (I have already granted that there are other senses in which all these arts are temporal.)

As well as relations of temporal order between constitutive elements of the work, the elements of a work that is temporal

---

[13] We can order textual elements temporally if we want to, for example, by time of composition. But neither that nor any other temporal order we could impose would tell us anything constitutive about the work.

in this sense may have (one-place) temporal properties of duration; the incidents that go to make up the fiction occupy a definite amount of time. When specifying what is constitutive of the work we may need to specify these temporal properties and relations in precise or in imprecise terms. It is constitutive of a certain movie that each shot lasts exactly a certain time. Specifications of duration for a play are vaguer because theatre is a performance art, and the duration of speech and incident is to some extent determinable by the makers of each performance – though in any actual performance each action or speech lasts a precise amount of time.

We get the second of this trio of kinds of temporality in art if we look, not for temporal relations within the work itself, but for a temporal ordering of the observer's experience of the work. I said that the constitutive elements of the novel are not temporally ordered. Sometimes this is denied; but what people seem to have in mind when they say that the text is temporally ordered is that the ordering of elements – nontemporal as it happens – induces a temporal ordering in the reader's *experience* of the novel.[14] And it is not just any old ordering of experience, because the layout of the text, together with the standard direction of reading, imposes a specific temporal ordering. So it is with at least some paintings, in that they require a temporally ordered looking, with certain elements to be looked at before others. They differ from literary works in that the preferred order of experience cannot simply be read off from any order of the visible elements themselves; those elements do not *have* an intrinsic order in the way that words and sentences do.

In this experiential sense, works of any kind can be temporal, though not all are; some paintings and some static sculptures are not: for them there is no preferred ordering of experience. If we are interested in whether a *kind* of art, rather than just a particular work of that kind, is temporal, there is a distinction worth making. Temporality in our first sense – temporality of

[14] As Gérard Genette says, "The narrative text, like every other text, has no other temporality than what it borrows, metanymically, from its own reading" (*Narrative Discourse*, p. 34).

the work, or "temporality$_w$" as I shall call it – is such that if it applies to any works of a given kind, it applies to all works of that kind. (At least, I cannot think of any art kinds which are counterexamples to this claim!) In this sense, temporality$_w$ inheres *strongly* in the kinds in which it inheres at all.[15] But experiential temporality – "temporality$_e$" as I shall call it – inheres strongly in some kinds but weakly in others; strongly in literature and film, since for any literary or filmic work there is a canonical temporal order of experience, but only weakly in painting and sculpture because, as we have seen, there is a preferred temporal order of experience for some works in these kinds but not for others. So there are three possible relations between any candidate for temporality and any art form: strong and weak inherence, and exclusion, when no work of that kind is temporal in the chosen sense.

I turn now to the third sense of temporality, which is concerned with the temporality of things represented rather than with the temporality of that which represents. Cinema is a time art in this sense also because time, or the passage of time, is one of the things film represents. But this does not yet distinguish cinema from any other representational art. All representational arts portray time in the sense that they portray temporal properties of, and temporal relations between, the events they represent. *Hamlet* portrays the deaths of Ophelia and Hamlet, and in such a way that it portrays the one occurring before the other. Painting does the same; Poussin's *Renaldo and Almeda* portrays Almeda gazing on Renaldo as he sleeps; the gazing and the sleeping are represented as simultaneous, and simultaneity is a temporal relation between events. There are less trivial examples of the representation of time in static pictorial arts. Pictures may represent time in a variety of ways: by encouraging the viewer to make an inference from what is explicitly depicted about what came before and what will come after; by juxtaposition of distinct static images, as when we are shown a series of temporally related photographs; by transforming temporal properties into spatial ones, as in Filippo Lippi's tondo in the Pitti

[15] On strong and weak inherence see the Introduction.

Palace, wherein events earlier in the life of the Virgin are represented deeper within the picture space; and by special techniques such as blurring and multiple exposure. Music, if it is a representational art, can surely represent spatial and temporal relations.

The capacity to represent the temporal – call it "temporality$_r$" – is one further good sense in which something can be a temporal art. But as the examples just given show, it is a relatively undiscriminating sense; it is hard to think of an art form capable of representation which is *not* temporal in this sense. Note, however, that it is not so undiscriminating as to make every representational work a work of temporal art. Paintings can lack the kinds of narrative contents and associations that would render them temporal$_r$; in terms of our earlier taxonomy, temporality$_r$ inheres only weakly in painting. Later, I shall ask whether it inheres weakly or strongly in cinema. But certainly it does inhere in cinema; cinema makes the representation of temporal relations *possible*. In fact the vast majority of films do represent temporal properties and relations.

3.5 REPRESENTING TIME BY MEANS OF TIME

So far we have three senses in which cinema is a temporal art; we can put them together to get another, and the result is the most significant sense in which cinema is a temporal art. The new sense I have in mind is not just the sum of the previous senses; that summative sense, being temporal in all those three ways, is a kind of temporality; but we get something more interesting by connecting the three more subtly.

Let us begin with this idea: that an art form is temporal in this connected sense – I shall call that "temporality$_c$" – if temporal properties of elements of the representation serve to represent temporal properties of the things represented. Cinema is temporal$_c$. What is distinctively temporal about film is not its portrayal of time, but the manner of its portrayal: its portrayal of time by means of time.[16] This easily generalizes: the represen-

---

[16] Is literature temporal$_c$? No: literary works take time to read, and the events

tation of spatial properties by spatial properties, colour properties by colour properties and so forth. Let us examine the general principles here.

An idea that Wittgenstein made much of in the *Tractatus* is that when two expressions refer to different objects, we can represent a relation between the objects by means of a relation between the expressions. And just as a name that represents an object need not be the same thing as that object, so the relation between names need not be the same thing as the relation between things named. One name's being to the right of the other might represent one of the things named being to the right of the other thing named, or represent the thing named on the right being taller than the thing named on the left, or represent some other relation between those things. Similarly for one-place relations or properties: Fred being red could be represented by writing an expression which refers to Fred ("Fred" say), and writing it, say, in green ink. The greenness of the ink refers to the redness of Fred. We might have arranged it so that the expression's being written in red represents Fred as red. In that case we have what I shall call *automorphic* representation: the representation's having property P represents the thing represented having property P. Automorphic representation is a special case of what I shall call *homomorphic* representation, where a property of some kind represents a property of that same kind. So the examples of the red and green ink are examples of homomorphic representation, since in both cases a colour represents a colour, but only the former is an example of automorphic representation. Of course the notion of homomorphic representation is subject to any relativity that attaches to the notion of a property kind. If what we group together as colours have no similarity in nature, then the green-red case can be no more than homomorphic *for us*. But I shall not be concerned here about

they describe take time, but the length of the time necessary to read the work, or part thereof, is not in general a guide to the length of time taken by the events narrated. Mieke Bal says that narrative writing is "iconic" because it resembles its content "since both contain a lapse of time" ("Description as Narration", in *On Story-Telling*, p. 116). But this iconicity is very weak compared with the rich temporal correspondence possible in film.

whether this is so, for perceiver-relative homomorphicity is as much as we shall need for present purposes.

Automorphic representation is subject to a somewhat different relativity. What constitutes automorphic representation on one occasion need not do so on another. Grant that the redness of the name represents the redness of the thing named; but if we don't care about precise shading, we shall not indicate the precise shading of Fred by the precise shading of the name; it is understood that having the name coloured some shade of red represents Fred's being some (possibly other) shade of red. And if *being some colour or other* is all that matters to us, then having the name written in some colour can represent Fred's being some colour. In that case, if the name is written in green and Fred is actually red we still have automorphic representation because it is not *being green* but *being some colour or other* that does the representing, and it represents itself. The lesson: judgements about whether we are dealing with automorphic representation are hasty if they are made in ignorance of the level of specificity at which we are operating.

Consider an ordinary kind of picture. Our picture contains, let us suppose, a representation of Fred; that representation has a part coloured red, and its being so represents Fred's tie being red. So pictures contain parts that represent things, but the pictures themselves represent states of affairs, though they do not always represent *actual* states of affairs. The states of affairs they represent may have temporal properties that are also represented, and there may be temporal relations between the states of affairs that are represented. Those temporal properties can be represented in various ways; that is, various properties of and relations between the pictures themselves can represent those temporal properties and relations. I have noted that it is common with painting for spatial relations between the picture's elements to represent temporal relations between the events depicted, as with the cartoon's progression from left to right, which denotes the progression of events from earlier to later. Within the same frame, on the same canvas, and indeed, as parts of the same picture, we may have several different events depicted, to be understood as occurring at different times, where spatial relations between the depictions denote temporal relations between the events depicted (as in Filippo Lippi's tondo). But with painting, temporal properties of events are not represented by *temporal* properties of representations, and the reason is clear: painting is temporal$_r$ but not temporal$_w$, so it does not have the capacity to be temporal$_c$.

While painting is not a temporal$_c$ art, cinema, as I have already noted, is; temporal properties of cinematic representations (images) serve to represent temporal properties of the events represented. It is temporal properties of the cinematic representation that we mostly observe and rely upon in order to figure out what temporal properties of the fictional characters and events are portrayed. Similarly, it is by detecting spatial properties of the cinematic representation that we determine the spatial relations between characters and things in the fiction represented. That way, film depicts space and time. Film's representation of time by time can be automorphic or merely homomorphic. The represented fight lasts five minutes, and its lasting that long is represented by the relevant representation onscreen lasting just that long. It is the default setting for cinematic interpretation that the representation of duration in cinema is automorphic; it is the assumption we start with, and from which we move only when some aspect of the narration, some clash with real-world belief or some combination of the two suggests we should. In Passolini's *Gospel According to St Matthew* the representation of the Sermon on the Mount lasts a few moments. But changes in background and lighting suggest that the whole performance lasted much longer and took place at various locations. Here the context of narration and real-world belief conspire to shift our understanding: the changes of scene were meant to indicate something, otherwise they would not have been made; landscape and lighting are, and are commonly known to be, by and large locally stable; so what is probably being suggested here is discontinuous shifting of place and time.[17]

---

[17] You might argue that what is represented here is not the whole sermon, but just a few parts of it, and thus we can preserve the default setting. But

Automorphic representation is standard for duration. Is it standard also for temporal relations of precedence, like *occurring ten seconds before*? It may seem not. In film, ten seconds between shots cannot usually be taken to imply that it is fictional that the events represented in the first shot took place ten seconds before the events represented in the second; jumps in time between shots are too common in film for that to be a safe inference. But remember that judgements about automorphism are sensitive to the intended specificity of description. If what is intended to be represented is the relation *occurring some time after*, then a representation that occurs ten seconds after another thereby occurs some time after it, and automorphism is preserved. Once again, however, the default setting can be abandoned, as when context suggests that the event represented next actually occurs *before* the event just represented. Then we have the flashback, about which there is more in Chapter 7.

Film has the capacity to represent the temporal by the temporal, so it is temporal$_c$. But film can represent the temporal in other ways; one way is to have a character or narrator say that this occurred twenty years after that, or for the words "twenty years later" to come up on the screen. Fades and dissolves function as qualitative representations of temporality, indicating some significant distance in time between successively narrated events, where context may or may not tell us roughly how much. A complication is that all fades and dissolves take place in time, so there is a temptation to say that what we have here is the joining together of temporal and other properties of the representation to represent temporal properties of the events represented – a kind of watered-down version of my temporality$_c$ condition. This may happen, but it is not generally so, and it would be a mistake to suppose that it is so simply because all cinematic effects take place in time. Suppose the dissolve takes two seconds, and the effect of the dissolve is to signal "some

to insist on this move in all cases would be, in effect, to identify what is represented with what is displayed, and that identification is hard to sustain. There is a similar device in Clouzot's *Wages of Fear*.

time later". The time taken for the dissolve can be considered to make a contribution to the representation of this temporal relation only if it can be thought of as operating *differentially*. That is, it must be the case that if the dissolve had taken less time or more time, then the dissolve would have signalled a correspondingly smaller or greater gap between the represented events. In certain cases, especially when there are several quick dissolves in succession, one can understand temporal representation to be working like that; a dissolve longer than the norm for this film, or longer than the last one, might indicate a proportionately greater time lapse. But if the sign saying "twenty years later" had been on the screen a few seconds longer than it was, that would have made no difference to the fact that there is twenty years between the represented events, and time consequently plays no representing role here.

So there are three kinds of cases: pure representation of the temporal by the temporal; pure representation of the temporal by nontemporal properties; and mixed (and, I believe, unusual) cases where the temporal and the nontemporal conspire together to represent the temporal.

Sometimes when an art form is said to be temporal, what is meant is that the form in question is especially adapted to the representation of the temporal, that its capacity for representing the temporal is peculiarly rich and subtle. The temporality$_c$ of cinema partly explains why this medium is said to be rich and subtle in its representation of time.[18] Homomorphic and especially automorphic representations of the temporal make for ease and flexibility. In film we get precise and detailed information about temporal duration and relations, and only in the most obscure narratives, like *Last Year at Marienbad*, does the quality of temporal information become significantly degraded. Yet even here there is, by comparison with, say, painting or the novel, a rich structure of temporal information concerning the

---

[18] Gerald Mast may have had something like this in mind when he said, "The cinema is the truest time-art of all, since it most closely parallels the operation of time itself." See Mast, *Film/Cinema/Movie*, p. 112. Quoted in Levinson and Alperson, *What Is a Temporal Art?*

duration of a remark, a gesture or a glance. It is relations of precedence that are the first victims of subversive narration in film, and they are the main casualties in *Last Year*.

This account of temporality$_c$ employs only two of our three basic notions of temporality; it omits consideration of the second, the temporality of the viewer's experience (what I called temporality$_e$). In fact temporality$_e$ is implicit in the account I gave, for I have been assuming that the temporal properties of the work – shot duration and temporal precedence between shots – is a guide for the viewer in working out temporal properties of what is represented. But that will be so only if there is coincidence between temporal properties of the work and temporal properties of the viewer's experience of the work. And so, in general, there are. The viewer's experience of the shot lasts just as long as the shot – assuming an attentive viewer. The representation of the temporal by the temporal works because of this coincidence, and if it started to break down in some systematic way – if cinematic images began to cause viewers to have brief, unpredictable and unnoticed periods of unconsciousness – that kind of representation would be undermined.

Earlier I raised the question: does temporality$_c$ inhere strongly or only weakly in cinema? Only weakly if it is possible for there to be a film in which temporal properties of representations do *not* represent temporal properties of what is represented; otherwise strongly. (Recall that this discussion is relativized to fiction films, and that abstract filmic compositions are not in question here.) I say that temporality$_c$ inheres strongly in film. Try to imagine a film in which the passage of screen time has no implications for the relations between events represented. Even if the temporal relations between what is represented in successive shots is in all cases obscure (Was that a flashback?), individual shots, so long as they last, must, in virtue of their own duration, imply something about the duration of events depicted, though the implications can be utterly trivial. If the film image focuses steadily on the Empire State Building for a period of time, we can infer that the building stood fixed and unchanging during that time. Shooting in slow motion throughout the duration of the film would avoid any automorphic representation, but there would still be homomorphic representation; temporal relations between events onscreen would be proportional to, but not identical to, temporal relations between events depicted. Film is a strongly temporal art; it cannot but represent time by means of time.

3.6 SPATIAL REPRESENTATION

Having decided on a significant sense in which cinema is a temporal art, we shall naturally want to know whether it is in the same sense a spatial art. Unfortunately, the answer to this is somewhat equivocal.

In cinema, spatial properties certainly are represented homomorphically; spatial properties of representations represent spatial properties of the things represented. It seems that spatial properties are not, in general, represented automorphically. It is rare for the screen image representation of a six-foot man to be six feet high, and the size of the representation varies with distance from the camera in a way that does not indicate any variation in the size of the character. One might respond by recalling my strictures on level of specificity: perhaps the representing property is not the actual height of the representation, but its height relative to other representations. And that relative-height property can be thought of as representing the same relative-height property of the representee. That way we would preserve automorphicity of representation.

But this answer misses something. It is not just relative size that is represented on the screen; if that were the case, then what appears on the screen should leave open all questions about absolute size, which it usually does not. We are not in any doubt, for instance, that the human characters in most cinematic fictions are of about the same absolute size as real people. Some films do include characters of exceptional size (*The Incredible Shrinking Man, Attack of the Fifty Foot Woman*), but here the representation of exceptional size is achieved by contrast with the size of representations assumed to represent what is normal for the human population. We must conclude that, at least in standard cases, certain absolute spatial properties are represented in film, but clearly not automorphically. How, then, are they represented?

I think that absolute spatial properties are represented by relative spatial properties of representations, taken in conjunction with background assumptions about what is normal by real-world standards. Thus the relative spatial properties of cinematic representations function automorphically to represent the relative spatial properties of what is represented, and nonautomorphically to represent absolute spatial properties.

This discussion should make it clear that the representation of spatial properties and that of temporal ones in film are differently implemented, and that the representation of space is more difficult than that of time. The representation of temporal properties is, for cinema, relatively straightforward, for two reasons. First, time's one-dimensionality means that keeping track of the duration and succession of onscreen events is relatively simple, whereas the representation of objects in three-dimensional space on a two-dimensional screen leads inevitably to a degradation of information. Worse, cinema imposes a *double* relativity on spatial properties, for it represents them perspectively; it is relative spatial properties *as perceived from a certain point of view* (namely, that of the camera) that are represented. When the actor advances towards the camera against a fixed background, the result is a representation of change in the *apparent* relations of size between character and setting that may not, and usually does not, represent any such actual change. Something vaguely like this can, and occasionally does, occur, for the presentation of time in film; I am thinking of Eisenstein's "stretching out" of the time it takes the soldiers to clear the steps at Odessa in *Potemkin*. Perhaps this is a representation of the time those events seemed to take for those participating in them: a time distinct from that which those events actually took.[19] But this capacity of film to represent time in a quasi-perspectival

[19] Perhaps, but actually I doubt it. In an earlier scene there is a similar, but very brief, stretching of time, when a sailor breaks a plate. That occurrence is not plausibly understood as representing the sailor's subjective perception of the time involved. Rather, it is done for dramatic effect; so, I imagine, is the scene on the steps.

way is a device that can be used or not used at will. It is not, like film's depiction of space, built into the very mechanism of cinematic representation. And this quasi-perspectival representation of time in film is not really parallel to the perspectival representation of space, for reasons to do with fundamental differences between the ways we perceive time and space. An object may recede from us, thereby coming to occupy a smaller area of the visual field than another nearer but actually smaller object; nevertheless, perception represents the more distant object as larger. Perception itself compensates for the effect of perspective; it represents objects as occupying roughly the amount of space they do really occupy. But if we see events "speeded up" or "slowed down", as film enables us to see them, we do not *see them* as occupying the amount of time they really do occupy; instead we have to make an intellectual adjustment: an inference from the (artificially compressed) time we perceive the events as occupying, to the time they really do occupy. There is, for beings such as us, no genuinely perspectival representation of time.

Cinema's capacity to represent space differs in three important ways from that of theatre. The first is that theatre represents absolute spatial properties automorphically; in general, an actor of a certain size represents a character of just that size.[20] Second, the representation of spatial properties in theatre is less perspectival than that of cinema, and has the capacity at least to be completely nonperspectival. A description of the representational content of the film image would have to specify the point of view of filming, but a description of the theatrical representation would not always be a description of what is visible from one particular point of view. It is true that, in conventional theatre with a proscenium arch, a class of roughly preferred perspectives would have to be specified, and sometimes the perspectival representation of scenery defines a single preferred viewing position.[21] But theatre in the round without perspectival

---

[20] There can be exceptions, as when the entire action takes place on Mount Olympus and all the characters are gods.
[21] See Bordwell, *Narration in the Fiction Film*, p. 6.

scenery achieves something like coordinate-free representation. (Of course any spectator always sees the action from a certain perspective, as indeed we always see the real world from a certain perspective, namely our own. But this is not to be confused with any supposed intrinsically perspectival nature of the medium itself.) The third difference between film and theatre concerns the mobility of the camera, which thereby provides a rich source of information about the spatial relations between objects and compensates somewhat for the limitations of perspective and failure to represent absolute spatial properties automorphically.

3.7 REALIST FILM STYLE

From what I have said about film's depiction of space and time, it follows that film has the capacity for realism not merely in its depiction of objects but in its depiction of spatial and temporal relations between those objects. When objects and events are represented onscreen within a single shot, we are able to judge what spatial and temporal relations the film represents as holding between those objects and events, by using our ordinary capacities to judge the spatial and temporal relations between objects and events themselves. We judge the spatial relations between objects represented in the same shot by *seeing* that they are spatially related thus and so. We judge the temporal properties of, and relations between, events represented within the shot by noting that this event took (roughly) so long to observe, while that one was experienced as occurring later than the other one. That is exactly how we judge the spatial and temporal properties of things and events as we perceive them in the real world.[22]

---

[22] Edward Branigan argues that the relation between the time of viewing and the time of the fictional events themselves is conventional, on the grounds that what one notices during the period of screen time varies across persons and occasions (*Narrative Comprehension and Film*, p. 149). But this undoubted fact has no tendency to undermine the claim that within a shot, the standard relation between screen time and the time of fictional events is identity, and its being so relies on no convention whatsoever.

It is in this way that the style called *long-take, deep-focus style* – a style which writers like Bazin have argued is inherently realistic – extends the possibilities for realism in film; it enhances our ability to detect spatial and temporal properties of the fiction by using the capacity we have to detect those properties of things in the real world. When discontinuous shots are edited together, and when depth of field is limited within a shot, our ability to exercise our visual capacity to detect spatiotemporal relations between objects themselves is correspondingly limited. As shot length and depth of field increase, that ability is given greater scope. (Length of take and depth of focus are independent of one another, and long take and deep focus do not always go together, as David Bordwell pointed out to me. But if I am right about their capacity to enhance perceptual realism in film, the combination of these two features constitutes something like a stylistic "natural kind". It certainly explains the close historical connection between them.)

In montage style, on the other hand, where there is quick cutting between very distinct spatial (and sometimes temporal) perspectives, these spatial and temporal properties and relations have, with greater frequency, to be judged by means of inference from the overall dramatic structure of the film. Of course, as my earlier remarks were intended to suggest, this is a matter of degree; long-take style is *more* realistic than montage style, and montage style can itself be said to be more realistic than some other modes of representation – certainly more so than linguistic description. Unqualified claims that long-take, deep-focus style is realistic should be taken as implicitly relative to the class of artistic styles with which it is most naturally compared, namely other cinematic styles, just as the claim that elephants are large is understood as relative to the class of mammals.

It is often remarked that deep-focus style is unrealistic in that it presents us with an image in which objects are simultaneously in sharp focus when they are at considerably different distances from the camera, whereas objects at comparable distances from the eye could not be seen in focus together.[23] But this does not seriously detract from the perceptual realism of deep-focus style. Deep focus, particularly when used in conjunction with wide screen, enables us to concentrate our attention on one object, then to shift our attention at will to another object, just as we are able to do when perceiving the real world. Since we are usually not very conscious of refocusing our eyes, the similarities between viewing deep-focus style and perceiving the real world are more striking than the differences. With montage and narrow-focus styles, on the other hand, we are severely limited by shot length and depth of field in our capacity to shift our attention from one object to another at will – though as I have said, this feature is not entirely absent in montage style.

To summarize: film is, in one sense, a realistic medium. It is capable of representing depictively, and thereby enables us to use our visual capacities to identify objects in order to know that those very objects are represented onscreen. Further, it is capable of representing spatiotemporal relations between objects in the same way; we use our capacities to identify spatiotemporal relations between things in order to know that those relations hold between the things represented onscreen. And long-take, deep-focus style is more realistic than some other styles in that it allows for more of this kind of representation of spatiotemporal relations.

3.8 THE RELATIVITY OF LIKENESS

Explicating the idea of film realism in terms of my generalized notion of depiction helps us avoid an error that has dogged theorizing about the cinema: that realism in film can be attacked on metaphysical grounds because it postulates an observer-independent world – an idea which is then further associated by some theorists with a politically conservative agenda of submission to prevailing conditions. But realism as I have explicated it here appeals to no such postulate (though

[23] See, e.g., Patrick Ogle, "Technological and Aesthetic Influences on the Development of Deep-Focus Cinematography in the United States".

one might argue that such a postulate is both philosophically respectable and politically neutral). The claim of Perceptual Realism is not that cinema presents objects and events isomorphic to those that exist in an observer-independent world, but rather that, in crucial respects, film watching is similar to ordinary perceptual experience of the world, irrespective of whether and to what extent that world is independent of our experience of it.

When I say "film watching is similar to ordinary perceptual experience of the world", I mean that film watching is similar to *our* ordinary perceptual experience of the world. There might be creatures as intelligent and perceptually discriminating as we are, but who experience the world differently. They might not be able to deploy their natural recognitional capacities in order to grasp what is depicted in film and our other pictorial forms of representation. Recall that bats might have visual experiences qualitatively similar to our own, but caused by their very different perceptual systems, which depend on bouncing sound waves off of solid objects. They wouldn't have any success detecting the spatial properties of objects as they are represented on a flat screen, and film would be a medium with little appeal for them. So there is a definite relativity about my conception of realism; what is realistic for us might not be realistic for other creatures. My concept of realism is what I have called a response-dependent concept; it is applicable to things by virtue of the responses to it of a certain class of intelligent agents, namely ourselves.[24]

Some people will find this relativistic concept of realism jarring, perhaps oxymoronic. Among them are those who object to realism because realism presupposes – so they think – some sort of absolutist conception of the world and all its aspects. They think that realism postulates a world describable without reference to any subjective point of view. But that is a mistake. Colours are real, relational properties of things – properties they have in virtue of our responses to them. For the record, let us give a tolerably precise characterization of Perceptual Realism:

[24] See this volume, Chapter 1, Section 1.5.

A representation R is perceptually realistic in its representation of feature F for creatures of kind C iff

(i) R represents something as having F;
(ii) Cs have a certain perceptual capacity P to recognize instances of F;
(iii) Cs recognize that R represents something as having F by deploying capacity P.

So what is realistic for us need not be realistic for intelligent bats or for Martians with their strange sensory faculties. Perhaps the Martians would not, even after a period of familiarization, be able to understand our cinematic narratives. But this admission of relativity does not support the claims of Christian Metz and others that there is a deep conventionality and cultural specificity in our cinematic depictions.[25] We have learned to be sceptical of those traveller's tales according to which humans from other cultures find our styles of pictorial representation alien and uninterpretable.[26] Indeed, the existence of substantial cultural barriers to the understanding of depictions would be surprising in the light of evidence which shows that creatures belonging to other species are capable of understanding the depictive contents of photographs.[27] And the undoubted fact that cinematic

---

[25] "What is called the analogy, the 'resemblance' . . . really lies within a whole group of highly elaborate mental and social organizations . . . and the apprehension of a resemblance implies an entire construction whose modalities vary notably down through history, or from one society to another. In this sense the analogy is, itself, codified" (Metz, "Cinematographic Language", p. 584).

[26] As Wollheim points out, people from other cultures would not be able to make the mistakes they are said to make about perspective in the Western-style pictures with which they are presented if they could not recognize representational features of those pictures (Wollheim, *Painting as an Art*, p. 53). Work by Hudson which purports to show that black southern Africans do not readily understand the depictive content of Western perspective has been severely criticized; see R. K. Jones and M. A. Hagen, "A Perspective on Cross-Cultural Picture Perception".

[27] In an experiment by Premack and Woodruff, a chimp, Sarah, was shown a film of an actor trying to reach some bananas suspended above him; she was then asked to choose from various photographs depicting further possible moves in the attempt. Sarah chose the picture that showed the actor piling

representations are different in various ways from what they represent – by being, for example, flat while the objects they represent are solid – does not itself make those representations conventional.[28] But convention is the subject of the next chapter, and I shall leave detailed discussion of it until then.

There is another sense in which what I have called Perceptual Realism can be interpreted relativistically. I have suggested that representations are perceptually realistic when they share perceptually significant properties with the things they represent. Perhaps that is too reminiscent of the view which metaphysical antirealists reject: that the world and the things in it have determinate features independent of our conceptualization, and that we depict the world right when we give our representations those same features. I happen to think that this view is not so very far from the truth, but its truth or falsity is irrelevant to the issue of Perceptual Realism, just as it was irrelevant to the issue of Illusionism. We need not state Perceptual Realism in terms of the sharing of properties. We can instead state it in terms of the appearance, for us, that things and their representations share properties. Perhaps, as some scientifically minded philosophers think, things really have no colours, and all our colour attributions are false.[29] Perhaps, due to some sceptical scenario, there isn't a real, mind-independent world out there at all. Perhaps creatures from radically different cultures would

crates underneath the bananas, thereby displaying her recognition that this was the correct solution. The central claim of this paper – that chimps have a theory of mind – must be treated with some scepticism, but the evidence on which the authors built their theorizing – the ability of chimps to sort photographs according to whether they represented a solution to the problem in hand – is not disputed. See D. Premack and G. Woodruff, "Does the Chimpanzee Have a Theory of Mind?"

[28] "The very necessity of depicting a bulky three-dimensional object as a flat, two-dimensional image testifies to a certain conventionality" (Juri Lotman, *Semiotics of the Cinema*, p. 6). A version of this argument can be found in almost every discussion of film semiotics. See, e.g., Robert Lapsley and Michael Westlake, *Film Theory: An Introduction*, p. 45. For more detail on the notion of a convention, see this volume, Chapter 4.

[29] See, e.g., Boghossian and Velleman, "Colour as a Secondary Quality". This view goes back to Galileo.

conceptualize the world in ways that are inconsistent or incommensurable with our own, and there is no rational way of choosing between these rival conceptualizations. But none of these possibilities – if that is what they are – is in any way inconsistent with Perceptual Realism. That doctrine need claim only that depictions in general and cinematic images in particular *appear to us* as in significant ways the same as the kinds of things and events they represent, and that it is their so appearing that enables us to identify their representational contents.

Chapter 4
Languages of art and languages of film

> ... the proper objects of sight are lights and colours, with their several shades and degrees; all which, being infinitely diversified and combined, form a language wonderfully adapted to suggest and exhibit to us the distances, figures, situations, dimension, and various qualities of tangible objects: not by similitude, nor yet by inference of necessary connection, but by the arbitrary imposition of providence, just as words suggest the things signified by them.
>
> *George Berkeley*

That the medium of cinematic images is in some sense pictorial is hardly controversial. But many will object to the sharp distinction I have drawn between the pictorial and linguistic, a distinction Berkeley apparently seeks to undermine in the quotation above. That distinction is rejected by almost every consciously theoretical writer on film, and on art and culture generally. The prevailing view is that picturing is a mode of representation at least very like linguistic representation, that images in general and cinematic images in particular operate by means of codes or conventions that are like the semantic and syntactic rules of a language. Berkeley's view that the appearances of things form a kind of arbitrary code, and that seeing is therefore a kind of reading, is one which, shorn of its theological trappings, many contemporary theorists of cinema would endorse.

This idea of the ubiquity of language is so entrenched that expressions like "the grammar of quattrocento painting", "the vocabulary of Gothic architecture" and "the language of film" do not strike us as peculiar or in need of justification.[1] Some of

[1] See also the chimerical "story grammar", aptly criticized in R. Wilensky, "Story Grammars Revisited".

these uses may be unexceptionable shorthand: talk of the vocabulary of an architectural style sometimes means just whatever devices are typically employed in that style. But sometimes the usage suggests possession of a linguistic theory that can turn casual connoisseurship into a powerful technique of analysis. The suggestion is spurious. Art, architecture, film and the rest have little in common with any of the uncontroversial examples of language that have shaped our recent linguistic theorizing. It is not likely, therefore, that linguistics will help us explain how it is we use, interpret and appreciate any of these things. So I claim, and so I shall argue with respect to the case of film.

This much is negative. But there is something important to learn about film and the comprehension of it by comparing its communicative aspect with that of language. That will prepare the way for a theory of the interpretation of film developed in Part III. So while this chapter rounds off the discussion of cinematic representation with the thought that it is not linguistic, quasi-linguistic or even remotely linguistic, much of its significance will not be apparent until we compare the interpretation of texts and that of film in Chapter 8.

4.1 FINDING THE THESIS

The hypothesis that there is a language of film is not the true but uninteresting claim that the language of *Citizen Kane* is English and that of *Rashomon* is Japanese. It is the hypothesis that there is a specifically cinematic language which can and sometimes does operate independently of accompanying words or sounds – that there is a language of cinematic images, their modifications and juxtapositions.[2]

The idea that there is such a language, along with comparable claims for painting, architecture and the rest, is part of the legacy of structuralism. But while structuralism has led us up one blind

[2] Sometimes advocates of cinema language seem to be asserting that there are many different such languages. The arguments I shall bring forward will be just as effective against that hypothesis as they are against the hypothesis that there is one such language. So I shall not bother to consider the multiple-languages hypothesis separately.

alley after another, the idea that structure is the key to understanding ourselves and our culture has proved surprisingly re-
silient; the grudging recognition one hears from time to time
that cinema is, after all, really rather different from anything we
would normally call a language goes along with an enduring
belief that, at some level, an underlying similarity will be found.

Where did the structuralists go wrong? Enthusiastic for universal principles in the human sciences, they fastened onto the
success of theoretical linguistics, hoping to explain other human
activities on the same basis. Thus the structuralist Tzvetan Todorov: "If we admit the existence of a universal grammar, we
must no longer limit it to language alone. It will have, evidently,
a psychological reality.... This psychological reality makes
plausible the existence of the same structure elsewhere than in
speech".[3] The structuralist's strategy was to explain our competence in nonlinguistic – or at least not obviously linguistic –
domains by appeal to those mental structures that underlie our
linguistic competence, and thereby to show that those other domains are, after all, basically linguistic in structure.[4] That strategy derives from a view of the mind as a unified or at least
highly interconnected mechanism in which basically the same
competencies apply across domains. I have already rejected that
view of the mind. I have argued that the mind is a complex, less
than fully integrated institution with relatively autonomous de-
partments dedicated to specific functions. Currently available
evidence suggests that language is a particularly good example
of this "vertical" structuring of the mind. A child's acquisition
of linguistic skills seems to be remarkably insensitive to variations in her other competencies, including perceptual ones. For
example, the use of personal pronouns emerges in congenitally

---

[3] Tzvetan Todorov, *The Poetics of Prose*, pp. 108–109.
[4] A kind of mirror image to this approach, deriving from the same universal-
izing conception of the mind, is Piaget's theory that linguistic ability is derived from other more primitive and general human competencies, in
particular from "sensorimotor" abilities. For a lively – if partisan – account
of the collapse of Piaget's program under pressure from Chomsky's linguistics, see M. Piattelli-Palmarini, "Ever Since Language and Learning: Afterthoughts on the Piaget–Chomsky Debate".

deaf children who employ sign language at just the same time as in hearing children, with both groups going through a period of pronoun reversal, confusing "you" and "I".[5] There just is no reason – apart from the initial plausibility and simplicity of the idea – to suppose that mental structures designed to accomplish one kind of task will be similar in any interesting way to other such structures, or that a structure used for one purpose will turn out to be used for others.[6]

If the view that there is a language of picturing is to be rejected, perhaps there is another hypothesis to be considered: that film is not to be analysed as a language, but as an example of the broader category of semiotic systems. In that case cinema falls within the scope of a more general theory that includes both natural languages and a great deal else: everything, in fact, that is a system of signs. If the hypothesis that cinema is a language is to be rejected, perhaps we should consider the weaker position of the semioticists – weaker because the hypothesis that cinema is a language entails but is not entailed by the hypothesis that it is a semiotic system. But I shall not confront the semiotic hypothesis in any detail. One reason is that the generality aimed for in semiotics has resulted in a great deal of taxonomizing but little identifiable as theory. It has also never been made clear what a "code" is supposed to be, though codes are what semioticists are apparently most interested in finding. Nor is it easy to read off a characterization from the examples offered. Among cinematic codes there are, we are told, "the complex system according to which the cinematic equipment (recording camera, film strip, projector) 'reproduces movement' ",[7] and "the representational code of linear perspective".[8] It is hard to think of a definition of code which would cover these two items and not cover everything else. So a critical assessment of the semiotic hypothesis would require us to figure out what the hypothesis is, exactly. Or, if there is no clear hypothesis available, we shall

---

[5] See L. A. Petitto, "On the Autonomy of Language and Gesture: Evidence from the Acquisition of Pronouns in American Sign Language".

[6] For more on Structuralism see Chapter 9, Section 9.4.

[7] Christian Metz, *Language and Cinema*, p. 191.

[8] Comolli, "Machines of the Visible", p. 135.

have to devise a plausible hypothesis as a target for criticism. That would be a lengthy undertaking, and I should like to avoid it.

It is not just the vagueness of semiotics that makes me unwilling to tackle it head-on. At least some of what I say in relation to the hypothesis that there is a language of cinema will count against semiotics as well. Semioticians seem committed to the "conventionality" of the sign systems they investigate; this assumption makes them hopeful they will discover a unified theory of signs.[9] And in the course of arguing against the idea of a language of film I argue that cinematic images are not conventional signs. I have no quarrel with the claim that cinematic images are signs, if that means simply that they are representations. But the nonconventionality of cinematic signs means that talk of a *system* of cinematic signs is vacuous.

4.2 CINEMA LANGUAGE AND NATURAL LANGUAGE

The language of cinema, if there is one, is in various ways startlingly different from any natural language. It is what we might call medium specific: it has its existence in cinematic images and their modifications, so it is conveyed to us through sight alone.[10] No natural language is medium specific in this way; natural languages can be spoken and they can be written, even if in fact some of them are not, so they are available to sight and to hearing. Braille makes a natural language available to the sense of touch, and a coding of English into olfactory sensations is possible, though it would be unwieldy in practice. Natural languages are available to us through all our senses.

Cinema language is not just medium specific: you could not even "translate" cinematic images into distinct visual images by, say, stretching, distortion or colour modulation and still have

---

[9] "Signs are correlated with what they stand for on the basis of a rule or a convention" (Umberto Eco, "On the Contribution of Film to Semiotics", p. 196).
[10] On the so-called medium-transferability of natural languages see John Lyons, *Language and Linguistics*, p. 11.

what advocates of cinema language would call "the same language", for those transformations would impose a change of meaning; any change in the appearance of what is on the screen is potentially significant for our decisions about the content of the story that is thereby presented. But with natural languages there is nothing special or privileged about any visually specific way of representing letters and words, as font and handwriting differences attest. And there are codes in which you can write English sentences using permutations of our alphabet, other alphabets, numerals or whatever.

Perhaps cinema language is so fundamentally different from natural languages that no significant properties of the one are attributable to the other. But if cinema language is so unlike natural language, what is to be gained from treating it as a language at all? True, we cannot conclude immediately from the fact that there are differences between natural languages and the supposed language of cinema that there is, after all, no such thing as a language of cinema. There are differences, some of them very striking, between the various natural languages. Ideally, we would distinguish accidental from essential differences, and if we found that cinema "language" differs essentially from natural language we would conclude that the former is not, after all, a language. But I do not know of any set of characteristics generally agreed to be essential for a language. We could try providing some, in the form of a definition, but that wouldn't settle anything. We don't decide questions about whether this or that is a cause by appealing to some definition of "cause", for we are at the stage with the concept of cause where we are testing definitions against cases, and not the other way around. So it is with language.

I suggest another method. Whatever disputes there are about whether this or that is a language, no one, so far as I know, has denied that *English* is a language, or that any of the other things we call "natural languages" are languages. Also, natural languages like English have been the objects of the most sustained and systematic theoretical investigation into language. Linguistics, in so far as it is a developed theory, is about these natural languages. The hope of those who say there is a language of cinema is that they will be able to make use of a well-developed theory – linguistics – in an area which is theoretically under-developed.[11] In that case the cash value of the claim that there is a language of cinema depends directly on the similarity between film and natural language. The less like natural language the cinema is, the less probable it is that linguistics will help us understand it, just as the difference between atoms and social customs makes it unlikely that physics will help us understand society.

I shall argue that, in crucial respects, film is very unlike a natural language. This will enable us to sidestep the definitional question. If someone agrees with my conclusions and still wants to say there is a language of film, I shall not argue with her choice of words. All that matters to me will have been conceded: that there is insufficient similarity between this "language" and any natural language for us to expect progress to be made in understanding the cinema by applying to it linguistics or any theory that adopts the principles and techniques of linguistics. The question I am raising here is about the transferability of a theory, not about the appropriateness of a word.

While I shall be sceptical throughout this chapter about the relevance of linguistics to film theory, I don't want to imply any comparable hostility to philosophy of language as a useful tool in this area. Much of what we class as philosophy of language is concerned with arguments and conclusions that are not, after all, specific to language, but which apply to linguistic and non-linguistic forms of communication alike. And while cinema is not a linguistic medium, it is essentially a mode of communication between a story-teller and an audience; more on this in Part III. Philosophy of language is not exhausted by any single theory, and within it there is fundamental disagreement about the nature of language and about the possibility of nonlinguistic thought and communication. My application of philosophy of

[11] Metz seems to have thought of it that way: "The methods of linguistics ... provide ... a constant and precious aid in establishing units that, though they are still very approximate, are liable over time ... to become progressively refined" (Christian Metz, "Some Points in the Semiotics of Cinema", p. 176).

language to film will be the application of a particular contestable theory. It will be important to bear this in mind in assessing my conclusions.

One important aspect of the argument to follow is that language and meaning are by no means coextensive; there can be meaning which is not linguistic meaning. The fault of those who find language everywhere is that they infer the presence of language from the presence of meaning.

4.3 THE SHAPE OF NATURAL LANGUAGE

I shall specify some salient features of natural language. My example will be English. The concept of cinema language has been able to thrive partly because it is never discussed with any precision, and I shall try to be as precise as I can be in describing what I take to be theoretically important aspects of any natural language. This will have at least the virtue that those who want to defend the applicability of linguistics to film theory will have to specify exactly where and why my description is wrong, or where I go wrong in claiming there is nothing in cinema that corresponds to the description. The account will be somewhat compressed, but the concepts appealed to should be familiar, and compression will help to give an overview; it is the logical relations between these concepts I want to emphasize. Nothing turns on the choice of example: trivial reformulations would fit the description to any natural language.

English displays the features of *productivity* and *conventionality*. Productivity means that an unlimited number of sentences of English can be uttered and comprehended; in fact many of the sentences we utter and comprehend every day have never been uttered, and so have never been comprehended, before. Whatever learning English involves, it does not involve learning meanings sentence by sentence; otherwise we would need instruction every time we heard a new sentence.[12]

---

[12] What I am here calling "productivity" is sometimes called "generativity", which, in the present context, might be confused with the notion of *natural generativity* to which I appeal in this and other chapters.

English is conventional in that what words and sentences of English mean is determined, not by relations of natural affinity between words and meanings, or because the human mind is specially apt to associate certain words with certain meanings, but by adventitious uniformities of practice adhered to because they aid communication. The differences between the various natural languages humans use (and these differences are small by comparison with those between all the logically possible languages) are mostly accounted for as differences between these uniformities of practice. These uniformities of practice are conventions. A convention, as David Lewis has shown, need not have its origin in agreement. There is a convention to the effect that a word has a certain meaning when there is a regularity of use among members of the speech community; they use that word intending to mean something, and they do so because they know others do the same, and desire to continue the regularity because by doing so they are able to achieve a coordination between what they mean by it and what hearers will take them to mean, a coordination necessary for successful communication. It does not much matter what word we use to express a given meaning; what matters is that most of us use it most of the time to express the same meaning. That way, we have some idea about what meaning others use it to express, and they have some idea about our use. And that way we are able to coordinate our communicative activities.[13]

Conventionality and productivity combine to set certain further requirements on the shape of language: Conventionality means that language has to be learned; if the meanings of words were, say, innately known, and speakers of a common language drew on that knowledge in making and understanding utterances, there would be no conventions necessary to connect words with their meanings. Productivity precludes the language

---

[13] See David K. Lewis, *Convention*. I have presented Lewis's account of convention in language as if it were of the conventionality of words. In fact there are problems in extending his account from whole sentences to sentential components. But these problems are, I take it, problems of detail rather than of principle. The best work I know on this is Timothy Irwin's unpublished M.A. thesis, *Meaning and Convention*.

being learned sentence by sentence, since in a language which displays productivity, speakers understand sentences to which they have had no previous exposure. So meanings in our language, if they are to be learned at all, must be specified *recursively*: we start with a set of conventions that assign meanings to a finite stock of words, and we combine words into further meaningful units (e.g., sentences) by rules of composition, which tell us how the meaning of the whole depends on the meanings of the parts.[14] Thus our language is *molecular*: its sentences are built out of independently meaningful units – what I shall call *meaning atoms* – by rules that assign meanings to complexes as a function of the meanings of the basic parts. Words are our atoms; they are meaningful, and they contribute to the meanings of larger units to which they belong, but they themselves have no meaningful parts.[15]

Since the atoms – words in English – are assigned meanings individually, and since the composition rules make the meaning of the whole a function of the meanings of the parts, meaning in our language is *acontextual*. The meaning of a given word is determined by its meaning convention – not by the meanings of other words, and not by anything else – and the meanings of sentences depend only on the meanings of the words in them.[16]

In sum, our language is productive and conventional, so its meaning-determining conventions are recursive, so it has meaning atoms, so it is molecular, so it is acontextual. A great deal in the argument that follows will depend on these entailments.

As I have already stressed, none of this is definitive of lan-

---

[14] I don't say we learn our language entirely from the bottom up. No doubt we start with simple sentences, shake out the word meanings by decomposition, and zigzag back and forth, continually expanding our competence in a way governed partly by trial and error. What is claimed is simply that if the meanings of linguistic units could not, in principle, be stated recursively the language would not be learnable.

[15] Not *every* word is an atom, as when a single word has a meaning that is a function of the meaning of other words and operators, as with "invalid".

[16] This account of meaning in natural language contradicts the structuralist's claim that linguistic meaning is wholly a matter of a sign's relations to other signs. That is as it should be; a change in the meaning of one term does not induce a change in the meanings of all terms.

guage; there might be languages that are either not productive, or not conventional, or neither.[17] But if there is, for cinema, anything that plays a language-like role, it would surely be productive; there is an unlimited number of things that can be conveyed by cinema images. New films do not simply recycle a fixed stock of images; they present us with new images which, by and large, we have no special problem understanding.[18] And the people who claim that there is a language of film emphasize the contingency and conventionality of that language, the degree of its social and cultural determination. (I shall suggest that there is some confusion on their parts about what this conventionality amounts to.) So advocates of cinema language will hold to the idea that this language, or any one of the possibly many cinematic languages, is both productive and conventional. But that, as I have argued, means that a language of cinema must also be recursive, molecular and acontextual.

I shall argue that there is nothing in cinema that satisfies all these requirements, or anything vaguely like them. One objection no doubt forming already in the minds of cinema-language advocates is that my account of meaning in natural language is too narrowly mechanistic to be plausible for the natural lan-

[17] Perhaps the language of thought, if there is one, is productive and nonconventional. Perhaps Wittgenstein's "block", "pillar", "slab", "beam" language described at the beginning of the *Investigations* is conventional and nonproductive. Productivity seems to be more important than conventionality for characterizing what is special about human languages. There is some evidence that chimpanzees can employ rudimentary systems of arbitrary symbols (see, e.g., D. Premack, "Minds with and without Language"; and S. Savage-Rumbaugh et al., "Spontaneous Symbol Acquisition and Communicative Use by Pigmy Chimpanzees *Pan paniscus*"), but their use shows little sign of productivity (see M. C. Corballis, "On the Evolution of Language and Generativity"). For an overview, see David Premack, *Gavagai! Or the Future History of the Animal Language Controversy*.

[18] If you doubt this, carry out an experiment recommended by Irving Biederman: 'Turn on your TV with the sound off. Now change channels with your eyes closed. At each new channel, blink quickly. As the picture appears, you will typically experience little effort and delay ... in interpreting the image, even though it is one you did not expect and even though you have not previously seen its precise form." "Higher-Level Vision"; page references are to the partial reprint, here and in note 29, as "Visual Object Recognition".

guage case, and so it cannot be the basis for any significant attack on the idea of cinema language. So I had better try to dispel at least some of the more obvious objections to the account of natural language just given.

4.4 OBJECTIONS REJECTED

It would be a mistake to suppose the account just given is inconsistent with the notable *vagueness* of linguistic meaning. The conventions that specify the meanings of many, perhaps all, of the words of a natural language fail to determine the extensions of those words precisely; there are times when we know all the relevant empirical facts, as well as everything relevant about the meanings of words, yet still cannot decide whether a certain object is properly called a hill rather than a mountain. When that is so, a word's meaning is vague, but that is no objection to the recursiveness of meaning; it indicates just that the recursive rules will import vagueness of meaning into any sentences that contain vague terms. While vagueness raises problems which cannot be ignored, it should not be used as an excuse for abandoning the project of giving a theory, perhaps a rather precise theory, about meaning, and about the transmission of meaning from words to sentences.

Further, the account I have given is not – and this point can easily be confused with the last – committed to what I shall call the *determinacy* of meaning. Is it literally correct to speak of the legs of chairs? Perhaps, but there was a time when this was not literally correct, and a later time when this usage could not properly be called either literal or figurative. The literal meaning of "literal meaning" is as vague as that of "hill". But just as vagueness is no objection to the claim that there are hills, so it is no objection to the claim that there are literal meanings. Consequently our theory is not committed to the *constancy* of literal meaning. Words have literal meanings at one time that they do not have at others. But this, again, is no objection to the thesis that words have literal meanings. Otherwise we should not be able to say that objects have shapes and colours.

The claim that there is such a thing as the literal, acontextual meaning of words is not the claim that the meanings of words and sentences are *infallibly known* to speakers of the language. We can be mistaken about what the literal meaning of an expression is, even when we understand the language to which that expression belongs. Since there is no upper bound to the potential length of sentences in a natural language like English, there are presumably many sentences of that language which are so long the human mind cannot process their meanings. And length is not the only problem: "No head injury is too trivial to be ignored" is a celebrated case of a sentence the literal meaning of which almost everyone misunderstands – until they do some hard work on figuring out what it means.

Nor is it an objection to the theory of language just outlined that many words, for example "bank", have more than one meaning; the sensible response to that is to say that some words have more than one meaning convention attached to them, and the rules of composition can be applied when one particular meaning is chosen.[19] As long as the rules can be seen to apply whatever meaning is singled out, ambiguity is no threat to the theory. There would be a threat to the theory if there were words that had infinitely many distinct meanings, for then we could give no recursive specification of meaning for a language containing such a word. But there is no reason to suppose that this is the case.

Another objection to the idea of context-free literal meaning is that what is conveyed by a sentence varies from one context of utterance to another. That is true, but it shows merely that what is conveyed by a use of a sentence is not always the same as the literal meaning of the sentence. What is conveyed by a use of a sentence (if we confine ourselves, for the sake of simplicity, to indicatives) is what the speaker asserts by uttering it. And a speaker can use a sentence which means one thing to assert more or other than what the sentence means. An utterance of "Harold is a snake", performed while witnessing some par-

[19] Alternatively we can say that in such cases there are two distinct but identically spelled words, each with its own (unique) meaning convention attached.

ticularly discreditable action of Harold's and as part of a conversation about Harold's character, might convey the thought that Harold is given to scheming self-aggrandizement. But the sentence "Harold is a snake" does not mean that.

But in that case, why postulate literal meanings? Why not be content with a single category of meaning: the context-dependent meaning of the utterance? Some literary theorists have recently taken that option.[20] But it is not a viable one. It is true that what we understand by an utterance is not a function *solely* of the meanings of the words uttered, since the same words uttered in different contexts can be used to communicate different things. But to conclude from this that literal meaning plays no role in explaining understanding would be like concluding that colour plays no role in our response to a picture because the same colour may look garish in this context and comfortably warm in that one. Take away the colour and you take away the response; take away literal meaning, and you take away understanding. Context matters for understanding, but it cannot be all that matters – otherwise I should be able to understand the native utterances of my Japanese friends just by understanding the contexts in which those utterances are made. I don't understand them, even when I know the context, because I don't speak Japanese; I lack knowledge of the literal meanings of Japanese sentences. You might insist that with the utterances in Japanese there are aspects of context I fail to grasp, but that would be just to repackage literal meaning under a new label: "context of utterance".

4.5 INTERPRETATION AND UTTERANCE MEANING

So there is a difference between the literal meaning of a sentence and the meaning of an *utterance* of that sentence. The meaning of a particular utterance depends, of course, in part on the meaning of the sentence uttered, which depends on convention; but

[20] See Stanley Fish, *Is There a Text in This Class?* and *Doing What Comes Naturally*. See also my "Text without Context: Some Errors of Stanley Fish".

it would be a mistake to say that utterance meaning is itself conventional. It cannot be supposed that we work out the meaning of an utterance by appealing to conventions of the form, "An utterance of sentence *S* in context *C* means *M*." There is an unlimited number of values for *C*, and contexts are not constructed recursively from a finite set of context constituents. But knowledge of utterance meaning is productive; we understand utterances in contexts we have not previously encountered. How so? When we figure out utterance meaning we apply the conventions of literal, linguistic meaning, together with nonconventional rules of rationality; we assume the speaker understands the language and the relevant features of the speech context, and is able to act appropriately – to choose appropriate words – so as to get us to realize what it is he intends to get across. The best hypothesis about that intention gives us the utterance meaning. This assumption of rationality, and the various specific subrules to which it gives rise,[21] are not conventions, because they are not assumptions to which there is any realistic alternative; they are assumptions the world imposes on us rather than ones we impose on the world. We cannot choose to regard a speaker as rational and so interpret his utterance one way, or choose to regard him as irrational and interpret it in another. If we do not assume him at least minimally rational we cannot come up with an interpretation – or rather we have no way of deciding among countlessly many of them.[22]

This account of how language functions suggests that the advocates of cinema language were too optimistic in assessing what could be achieved for interpretation by way of convention alone. Literary interpretation is largely a matter of figuring out utterance meaning; what story the text has to tell is not just a matter of the literal meanings of the words on the page, which often have to be taken nonliterally, and even then can sometimes be thought of only as hinting at the events of the story. Figuring out the events of the narrative is a matter of figuring out, on the

[21] On which see Paul Grice, "Logic and Conversation".
[22] This is not Davidsonian charity, which would have us regard the speaker's utterances as (largely) true – clearly a pointless injunction in the case of a fictional utterance.

basis of your understanding of the language and of the principle of rationality, what story would most likely have been intended by someone who had chosen to write those words with those meanings: so I shall argue in Chapter 8. Even if there is a language of cinema, and it functions in the presentation of cinematic narrative in something like the way language functions in literary forms, film interpretation is still going to be largely a matter of calculating intentions; understanding the language of a text or (if there is one) of a film is just the first step in getting to an interpretation. Cinema theorists often write as if cinema language is the key to understanding cinematic narrative. If the analogy with natural language held, discovering that language would be more like being told which shop the key was in.

So if there is a language of film, it won't provide an answer to the problem of interpretation. It might, on the other hand, be a precursor to an answer, and therefore worth having. It's time to see that there is no such thing to be had.

4.6 CONFUSIONS ABOUT CONVENTION

I have described some crucial features of the way meaning is articulated and communicated in natural language. We now have to decide how far the functioning of cinematic images is like that of a natural language in these respects. We can say, first of all, that the function of cinematic images in the fiction film is to tell a story, just as the function of the words and sentences in a fictional text is to tell a story. So the question we need to ask is this: Do these images perform their story-telling function in the way that sentences of the literary text do?

Some who are sceptical of the idea of cinema language have argued that they do not, on the grounds that cinematic images function contextually, and therefore in a way different from words and sentences which function, as we have seen, acontextually. Thus George Wilson argues that the meaning we give a particular sequence of shots depends on how coherently that sequence, so interpreted, fits into the rest of the film. Whether, in *The Lady from Shanghai*, the juxtaposition of a hand pressing a button and a car crashing is to be taken as signifying a causal relation between the two depends on whether there is elsewhere in the film evidence for this peculiar causality. This suggests, says Wilson, "the holistic character of all interpretive work".[23]

Wilson is right that what the cinematic image tells us about the fiction depends on the surrounding context of other images. But that is true also of words and sentences in a text, where there is no dispute about the presence of a language. What kind of relation between described events is suggested by one bit of text depends upon the role that bit of text is seen to have in the context of all the other bits. If the text says, "Her hand pressed the button just before the car crashed", it is then a matter of interpretation, which will have to take account of the rest of the text, as to whether it is part of the story that the pressing caused the crash. Even if the text were more explicit, and said, "Her pressing of the button caused the crash", we would have to decide, on the basis of our overall assessment of the rest of the text, whether this should be taken as a reliable guide to the story, rather than, say, the suspect utterance of an unreliable narrator. So the context dependence of interpretation applies to literature as much as to film, and it cannot on its own be an argument against there being a language of the cinema.

How is the context sensitivity we find in literary interpretation compatible with the fact that linguistic meaning is acontextual? What words and sentences mean is determined by the conventions of the language, and these conventions provide, as we have seen, for the acontextuality of meaning. What a speaker asserts by uttering words and sentences with those meanings depends on more than meaning-determining conventions. It depends, exactly, on context, together with assumptions about rationality. The context sensitivity of interpretation is a further indication that the target of interpretation is the speaker's meaning rather than the literal meanings of words and sentences.

So perhaps the language of film enthusiast can meet Wilson's challenge to the idea of cinema language by drawing a distinction between the literal meanings of cinematic images and the

---

[23] Wilson, *Narration in Light*, p. 203.

meaning we attribute to the act of "uttering" – that is, producing and displaying – them. He would have to show that the literal meaning of these images preserves a language-like acontextuality, while appealing to their utterance meaning to explain contextual dependence. If he could show that this literal meaning, whatever it is, is in theoretically important ways analogous to literal meaning as it appears in natural language, his task would be complete. I shall argue that this last and most important step is one he cannot take.

The argument hinges crucially on the following claim: it is not possible to identify any set of conventions that function to confer meaning on cinematic images in anything like the way in which conventions confer (literal) meaning on language. This is the fundamental disanalogy between language and pictorial modes of representation. And the argument for this claim is that the meaning of a cinematic image is nonatomic and so nonrecursive. There are no atoms of meaning for cinematic images; every temporal and spatial part of the image is meaningful down to the limits of visual discriminability. When a spatial part of the image has distinguishable spatial parts within it, the viewer who can identify what is represented by the larger spatial parts will be able to identify what is represented by the parts within it. To see a part of the image as representing a face is necessarily to be able to recognize parts within that image part which represent facial features, however indistinctly. And the principle holds for image parts that have no internal discriminable structure. A part of the image of the tiger represents one of his stripes, and represents it as uniformly black, in virtue of that image part itself being uniformly black. Still, once it is acknowledged that this uniformly black image part represents a stripe, it will be understood that any subpart of that image part represents a subpart of the stripe.[24]

Despite being nonatomic, film images are productive: there is an unlimited number of visible scenes that cinematic images can represent, and we generally have no trouble grasping the repre-

[24] Virtually the same point is made by Roger Scruton in *The Aesthetic Understanding*, p. 107.

sentational properties of cinematic images we have never seen before. Being without meaning atoms, and therefore nonrecursive, and being at the same time productive, the meaning of cinematic images cannot be conventional. It is natural meaning. With images, productivity is natural generativity, and we explain that in terms of natural recognitional capacities. As I argued in Chapter 3, we understand what is depicted onscreen by employing our visual capacities to recognize the entities depicted.[25]

To say that the meaning of a cinematic image is naturally rather than conventionally determined is not to say that this meaning has nothing to do with convention. How things are placed before the camera will be influenced by social institutions like styles of dress, composition and decor, as well as by considerations of decorum; these things, or some of them, count as conventions. But this is not grounds for saying the meaning of the image is *itself* conventional in the sense that meaning in natural language is. To be conventional in the way language is there would have to be a set of conventions governing the meanings of all the image atoms, and since there are no image atoms there are no such conventions.

This nice distinction – between what is conventional and what is influenced by convention – is overlooked by those who are content to appeal to a vague, impressionistic and all-purpose notion of convention to support their claims about the conventionality of images. Umberto Eco gives the example of an image from Fritz Lang's *M*, in which the girl's balloon is caught in overhead wires. This image, he says, "stands for" the capture of the girl by the murderer, but it does so only by convention; that is, it does so only because in our culture "wires recall ropes, ropes capture, and so on".[26]

The example isn't helpful to Eco's case, since there really are no conventions associating wire with ropes and ropes with capture. Wires and ropes are alike in their function and appearance, which is nothing to do with convention, and it is by no kind of

---

[25] See Section 3.1 in the previous chapter; and Schier, *Deeper into Pictures*. See also Sartwell, "Natural Generativity and Imitation", especially pp. 186–187.
[26] Eco, "On the Contribution of Film to Semiotics", p. 207.

convention that ropes are useful for capturing things. A better example would be a case where the image of a red traffic light is a metaphor (not, I grant, a very imaginative or subtle one) for the end of a love affair. A red traffic light is suggestive of endings because there is a convention which associates the colour of the light with the instruction to stop. But still, there is no *conventional* meaning possessed by this image of the traffic light, as it appears in our imaginary film. One thing the image can be said to mean is what it depicts, which is a traffic light. It does that in virtue of being a cinematic image of a traffic light, and not by convention. The image might have meaning in virtue of being a metaphor for, or suggesting, the end of the affair. That isn't conventional meaning either. An image, like a word or a sentence, can suggest or be a metaphor for any number of things depending on context. No convention associates a real red traffic light with endings of relationships, and no convention associates the phrase "a red traffic light" with such endings. For that association to be conventional, there would have to be a uniformity of practice in the community to use the one as a sign of the other, or an agreement to use the one for the other if appropriate circumstances arose. I'm not sure I have ever seen a traffic-light image used in film in just the way I have described, but if I had, I think I would have understood its metaphorical significance without drawing on, or making an inference to, any practice of using traffic lights that way, or any agreement to use them that way. Metaphors don't work by convention; understanding them involves understanding intention, and we see the traffic lights as suggestive of ending when we see that the image of the traffic lights has been placed in the film just at this point with the intention of suggesting an ending.[27] Metaphor has to be explained in terms of utterance meaning, not in terms of literal (i.e., conventional) meaning.

In another place, Eco has argued for the conventionality of images generally on the grounds that our images tend to be,

---

[27] See the comments critical of Eco's conception of convention in Gilbert Harman, "Eco Location", in the second edition of *Film Theory and Criticism*. See also his "Semiotics and the Cinema: Metz and Wollen", in the same volume. Both are, unfortunately, omitted from subsequent editions.

and perhaps inevitably are, affected by our social practices: a picture of a lion was once praised for its lifelikeness; we can now see how much it owes to the conventions of heraldic representation.[28] Again, this argument simply conflates two kinds of conventions, those that facilitate meaning and those that determine it. From the fact that the characteristics of a sign are affected by convention it doesn't follow that the sign is a conventional sign. A sign is conventional only if there is a convention which determines its meaning.

An analogy may help. Colonel Smith asks Colonel Jones if Colonel Jones will kindly have the barracks cleared up after last night's party. Smith's request depends for its satisfaction on the giving of certain orders by Jones. But Smith's request is not itself an order; Smith is not in a position to order Jones to do anything. In general, what depends on Xs for its fulfilment is not itself thereby an X.

It may sound as if I am winning this argument by stipulation, insisting that images are not conventional in a quite idiosyncratic sense. Not so. Although I believe I am using the word "convention" in at least one of its ordinary senses, I agree that there are other senses my usage does not cover, and that in some of these senses, cinematic and other images may be said to be conventional. You may use "convention" in any of these other senses, or give to it any sense you like, but please use it only in one way, and make sure you have in your vocabulary other words, one for each distinguishable concept we need in this inquiry. One of those concepts is what I have called "conventionality", and it applies to words in English because their meanings are determined by a coordinated practice based on mutual expectation. That is the target concept, whatever you choose to call it, for anyone who wants to argue that cinematic images have much in common with the items studied by linguistics. This target concept does not, and could not, apply to the relation between cinematic images and their meanings, and the whole argument just given could be restated without using the word "convention" at all.

---

[28] Eco, *A Theory of Semiotics*, p. 205.

4.7 RELATIONS BETWEEN IMAGES

Perhaps the claim that there is a language of cinematic images is not the claim that these images themselves have a language-like structure, but rather that these images enter into language-like combinations with each other. In films, there are combinations of images; sometimes these combinations form identifiable and recurrent patterns, and these combinations can have a meaning which partly depends on the manner of their combination. Isn't there something here like the articulated structure of a sentence? No. As many film theorists have recognized, the representational content of a cinematic image cannot be equated with that of a name, predicate or other sub-sentential part of speech. If these images line up with anything in language it is with sentences themselves; images, like sentences, represent events, situations and states of affairs. They are not like names and descriptions, which pick out particular objects. So we cannot hope to find in the articulation of images anything like the internal syntactic structure of a sentence. The most we can hope to do is to latch onto the linguistic model at the point where *sentential* connectives and operators are introduced: the familiar truth functions like "and" and "not", together with intensional operators like "because", "causes" and the rest. Even if there were a genuine parallel discoverable at this point between the articulation of images and that of sentences (I shall argue that there is not one) it would not vindicate the idea that a theory of language comprehension will explain the comprehension of cinema. A theory of the sentential operators tells us how our understanding of sentence combinations depends on our understanding of the sentences which make them up. To account for our comprehension of the sentential components we need a prior theory about how we understand "atomic" sentences – those which do not have sentences as parts. This very basic part of linguistic theorizing tells us about the conventions which assign meanings to individual words, and about the rules for combining words into significant sentences. This part of the theory has, as I have argued, no counterpart in any theory of how we understand images.

Are there, in fact, any significant parallels between the connections we find in cinema between images, and the connections we find in natural languages between sentences? Note that sentential connections are indicated by means of convention: it is a convention, with us, that we indicate, by the use of "and" to join together two sentences, that the resulting combination is true only if both of its sentential components are true. Consider a fairly standard and familiar image combination in film: one image is connected to the next by means of a fade out and in. Typically, this represents there being a significant lapse of time between the events depicted in the first image and those in the second. This may reasonably be called a convention: other ways of connecting the images would do as well, or nearly as well, to indicate the desired relation. Perhaps other cinematic techniques, like shot–reverse-shot editing and eyeline matches, are conventions, though we might need a fairly generous account of convention to make them so. But still, these conventions, if that is what they are, do not amount to anything like the systematic, articulated set of conventions that govern a natural language. At most they enrich the meaning of an already nonconventionally meaningful structure; joining two shots or sequences by means of a fade adds meaning to that already present in the two shots taken individually; it may even alter that meaning. But if there were no nonconventional meaning there already, the fade would add none. With language it is the other way about; without convention there is no meaning at all, and two meaningless sentences cannot be joined to give a meaningful combination. Nor do the cinematic conventions I've just described form any kind of system. There are no rules, recursive or otherwise, by which meanings are built up by, say, the interpolation of a fade between the members of a shot–reverse-shot pair and according to which certain such combinations are meaningful or grammatically correct. All one can say of such a combination is that it does, or does not, work effectively to indicate some intended relationship between what the images themselves represent.

In just one way, the conventions of film are like the conventions of language: they set constraints on what the film maker can communicate to her audience about how the film is to be interpreted. Wittgenstein asked why you can't say "It's hot" and mean "It's cold". The answer is that in certain circumstances you can – for example, where you can count on your utterance being understood as ironic. But these circumstances do not always prevail, and we simply cannot use words however we like (or if we do, we won't be understood). Just so with film. The film maker cannot combine a pair of shots with a fade and mean anything she likes by it, and a shot–reverse-shot pair combined by means of a fade is likely to produce puzzlement unless there are strong contextual cues about what might be going on. What the film maker can communicate to viewers about how they are to interpret the images is limited by the conventional use to which the fade and other devices are put. *In no respect other than this is the combination of film images like a language.*

4.8 A LANGUAGE OF VISION?

An enthusiast for the language of images might try one last line of defence. According to my argument, we understand the depictive content of images by deploying the capacities we have to recognize the objects depicted. How, in fact, do we recognize those objects? How, in other words, does ordinary vision work? The answer is, I'm afraid, that we do not know. But one recent, plausible and to some extent empirically supported hypothesis might give hope that we are on the verge of discovering a language of vision. The hypothesis in question is that "a given view of an object is represented as an arrangement of simple primitive volumes, called *geons*".[29] Geons are volumes which belong to a larger set of volumes called generalized cones; geons include cubes, cones, pyramids, cylinders and other simple and familiar geometrical shapes in three dimensions. According to this hypothesis (sometimes called "recognition-by-components") combinations of two, or at most three, geons are sufficient to specify just about any object people typically are able to identify (there are currently estimated to be about thirty thousand of them).

[29] Biederman, "Visual Object Recognition", pp. 12–13.

One distinct advantage of the geon model is that it explains how people are able to identify an object when viewed from a variety of positions, even when they have not previously seen the object from that position.

Sometimes representing a seen object as a combination of geons in certain spatial relations is called "parsing", suggesting an analogy with the decomposition of sentences into their sentential parts. Might the geons and their combinations constitute something like a language of vision? I say not. The mind's stock of geons, if it has one, is nothing like the lexical knowledge of the speaker of a natural language. The geons are not representational devices conventionally connected with what they represent. They just are the shapes they are, and an object either does or does not, as a matter of fact, have the shape of a certain articulated set of geons. There is nothing conventional about the relation between geons and the objects they help us to recognize. Nor is there anything corresponding to a grammar of geons. While there may be compositions of geons which, contingently, don't correspond to the shape of anything we see in the world, there are no combinations of geons which "don't make sense", or are ungrammatical. Any articulation of geons corresponds to a perfectly coherent shape; there just might not be anything which has that shape. The recognition-by-components hypothesis suggests one way that objects in the world can be thought of as structured. There is no reason to think that their structure has anything in common with that of a language, and no reason to think that the skills we employ in analysing that structure bear any interesting relation to linguistic skills.

Part II

Imagination

FICTIONS, cinematic and other, engage the imagination. I present a theory according to which the imagination is a mental mechanism with certain uses and characteristics which can themselves shed light on the psychology of fiction. I develop a theory of visual imagining appropriate to the cinematic case.

Chapter 5

Imagination, the general theory

Imagination, without inducing the experience I imagine, delivers the fruits of experience.

Richard Wollheim

I have argued that it is a mistake to suppose that fictions, cinematic and other, create an illusion of reality. Fictions, I will argue, appeal not to belief, but to the faculty of imagination. We shall see that I mean talk of a faculty quite literally here. The imagination I believe to be a purpose-built system within the mind, and one subject to selective damage in the way that vision and the components of vision are.

Imagination has been low on the agenda of recent analytic philosophy, perhaps on account of its presumed frivolity. Possibly by way of a reaction, the philosophical writing we have on the imagination has often been driven by a concern with psychopathology, certainly evident in the work of Wollheim, and in the otherwise very different (and generally less rewarding) work of film theorists influenced by Lacan.[1] We need a psychopathology of imagination. But if we seek a naturalistic, biological explanation of imagination, we cannot rest with psychopathology; it is hardly credible that so complex and subtle a mechanism as the imagination should have developed and been

[1] See, e.g., Richard Wollheim, "Imagination and Identification", especially the later part. It is noticeable that when occasionally a writer on film seeks a theoretical alternative to the Lacanian framework, the alternative is still located within the realm of theorizing about the psychopathological – as with Gaylyn Studlar ("Masochism and the Perverse Pleasures of the Cinema"), who turns to Gilles Deleuze's *Masochism: An Interpretation of Coldness and Cruelty*.

sustained if it served no positive purpose. So we need an account of what is sometimes called the proper functioning of imagination: a biologically oriented theory that explains the adaptive benefit we gain from having the capacity to imagine. But from this point of view, imagination is puzzling. If we think of the development of mind in evolutionary terms, we might expect mechanisms of mental representation to be selected according to their reliability, and a mechanism that systematically misrepresents the world, as the imagination surely does, would seem to have enormous costs and no obvious benefits; for what we imagine often bears no systematic relation to what actually is.[2] As we shall see, the capacity for imagining does serve important cognitive, information-gathering goals. One effect of this turn towards science will be, I hope, the long-due recognition that we cannot answer all the philosophically interesting questions about imagination by a combination of introspection and a priori analysis.[3]

5.1 PERSPECTIVE SHIFTS

Between roughly the ages of three and a half and four and a half, children normally undergo an important shift in their understanding of the relation between themselves and others. Before the shift, children find it difficult to understand that someone's beliefs can be different from their own; the shift occurs when they come to understand this. Here's an experiment which illustrates this rather vividly.[4]

Sally, a puppet, is seen to hide a sweet in box A. She leaves the room. Another puppet is seen to move the sweet to box B.

---

[2] This problem was pointed out by Alan Leslie, "Pretence and Representation: The Origins of 'Theory of Mind' ". But I reject Leslie's solution. See my "Imagination and Simulation: Aesthetics Meets Cognitive Science".

[3] Occasionally, governments cotton on to the power of imagination. According to the *Guardian* (August 2, 1992), "Imagining the president's death is in Kenya a crime punishable by death."

[4] The experiment was devised by Hans Wimmer and Josef Perner. See their "Beliefs about Beliefs: Representation and Constraining Function of Wrong Beliefs in Young Children's Understanding of Deception". Their result has been replicated in a great variety of settings.

Sally returns. Question: where does Sally think her sweet is? Three-year-olds say "box B". The child thinks the sweet is in box B, having seen it moved there. The child then credits Sally with a belief the same as his or her own. By four and a half, most children realize that Sally did not see the sweet moved, and that her belief will consequently differ from the child's own. Before the shift, the child attributes to others his or her own perspective on the world. After the shift the child is able to calculate how a different perspective will lead to different beliefs.

Perhaps "calculate" isn't quite the right word here. Calculation suggests that the child possesses some sort of theory – perhaps a tacit theory, not consciously understood – and applies the theory to work out, in a particular case, what the other person's belief will be. For instance, the child might, in responding to the Sally experiment, apply the principle that if someone does not see something happen they will generally not know that it has happened, concluding that Sally does not know that the sweet has been moved. Many psychologists and philosophers working in the area of cognitive science think that this is, in fact, what the child does. They think that the shift in understanding I have just described occurs when the child acquires a new theory or part of a theory, a theory of mind, or acquires the ability to access and apply that theory.[5] But that is not the only possible view. One can suppose instead that the shift comes about through the acquisition of an ability, not through the acquisition of a theoretical principle, albeit a rough-and-ready one. On this view, the shift is a matter of *knowing how* rather than *knowing that*.[6]

[5] See, e.g., S. Baron-Cohen et al., "Does the Autistic Child Have a Theory of Mind'?"; Leslie, "Pretence and Representation"; and S. Stich and S. Nichols, "Second Thoughts on Simulation". On some views, Leslie's for example, the theory in question is presumed to be innate. According to others it is learned. See, e.g., Alison Gopnik, "What Is It if It Isn't a Theory?"

[6] Alvin Goldman, "Interpretation Psychologized"; Robert M. Gordon, "Folk Psychology as Simulation"; Jane Heal, "Replication and Functionalism"; and the articles in a double issue of *Mind and Language*, 7, nos. 1–2 (1992) devoted to simulation theory.

5.2 SIMULATION

On the knowing-how view, our basic mode of access to the minds of others works like this: I imagine myself to be in the other person's position, receiving the sensory information the other receives. Having thus projected myself imaginatively into that situation, I then imagine how I would respond to it: what beliefs and desires I would have, what decisions I would make and how I would feel having those perceptions, beliefs and desires, and making those decisions. But, crucially, this process of "imagining how I would respond" is not a matter of my *calculating* how I would respond by appeal to rough-and-ready principles of mental functioning. Imagining having certain beliefs and desires is not a matter of considering the proposition that I have those beliefs and desires, and then deducing, on the basis of a theory, what I would do as a consequence. Rather, I simply *observe how I do respond in imagination*. To imagine having those beliefs and desires is to take on, temporarily, those beliefs and desires; they become, temporarily and with other qualifications I shall describe in a moment, my own beliefs and desires. Being, thus temporarily, my own, they work their own effects on my mental economy, having the sorts of impacts on how I feel and what I decide to do that my ordinary, real beliefs and desires have. I let my mental processes run as if I really were in that situation – except that those processes run "off-line", disconnected from their normal sensory inputs and behavioural outputs. In that way I use my own mind to simulate the mind of another.

For example, I might start off my imagining by taking on in this way the beliefs and desires, and also the perceptions, of someone who sees a lion rushing towards him. These beliefs and desires then operate on me through their own natural powers; I start (if my imagining is vivid enough) to feel the visceral sensations of fear, and I decide to flee. But I don't flee; these beliefs and desires – let us call them pretend or imaginary beliefs and desires – differ from my own real beliefs and desires not just in being temporary and cancellable. Unlike my real beliefs and desires, they are run off-line, disconnected from their normal perceptual inputs and behavioural outputs. I start my simulation without requiring that the causal chain be initiated by actually seeing a lion, and end it at the point where the decision is made, but before that decision is translated into action. The function of the simulation is not to save me from a lion, since I am not actually threatened by one, but to help me understand the mental processes of someone so threatened. If my own mind is a reliable model of the other person's mind, then this process of mental simulation is a good guide to the mental states of the other. I can simply note that I formed, in imagination, a certain belief, desire or decision, then attribute it to the other. Let us call the hypothesis that we do, at least sometimes, come to a view about other people's mental states in this way, the *Simulation Hypothesis*. On this hypothesis, the shift which takes place when a child is able to comprehend another's belief which is, by her own lights, false, occurs like this: before the shift, the child is unable to project herself imaginatively into the position of the other; the shift occurs when the child becomes able to run a simulation which takes as initial conditions a perceptual state different from her own. Prior to that point, that child can attribute belief only by directly attributing to the other her own belief, and she is therefore unable to cope with differences of belief.[7]

An analogy may be helpful in understanding what is at stake between the knowing-that view (what is sometimes called the "theory theory") and the knowing-how view, which I have called the Simulation Hypothesis. Suppose you wish to know whether a bridge will withstand a certain kind of stress. One way to find out would be to have a theory about the strengths of materials and the way forces act on them, and to calculate,

[7] The problem for the child at three years old is not that she lacks the concept of a belief different from her own ("false belief", as this is sometimes called in the literature). For children at this age can, in certain circumstances, exhibit an understanding of false belief – citing, for example, an agent's false belief that the cat is in the garage in order to explain the fact that the agent is searching in the garage instead of under the table, where the cat really is (see H. Wellman and K. Bartsch, "Young Children's Reasoning about Beliefs"). The three-year-old's problem seems rather to be that she finds it difficult, without substantial prompts, to correct for false belief when imaginatively projecting herself into the agent's position.

on the basis of the theory, whether the bridge will withstand the stress. If you don't have such a theory, but instead have a reliable model of the bridge, you can answer the question by subjecting the model to just those stresses (assume that there are no scaling calculations to do). The Simulation Hypothesis says that we do have a reliable model of the mental processes of others, namely our own mental processes run off-line. Using the model, we are able to draw conclusions about other minds without having a theory of how minds, including our own, work.

But what reason is there to think that my own mind is a reliable model of the minds of others? To be a reliable model it needs to be similar to the minds of others. How similar are our minds? Roy Sorensen has argued that if simulation theory is correct, we may expect agents within a given population to be mentally similar, because being mentally average will confer a selective advantage.[8] The more like others I am, the more reliable will be the process of mental modelling I engage in, the more I will be able to work out what others believe and desire, what they believe I believe and desire, and what they desire I believe and desire. That way, I shall be better able to cooperate with them when cooperation suits me, and to compete with them when it does not. That way I have a better chance of surviving and breeding. And as people's minds bunch more closely around the average, the pressure to be average increases, because by being average there are more and more people I can successfully simulate. On this view, we may expect an accelerating tendency towards mental homogeneity.

Sorensen's argument is not in favour of the Simulation Hypothesis. That is, it does not provide a reason for saying that we are simulators rather than theorists when it comes to understanding the mental states of others. Rather, it is a defence of the Simulation Hypothesis against an objection to it. Sorensen's point is that, if we are simulationists, we can expect that evolution will have made us mentally similar enough for simulations to be successful a significant proportion of the time, and

---

[8] Roy Sorensen, "Self-Strengthening Empathy", unpublished.

so it is no objection to the Simulation Hypothesis to say that simulation would not deliver the desired result because of mental diversity.

I believe that the Simulation Hypothesis is very important for our understanding, not just of how we comprehend other minds, but of how we engage with fictions, including cinematic fictions. I say that fictions are devices which encourage and guide the imagination; fictions tell stories, and the things which are parts of the stories they tell are things which those fictions authorize us to imagine.[9] *Clouds of Witness* authorizes us to imagine that Lord Peter establishes his brother's innocence, for that is part of the story it tells; conversely, it prohibits us from imagining that his brother is hanged for murder, for it is part of the story that he is not hanged. (Sometimes, of course, our decisions about what we are authorized to imagine are more complex and controversial.) We can, of course, improvise our own stories, providing ourselves with spontaneous fictions that encourage us to imagine ourselves in interesting and colourful situations. But we often enjoy having our imaginations guided by an external source – the work of an author whose skill in story construction may be superior to our own and whose outcome we can't predict in advance. Such an external source, however encoded and through whatever sensory channels it is received, is a fiction, in my sense.[10] Films are encoded in visual and auditory depictions, and are received through the senses of sight and hearing. Novels, while normally received through the sense of sight (we normally read with our eyes) are encoded not in visual depictions, but in linguistic symbols accessible to sight. Both are forms of fiction.

"Imagination" has a number of senses, none of them very clear. But one kind of imagining is, I believe, the process of running our mental states off-line. That is the kind of imagining which takes place when we engage with fictions. So far, I have described off-line simulation only in the context of our attempts to comprehend the mental states of another. But that is simply one function of simulation. Simulation itself occurs when, for

---

[9] See Walton, *Mimesis as Make-Believe*, p. 51.
[10] See my *Nature of Fiction*.

whatever reason, we run our mental states off-line. One reason we can run our mental states, in particular our belief–desire system, off-line is to engage with a fictional work. That happens when the fictional story itself provides the inputs to the simulation.

Consider first a nonfictional work: a newspaper article or television documentary. If we think the work reliable, we shall form certain beliefs based on the information the work conveys. We may also acquire certain desires: documentaries about the dangers of smoking can make you want to give up, and travel articles extolling the virtues of an exotic location can make you want to go there. (So as to simplify things, I'll concentrate on the case of belief for the moment.)

A fictional work, assuming we know that it's fiction, can have effects on our mental processes similar in various ways to the effects of nonfiction. Fictional works can engage our attention, and they can have what is, on reflection, a surprising capacity to move us. But we do not acquire from them beliefs in the straightforward way that we acquire beliefs from nonfiction. With fictions, our mental processes are engaged off-line, and what we acquire instead of beliefs is *imaginings* which simulate belief. When I work out what Sally believes about the location of her chocolates, I mentally simulate Sally's mental processes, her having certain perceptions and thereby acquiring certain beliefs. In other words, I imagine being in Sally's situation, responding as she responds. When I engage with fiction I simulate the process of acquiring beliefs – the beliefs I would acquire if I took the work I am engaged with for fact rather than fiction. Here I imagine myself acquiring factual knowledge. In the Sally case I imagine being in the situation someone else actually is in; in the fiction case I imagine being in a situation I could be in but actually am not in. In the first case the imagining is an instrument to a further purpose: to inform me of the mental processes of someone else. In the second case the imagining has no such further purpose: the simulation provoked by the fiction I read is simply something I enjoy.[11]

[11] Simulations engaged in in the course of reading or watching fiction *might*

We can think of beliefs and desires as states with two aspects: a representational and a functional aspect. A belief and a desire might have identical representational contents. I believe that it will rain, and I hope that it will. Here, the content is the same: that it will rain. But despite their sameness of content, the belief and the desire are distinct kinds of states. While they do not differ in representational content, they differ functionally, that is, in terms of causes and effects. Believing that it will rain tends to be caused by kinds of sensory and other experiences different from those which tend to cause desiring that it will rain, and believing that it will rain will tend to have consequences for my behaviour different from the behavioural consequences of desiring that it will. Belief and desire are different attitudes, and their being different in this regard is a matter of the functional differences between them.[12]

I said that what makes something a belief rather than some other kind of state is its causes and effects. In that case there is something unsatisfactory in my description of simulation as "running beliefs off-line" (I'll come to the issue of desires in a moment). Running off-line is, exactly, a matter of severing the connections between our mental states and their perceptual causes and behavioural effects. A belief run "off-line" isn't really a belief, just as a monarch who has been deposed is no longer a monarch. Revolutions transmute monarchs into ex-monarchs. Simulation transmutes beliefs into imaginings. Just as a belief and a desire may have the same content but differ functionally, so may a belief and an imagining. Believing that it will rain has certain connections to perception and to behaviour which, when they are severed, transmutes that belief into a case of imagining that it will rain.

Since imaginings are states run "off-line", does that mean that imaginings completely lack a functional aspect, being, as it were, pure representations? No. While they lack the connections of

have a further purpose: to help me pass a literature or film-studies exam, for example. My point is that they need not have any further purpose in order to seem worthwhile to us.

[12] For an attempt to account in functional terms for the difference between belief and desire see Jamie Whyte, "The Normal Rewards of Success".

belief to the external world via perception and behaviour, they retain some internal connections. With off-line simulation, states of imagining function as internal surrogates of beliefs because they retain belief-like connections to other mental states and to the body. Imaginings, like beliefs, can lead to decisions, and can cause certain kinds of bodily sensations. Compare believing that you are confronted by a dangerous bear with imagining that you are. Imagining there is a bear in front of me, just like believing there is one, may cause a decision to flee. But in the imagining case the decision itself is an imaginary one; it is something that stands to real decision as imagining stands to belief. And vividly imagining there is a bear there will cause me to have some of the unpleasant visceral and other bodily feelings that believing there is a bear there would, though perhaps less intensely. Note that in this case what is caused by the imagining is a real state of feeling and not an imaginary one. Imagining yourself in danger causes you really to feel disturbed; it does not merely cause a state of imaginary disturbance. The reason for that is that feelings are states identified, not in terms of their function, but in terms of how they feel. A state which feels like a bodily sensation really is one.

I have been discussing the relation of imagining to belief, and I said I would bring desire into the picture. If mental simulation is how we understand the minds of others, there must be states that stand to desire as imaginings stand to beliefs; for us adequately to simulate the mental states of others, we must simulate their desires as well as their beliefs. So as well as pretend or imaginary beliefs – what I have been calling imaginings – we need pretend or imaginary desires. Fictions provoke imaginary desires just as they do imaginary beliefs. Reading the story, I want the hero to succeed. Or do I? After all, I am perfectly aware there is no hero to be the object of my desire. How can I desire something for an entity I don't believe in?[13] What's really happening is that desires are being run off-line, in tandem with

[13] For more on this absence of belief problem, see my *Nature of Fiction*, chapter 5. See also this chapter, Section 5.4.

pretend beliefs. I have a pretend desire that the hero succeed, backed up by a pretend belief in his existence.

Couldn't we be more economical here, supposing that there is one unified state of imagining, and that what we might neutrally call "pretend beliefs" and "pretend desires" are accounted for by saying that in the one case we imagine that we believe something, and in the other that we imagine that we desire it? That way we get by with three categories – belief, desire and imagining – instead of my four – belief, desire, pretend belief and pretend desire. But this admirably economical move has problems. It would not then be possible simply to imagine (in the intuitive sense) that some state of affairs occurred; I would have to imagine that I believed that it occurred. Now consider the case of imagining that something occurred and that no one knows anything about it (cases of this kind will recur when I discuss imagining in response to film). That would require me to imagine that I believe that it happened and that no one else believed that it did. The content of my imagining would in that and similar cases be paradoxical. But it does seem that I can imagine that something happens that no one knows anything about, without thereby imagining something impossible. So imagining something cannot, in general, be equivalent to imagining believing it.[14] In that case we really are going to need recourse to what I have called "pretend desires" as well as to pretend beliefs, in order to explain important aspects of mental processing.

It is important to see what sort of claim I am making here about the relation between imagination and mental simulation. In saying that imagination is simulation I am not, for example, offering a piece of conceptual analysis that might serve to introduce the concept of imagining to one who lacked it. On the contrary, it may well be that, to get a grip on the notion of simulation, one

---

[14] Also, of course, I can imagine that no one is doing any imagining, but I trust there is nothing even apparently paradoxical about what I am imagining in that case.

needs already to possess the concept of imagining. My proposal has closer methodological affinities to such essentialist identifications as the claim that water is H_2O. This is not to be understood as offering an analysis of the concept of water; the claim is rather that water has a hidden inner structure that is explanatory of its more evident surface properties, and which may bring with it some surprising consequences – that water is not really a continuous substance, for example. Likewise, the cash value of the claim that imagining is simulation lies in its explanatory power. The rest of this chapter is designed to give a brief indication of that power.

5.3 FICTION AND TWO KINDS OF SIMULATION

I introduced the idea of imagining-as-simulation by describing our simulation of the mental states of other real people. I then suggested that the capacity for simulation is something we apply to fictional works, and that these two functions of simulation are quite different. Perhaps they are not always so different. Might it be, for example, that fictional works sometimes require or encourage us to simulate the mental states of their *characters*? I believe the answer is yes: understanding, appreciating and learning from a fictional work (it might be a cinematic or other kind of fictional work) sometimes requires that we simulate the mental states of a character within the fiction.

I want to make a distinction between two kinds of imaginings that fictions encourage. There is, first of all, imagining what is fictional in a story. Part of engaging with a fictional work consists of imagining those things which it makes fictional, as *Anna Karenina* makes it fictional that Anna commits suicide.[15] Cases where we imagine what is fictional, I call *primary* imaginings. *Secondary* imagining occurs when we imagine various things *so as to* imagine what is true in the story. Frequently, secondary imaginings are not required for primary imagining to take place:

---

[15] On this see my *Nature of Fiction*, chapter 2; and Walton, *Mimesis as Make-Believe*, chapter 2.

the story has it that a certain character walked down a dark street, and we simply imagine that. Then we have primary imagining without the need for secondary imagining. Primary imagining most notably requires secondary imagining in cases where what we are primarily to imagine is the experience of a character.[16] If the dark street hides something threatening, the character who walks it may have thoughts, anxieties, visual and auditory experiences and bodily sensations that it would be important for readers to imagine something about. The author may indicate, to a greater or lesser degree of specificity, what the character's experience is. But it is notoriously difficult, and in some cases perhaps impossible, for us to describe people's mental states precisely. Authors who adopt stream of consciousness and other subjective styles have failed to do it, and so have film makers like Hitchcock who try to re-create a character's visual experiences onscreen. Anyway, the attempt at full specificity and precision in this regard would usually be regarded as a stylistic vice, leaving, as we significantly say, "nothing to the imagination". What the author explicitly says, and what can be inferred therefrom, will constrain our understanding of the character's mental state. It will set signposts and boundaries. But if these are all we have to go by in a fiction, it will seem dull and lifeless. It is when we are able, in imagination, to feel as the character feels that fictions of character take hold of us. This process of empathetic reenactment of the character's situation is what I call secondary imagining. As a result of putting myself, in imagination, in the character's position, I come to have imaginary versions of the thoughts, feelings and attitudes I would have were I in that situation. Having identified those thoughts,

[16] I am using the term "experience" here in a very broad sense. In my sense, what a character experiences includes visual, auditory, bodily and other sensations, and also the beliefs, desires and intentions it is fictional that she has, in so far as they are accessible to her consciousness. Some people argue that states with propositional content like beliefs and desires are accessible to consciousness exactly because they have a characteristic feel in the way that sensations do (see, e.g., Alvin Goldman, "The Psychology of Folk Psychology"). But this is very much a minority opinion, and I do not want to judge this issue one way or the other here.

feelings and attitudes ostensively, I am then able to imagine that the character felt *that* way. That is how secondary imagining is a guide to primary imagining.[17]

Novels with characters into whose mental lives we readily project ourselves are not works in which we ourselves are characters. While I may simulate the situation of the character, imagining being in his situation, that piece of imagining does not correspond to anything which the novel makes fiction. It is, exactly, secondary imagining – imagining undertaken because it will put me in a position where I will be able to imagine something the novel makes fictional: that the character has certain thoughts and feelings in response to his situation. It is that further imagining which is primary.

Being able to construct fictions with characters whose mental

[17] There are times when secondary imagining fails us, because our minds are not attuned to the task at hand. Robert Gordon drew my attention to the following passage from *Time* magazine (May 9, 1994), by John Skow, entitled "Harold Brodkey's New Novel Is Erotic – But Not to Everybody": "We respond to stories with astonishing versatility of imagination. The three-year-old listening to his grandmother momentarily becomes Peter Rabbit; the geezer reading Patrick O'Brian's sea stories feels scared on the quarterdeck of a storm-blown frigate. But the distinction between what the reader imagines and what he actually experiences remains solid – the geezer does not actually get seasick. Over the whole range of literature, only erotica functions differently. If it works, sexual arousal is real, not imaginary. And if it doesn't work? The most recent example is Harold Brodkey's novel *Profane Friendship* (Farrar, Straus & Giroux; 387 pages; $23). The author tells of a long, intensely erotic affair between the narrator, an American novelist named Nino, and an Italian named Onni. The names are anagrams of each other – different stirrings of the same ingredients, including the same sex. If the drama is to succeed, the passion must not merely engage the reader intellectually; it must arouse him. For this heterosexual male, who has imagined himself to be Moll Flanders and Jonathan Livingston Seagull, the failure is total. Such a statement will surely be called homophobia, but fear and disapproval are not operating here. In fact, nothing is operating. The reader's reaction is vague exasperation. His mind simply does not have the software to induce the intended physiological response to the author's erotic obsessions, and these are the essence of the book. Such thoughts, of course, must occur regularly to gays when they read about hetero sex. You don't have to be a rabbit to enjoy Beatrix Potter, but you may have to be either gay or straight to appreciate gay or straight erotica."

lives readily lend themselves to simulation is not a capacity every fiction maker possesses or wishes to exploit. Through incompetence and sometimes through design, the characters of fiction resist simulation: their responses to situations, their words and even their thoughts (in so far as the author lets us know what they are) seem not to be those we would have in their situations. In these cases, when we engage with the fiction, trying to guess what will happen, trying to fill in its background of unstated presuppositions and undescribed events, we may have to rely more than usual on inferences we make concerning the author's intentions or about the constraints of form and genre the work conforms to. A rough guide to the degree of naturalism in a work of fiction is the extent to which we can let our own minds model those of the characters. To the extent that these minds are opaque, not merely in the sense of being underdescribed by the author, but in that of resisting simulation, we make a work that rejects the standards of naturalism.

Is it just an historical accident that most of our fiction is naturalistic in this sense? Despite frequent calls for, or announcements of, the death of naturalism, I think it unlikely. The drive to simulate seems to be a very powerful one. And with good reason; I shall argue in the next section that the disastrous effects of simulative failure are evident in the aloneness and multiple incompetencies of autism. The close historical association between fiction and psychological naturalism suggests that fictions have thrived exactly because they give us opportunities to exercise our capacity for simulation. Fiction may not be logically tied to psychological naturalism any more than painting is logically tied to naturalistic representation, but in both cases the psychological connection seems to go very deep.

5.4 CONSEQUENCES

Identifying imagination with simulation has interesting consequences; some of these concern features of imagining generally agreed on, while others require us to attribute to imagining features that can seem counterintuitive but which I believe to be correct. I want to point out some of those features.

First, given the characteristics of off-line simulation I have described, we can now explain certain features of our experience when we are engaged by fictions. While fictions do not cause us to believe in the reality of the fictional story, they can engage us to the extent of causing within us the sometimes pleasant and sometimes unpleasant bodily states we associate with being emotionally moved by events. If fictions encourage simulations, and simulated beliefs and desires retain their internal connections to our bodily states, that is exactly what we would expect. The anxiety that watching horror movies induces in me does not cause me to call the police, but it does cause me to *feel* afraid.

Second, the idea that imagination is simulation explains one peculiarity of imagining in relation to belief and desire: that there is no such thing as *dispositional* imagining. With belief and desire we have the distinction between dispositional and occurrent states. I may believe something I have never thought about and which plays no role in explaining my past or current behaviour. Similarly for desire. In these cases we say that the belief or desire is dispositional rather than occurrent; the state is possessed in virtue of the fact that if a relevant situation were to arise you would be likely to behave in a way that would betray the belief or the desire. But there is no comparable category of dispositional imagining, and all imagining is occurrent (though not necessarily conscious, as I shall argue). And while I may be disposed to imagine certain things, the possession of such a disposition does not constitute my dispositionally imagining them. But it is easy to see that with simulation there is also no dispositional–occurrent distinction to be made. You are either running a simulation or not, and being disposed to run a certain simulation does not constitute dispositionally simulating – no more than being disposed to run a mile means you are dispositionally running one.

Third, in identifying simulation and imagination we vindicate the intuition that imaginings are somehow secondary or derivative states. Imagining something may be different from believing it, but it does seem as if there is an asymmetrical dependence of imagining on belief. We can imagine a creature which has beliefs but lacks the capacity to imagine. Indeed, there may actually be cases of this in our population. People suffering from autism show a pattern of disabilities strikingly suggestive of the hypothesis that what they lack is, literally, imagination.[18] The condition is marked by a considerable degree of inflexibility and isolation in social relations; there is no spontaneous enthusiasm for games of imagination and pretence, and there is considerable difficulty in verbal communication, though high functioning autistic individuals often have functional mastery of language. Sufferers, even those few of high ability who hold responsible jobs, have difficulty understanding that other people have different knowledge, beliefs, desires and generally a different mental outlook on the world from themselves; and autistic children typically fail tests of understanding of false belief, such as the "Sally" test already described.[19] This inability to understand the mental states of others may explain why autistic subjects fail to provide relevant background information in their speech, fail to notice that others are bored by their own favourite topics of conversation, fail to understand that their own behaviour has caused offence. Often they seem to lack the ability to deceive, or even to understand the concept of deception.

This inability to comprehend mental states, together with the

---

[18] Autism was first identified by L. Kanner ("Autistic Disturbances of Affective Contact"). The condition often goes with a greater or lesser degree of general mental retardation, but 20% of autistics are in the "normal" range.

[19] In a version of Wimmer and Perner's false-belief experiment conducted by Baron-Cohen and colleagues ("Does the Autistic Child Have a 'Theory of Mind'?"), three groups of children were tested: clinically normal four-and-a-half-year-olds, a group of Down's syndrome children (mean IQ = 64, mean age = eleven years) and a group of autistic children (mean IQ = 82, mean age = twelve years). The success rate in the normal and Down's syndrome groups was high: 85% and 86% respectively, while the success rate in the autistic group was only 20%. See also D. Roth and A. Leslie, "The Recognition of Attitude Conveyed by Utterance: A Study of Preschool and Autistic Children". About 30% of autistic subjects pass the false-belief test and its variants. When set a task that tests understanding of higher-order belief (belief about belief) which normal six-year-olds pass, these autistic subjects fail (S. Baron-Cohen, "The Autistic Child's Theory of Mind: A Case of Specific Developmental Delay"). For a simulative account of autistic problems on so-called false-belief tests see my "Simulation-Theory, Theory-Theory and the Evidence from Autism".

lack of interest in pretence and the fictional, when taken in conjunction with the idea that we understand other people's mental states by an act of imaginative projection, strongly suggests that the basic deficiency of autism is a lack of imagination. But undoubtedly, autistic people have beliefs and desires. On the other hand, it is difficult to imagine a being who had the capacity for imagining, but not for belief. The Simulation Hypothesis explains this asymmetry. Since simulation runs the belief–desire system off-line, imagining is parasitic on these other mental states.

If imagining is simulation, then I think we have an explanation, or the beginnings of one, for a puzzling phenomenon: our ability to empathize with fictional characters and their situations. A familiar formulation: how can we pity Anna Karenina when we know that she does not exist? There are problems here of different kinds, one of which is logical: if emotions require certain kinds of beliefs (not merely causally but constitutively) how can we have emotions directed at fictional characters when we lack the relevant beliefs? But putting aside the logical problem which I have discussed elsewhere,[20] let us concentrate on the psychological issue: why do we get so involved with, distraught and caring about, people whose existence is merely imagined? I suggest that it is at least an insight into this problem to acknowledge, with the simulation theorists, that the basic mechanism by which we make emotional contact with other (this time real) people involves imagination. We come to understand, not merely in propositional terms, but in an emotionally attuned way, their situations; to feel as if we were in their situations by simulating their situations, or, if I am right in the basic identification of this chapter, by imagining. Empathizing with fictional characters would then just be an extension of this imaginative project; we imagine not merely that we are in someone else's shoes, but someone in whose shoes we then imagine ourselves.

Another feature of imagining which needs explaining is the collapse of iterativity: a puzzle related to a problem that David

---

[20] See Currie, *Nature of Fiction*, chapter 5.

Lewis has called the problem of the flash stockman.[21] Try imagining someone else imagining something; what tends to happen is that you end up imagining the something yourself. And with those fictions, like *A Thousand and One Nights*, where what is fictional is that someone is telling a fictional story, we very quickly move to the position where we are imagining the story told, not the telling of it. Why does imagining that someone imagines *P* tend to collapse into imagining *P*, whereas, for example, believing that someone believes *P* rarely collapses into believing *P*? If imagining is simulation, then imagining someone's imaginings is a matter of simulating her simulation. How would that work? Consider first the ordinary case: I simulate her beliefs and desires rather than her imaginings. Simplifying, suppose she believes *P* and desires *Q*; I then give myself appropriately off-line versions of *P* and *Q*. *P*, for me, is a case of pretend belief, and *Q* is a case of pretend desire. In this case I simulate the having of belief *P* and desire *Q*. Now consider the more complex case: I simulate her imagining, that is, her pretend beliefs and pretend desires. Suppose she has *P* as a pretend belief and *Q* as a pretend desire; she is, in other words, running off-line versions of *P* and *Q*. To model her mental processes in my own mind (in other words, to simulate her), what must I do? The answer is that I also must run off-line versions of *P* and *Q*. But we have seen, from an examination of the simple case, that this – running off-line versions of *P* and *Q* – is what counts for me as having *P* as a pretend belief and *Q* as a pretend desire. The attempt to simulate her simulation has resulted in my simply imagining what it is she imagines, and not her imagining of it.

In this chapter I have simply asserted a claim I have argued elsewhere – that we engage with a fictional story by imagining its content, or what is "true in the fiction".[22] An objection to this is that a good deal of the content of a fictional story is true, and known to be so by the audience. Thus what happens in fiction often happens against a background of real locations correctly

[21] See David Lewis, postscript to "Truth in Fiction", *Philosophical Papers*, vol. 1.
[22] See Currie, *Nature of Fiction*, chapter 2.

described and often includes historical incidents. But is it not at least very odd, goes the objection, to say that we imagine things that we believe to be true?[23]

In reply I say that, while this may sound odd, it is just what the identification of imagination with simulation would predict about our capacity to imagine. If I want to figure out what decision someone else will come to, I shall start by feeding into the simulation as initial conditions some assumptions about what the person believes. These (putative) beliefs will then be run off-line – thereby becoming imaginings – leading to a modelling of the other's decision-making process. But given that a lot of what other people believe I believe myself, there will be occasions when I shall have to feed in assumptions about what the person believes which coincide with what I believe. In such a case I shall have to run my own beliefs off-line, thereby bringing about a situation in which I imagine what I believe.

There is, in addition, a lot of independent evidence that people imagine what they believe to be true. Let us assume, plausibly, that imagining is what drives childhood games of pretence. Indeed, without this assumption, it would be difficult to see how pretence could be distinguished from mere confusion. The difference between the child who pretends the rocking horse is a horse and the child who thinks the rocking horse really is a horse might well not show up in behaviour. The difference is that in the first case, the child's behaviour is caused by her imagining the rocking horse to be a horse, and in the second case by her believing that it is. But it is clear, both from casual observation and from controlled experiments, that children incorporate a great deal of factual belief into pretence. Thus it might be part of the pretence that, as a result of someone's pouring activity, some cups are empty and some are full. In fact, no real pouring has been done, and so all the cups really are empty. Yet the child's pretence discriminates between empty and full cups, and so a component of the pretence is that something is true which *is* true: that this cup is empty. But if the behavioural pretence is driven by imagining, it is difficult to

[23] Noël Carroll, review of *The Nature of Fiction*.

avoid the conclusion that the child is imagining something, part of which is true.

Could we explain the behaviour by saying instead that it is the outcome of a combination of imagining and belief? That is, the child imagines that these two cups (which as it happens are empty) are full, and believes that these other two cups are empty. But what is the explanation of the fact that other beliefs of the child do not influence the pretend behaviour? The child believes that all four of the cups are empty, but only treats two of them as if they were. The simplest and most natural explanation seems to be that the belief that these two are empty does become part of what the child imagines, while the belief that all four are empty does not. And there are other cases where pretence seems to coincide almost entirely with belief – as with the case reported by Vygotsky of two sisters pretending to be sisters.[24]

One final and rather startling implication of the assimilation of imagining to simulation is that imagining should not be thought of as always and automatically a conscious or even an intentional action, since simulation, if it really does help us to understand the minds of others, must be done unintentionally, mostly at a subconscious level. For me that is a welcome result. If, as I have argued, fictions function to drive imagination, they do so in ways of which the subject is sometimes unaware, and over which the subject rarely exerts conscious control. But there are those who have argued that it is a priori of imaginative pretence that it is engaged in consciously and intentionally.[25] This claim seems to me symptomatic of a residual Cartesianism that has not yet been dislodged from this underdeveloped part of the philosophy of mind. If hitching the concept of imagination to simulation theory helps us to abandon it, so much the better.

---

[24] Alan Leslie discusses the issue of pretending what is believed in his "Pretending and Believing: Issues in the Theory of ToMM". I owe the reference to Vygotsky to Leslie's paper (see L. S. Vygotsky, "Play and Its Role in the Mental Development of the Child"). For criticism of Leslie's theoretical approach to the issue of pretence, see my "Imagination and Simulation".

[25] See, e.g., Noël Carroll, *The Philosophy of Horror: Paradoxes of the Heart*; and Anders Pettersson, "On Walton's and Currie's Analysis of Fiction".

5.5 THE DANGERS OF IMAGINING

Fictions, especially cinematic ones, are sometimes identified as the source of violent or otherwise undesirable behaviour, and as encouraging destructive attitudes. Whether and to what extent they do any or all of these things is a question to which empirical studies have not given a clear answer. However, in light of the identification of imagination with simulation, it is not hard to postulate a mechanism whereby fictions may do moral damage.

Suppose I am right in thinking about imagination in terms of off-line simulation. Imagination enables us to respond to the world not merely as it actually is and with the beliefs and desires we actually have, but as it might be, will be or was, and to experience it as we would with beliefs and desires other than our own. Imagination does this, according to the simulationist, by running our belief–desire system off-line, disconnected from action and behaviour. It must involve, therefore, some inhibiting mechanism which effects the disconnection. But there is a danger in this. An inhibiting mechanism might go wrong, or at best be unreliable; that is frequently how it is with mental mechanisms. That way, imagination would have a tendency to spill over into belief: what starts as an act of imagining might turn into a real belief or desire by being brought, inadvertently, on-line. In small ways this happens all the time: old Mr Harding's tendency to play a nonexistent cello at times of stress might be an example from literature, and most of us have a tendency to reach for the relevant body part when imagining a painful injury. Perhaps this also happens less often in more serious ways. There are people of whom we want to say that they are living a fantasy life, that they are in the grip of beliefs and desires which derive from fiction or fantasy rather than from experience or from sober reflection. Perhaps their inhibitory mechanisms are more than usually impaired, and their boundary between fact and fiction has genuinely started to blur.

In some ways, this blurring has a tendency to be corrected by the force of external reality. I imagine I am floating pleasantly in a warm swimming pool, but if such an imagining were to show any signs of breaking down the barriers provided by my inhibitory system and transmuting itself into a belief, the evidence from all my senses would quickly come to the rescue. No such belief could long survive its evident falsity.[26] But desiring is under no such tight ecological control. There is, certainly, a connection between perception and desire; perception influences, in various ways, what we desire. But the connection is much more tenuous than that between our empirical beliefs about the world and our perception of it, and perception does not provide the powerful second line of defence against renegade imaginings in the desire case that it does in the belief case. So, by imagining ourselves in the situation of a character with destructive, immoral desires, and thereby coming to have, in imagination, the desires of the character – what I have called secondary imagining – we may be in danger of really acquiring those desires through failure of the inhibitory mechanism.[27]

This chapter has provided a general theory of imagination. The next will develop a theory of specifically cinematic imagining.

---

[26] Perhaps hallucinations, or some of them, are produced by really spectacular blowouts in the inhibitory system.

[27] There is experimental evidence that children can come to believe, or be prone to believe, things which they have initially been asked merely to imagine being the case. See C. N. Johnson and Paul L. Harris, "Magic: Special but Not Excluded"; and Jacqueline D. Woolley and Katrine E. Phelps, "Young Children's Practical Reasoning about Imagination". For interesting evidence of leakage the other way – from beliefs and desires to imagination, see Nigel Harvey, "Wishful Thinking Impairs Belief–Desire Reasoning: A Case of Decoupling Failure in Adults?" The idea that there might be breakdowns in the mechanism of inhibition governing an off-line process may be useful in other areas. Jeannerod has recently suggested that certain kinds of compulsive imitative behaviour may be explained by a breakdown in the inhibitory control which governs motor imagery; in these cases, imagining performing a movement leads inevitably to actually performing it (M. Jeannerod, "The Representing Brain: Neural Correlates of Motor Intention and Imagery", p. 200).

Chapter 6
Imagination, personal and impersonal

A film makes us feel like eye-witnesses of the events
which it portrays.

Victor Perkins

Cinema is a medium in which fictions are presented pictorially.
In this way, its fictions differ from those of the novel and other
linguistic forms. But to characterize the difference between the
pictorial and the linguistic just at the point of *delivery* would be
to leave us with something important unexplained: the distinctive experience of pictorial, and in particular cinematic, fictions.
Watching movies is very different from reading novels. It is also
different from watching plays. Any adequate theory of cinema
will have to account for the differences. That theory must tell us
not only what is distinctive about the delivery of cinematic fictions but also about their reception – and about the connection
between the two. It will not be sufficient simply to say that viewers of a film are required to imagine various things, and that the
film is constructed so as to guide them in their imaginings, for
that is true of all fictions in whatever media. I have my own
story to tell about what is distinctive about cinematically induced imaginings, but it will appear strange and unmotivated
unless it is arrived at by the elimination of more familiar and
perhaps initially more plausible rivals. So I begin with what I
take to be the main rival account which I distil, by a process of
rational reconstruction, from the writings of film theorists of various times and persuasions. When we see what is wrong with
that account we shall have reason to look on my own proposal
with some favour.

6.1 THE CLASSICAL THEORY

By the term "classical film theory" I mean the kind of theorizing developed during the period of tumultuous development in the cinema through the thirties, forties and fifties. Considered as a period, it is generally regarded as having ended in the early sixties with the work of Jean Mitry, though there are people writing today who share significant doctrinal or methodological assumptions with the classical theorists. Its greatest exponent was André Bazin. The theorists I call classical often disagree about a great deal, and perhaps it is only by contrast with more recent developments in semiotics and the psychoanalytic exploration of the cinema that we can see the classical theorists as having anything much in common. However, there is one substantial doctrine which most of them hold. We have come across a version of it already when discussing the doctrine of illusionism. The classical illusionistic theory of cinema claims that the viewer is made to believe that he or she is a spectator at a real action, watching from within the space of the action, situated where the camera is. We have seen plenty of reason to reject that view. But perhaps we ought to consider whether some weakened version of it is true. And indeed, there is a weaker version of it which classical film theorists can be read as supporting, though it is sometimes hard to know whether they really have a strong or a weak version in mind. This weaker version substitutes for the notion of belief the notion of imagining. Instead of claiming, implausibly, that the viewer is made the subject of an illusion and is caused to have false beliefs about his or her situation, we might say this: that the viewer merely *imagines* that he or she is within the space of the action, watching real events from the position of the camera. Thus when Jean Mitry says, "I know that I am in the movie theatre, but I feel that I am in the world offered to my gaze, a world that I experience 'physically',"[1] we might take the phrase "feeling I am

---

[1] Jean Mitry, quoted approvingly both in Wilson, *Narration in Light*, p. 55, and in Charles Affron, *Cinema and Sentiment*, p. 7. The quotation is from *Esthétique et psychologie du cinéma, I: les structures*, p. 179.

in the world offered to my gaze" as meaning *imagining* that I am in that world, and imagining yourself in the fictional world is consistent with knowing you are actually in a movie theatre. George Wilson, a philosopher/film theorist, is quite explicit about the role of this kind of imagining in film: "The spectator *knows* that he is in the [movie] theatre, but *it is make-believe for him* that he is watching from within the space of the story."[2] It would be appropriately charitable to theorists like Balázs, Bazin and Panofsky to interpret them as offering a thesis compatible with Wilson's claim. Unlike the view that we literally believe ourselves to be within the space of the action – the view I criticized in Chapter 1 – Wilson's view is not obviously wrong. Nonetheless, I think it is wrong.

In criticizing this view, I am not going to be attacking the idea that the film viewer imagines various things; I have been arguing that that is exactly what fictional works, including cinematic fictional works, encourage. What I shall object to is the idea that cinematic works encourage us to imagine ourselves to be observers of the fictional events, placed within the world of the fiction. It will be useful to have some terminology with which to mark a distinction I am going to be using here. When I imagine merely that such and such happens, without imagining that I see (or have other kinds of epistemic contacts with) what happens, we have a case of *impersonal imagining*. When imagining involves the idea that *I* am seeing the imagined events, we have a species of *personal imagining*. (There are other kinds of personal imaginings: imagining that I am hearing something, etc.) More specifically, it is a case of *imagining seeing*. In the light of my earlier identification of imagination with simulation, this distinction seems unexceptionable. If imagination consists of running our beliefs off-line, then any distinction that holds among beliefs should hold among imaginings, and there surely is a distinction between believing that an event occurs and believing that you are seeing that event occur. I shall call

[2] Wilson, *Narrations in Light*, p. 56, italics in the original. Wilson uses the phrase "it is make-believe for him" rather than saying the viewer imagines, but that is certainly one plausible interpretation of his words, and it was, as Wilson confirmed in discussion, the intended one.

the view that the imagining appropriate to film is imagining seeing the *Imagined Observer Hypothesis*.[3] That is the thesis we can most charitably attribute to the classical theorists, and that is the thesis I reject.

If the thesis is right, there is something very special about the movies as a medium of fictional presentation; they put us, in imagination, right there with the characters in a way that novels and certain other media cannot do (I'll say more about plays in this regard in a while).[4] My view is that, in respect to narrative structure, movies are much more like novels than the Imagined Observer Hypothesis would have us believe. Still, there are obvious differences between literature and the movies which no theory can ignore. I'll try to show that we don't need the Imagined Observer Hypothesis to account for these differences.

On the whole, the classical theorists seem not merely to have assumed that film is special in the way just described – that it puts us in the picture – but to have approved and sometimes celebrated this capacity. More recent theory, or a good deal of it, can be seen as reacting against this approval and as arguing that film must strive to overcome this tendency. But new and classical theorists seem to have agreed that putting us in the picture is something that film naturally succeeds in doing unless "distancing" or "alienating" measures are taken by the film maker to prevent it. Since I shall argue that film does not have this capacity to any marked degree, I shall argue against classical and new theorists alike.

I noted kinds of personal imagining besides imagining seeing. Hearing is the most obvious case, but let us not forget the work of path-breaking auteurs like John Waters and William Castle, who gave us, respectively, Odorama and electrified seating.[5] If

---

[3] This thesis, or something like it, seems to be implicit in the work of early theorists like Münsterberg and Pudovkin.

[4] "In cinema it is not possible to speak, in the strict sense, of a *narrator*. The film does not narrate, but rather it places the spectator directly without intermediaries, *in the presence* of the facts narrated" (Julio Moreno, "Subjective Cinema: The Problem of Film in the First Person", p. 354. Quoted in Branigan, *Narrative Comprehension and Film*, p. 144).

[5] As I noted earlier, viewers of Waters's *Pink Flamingos* are sometimes provided

we can imagine that we see fictional things, presumably we can imagine that we smell and feel them, that we have sensory contact of all kinds with them. We can imagine other, nonsensuous modes of contact with them: that we know, like, distrust or admire them. But I shall confine my remarks to vision: it is perhaps the most interesting case because of the highly structured and complex nature of visual experience, and it is naturally the case most frequently discussed in connection with cinema. What I say about the case of seeing will be easily applicable to the other senses.

To repeat: I take it to be a distinctive thesis of classical film theory that cinema encourages a certain kind of imagining which I have called imagining seeing: imagining that you are seeing the fictional events of the film, and seeing them from the point of view of the camera.

6.2 CINEMA, THEATRE AND OTHER VISUAL FICTIONS

What of theatre? You may argue that the theatre-goer imagines that he sees Othello when he sees the actor playing Othello on the stage. But there's a difference between the theatrical and the cinematic case that any theory will need to accommodate. The view I ascribed to writers like Panofsky and Mitry is that we imagine not only that we see the characters in the film, but that we do so by occupying a certain position within its "space" or "world", and the position we occupy is that of the camera. What makes that a plausible hypothesis is that the role of the camera gives the movie what we might call an *intrinsic* point of view, a point of view that shifts quite independently of the actual position of the viewer, but which the viewer can imagine himself to occupy. A theatrical performance, obviously enough, has no intrinsic point of view.[6] Recognizing this, writers on theatre

with odour-producing scratch cards. Castle arranged for some of the theatres showing his *Tingler* to give mild electric shocks to the audience at appropriate moments during the program.

[6] A theatrical performance may implicitly define a point of view by being

have tended to emphasize the distance – and the barriers – between the audience and the fiction presented on stage. Haig Khatchadourian explicitly contrasts plays and movies in this respect: "It is probably true that we cannot experience the action of a play from 'within' its space time *in the way* we can in film."[7] Bernard Williams says that the theatrical audience "see what they may well describe as, say, Othello in front of a certain palace in Venice. . . . But they are not themselves at any specifiable distance from that palace". As members of the audience, they "are spectators of a world they are not in".[8] I assume Williams means that spectators imagine they see the palace (they can't really see a palace which isn't there), but they don't imagine being any particular distance from it. They do not imagine that they stand in any perspectival relation to the palace.

Later I shall address the question whether this idea of imagined nonperspectival seeing makes sense. For the moment I want to ask whether the idea of imagining seeing – perspectival or not – could be the key to identifying a broad class of visual fictions: a class which would include film, theatre, painting and certain other forms. The proposal is this: a fiction is visual, or belongs to a visual medium, if the kind of imagining it makes appropriate is imagining seeing. Kendall Walton thinks that painting is a visual medium in this sense. On his view, it is central to our interpretation of paintings that we engage in various visual imaginings with respect to them: we recognize the picture as a picture of a deer, he says, when we notice ourselves imagining that we are seeing a deer when we look at the picture.[9]

Painting, theatre and film certainly are visual media. The question is whether this is because they encourage imagining seeing. The idea is not implausible. It offers a neat contrast with another

staged to favour a certain viewing position. But this does not give it an intrinsic point of view in the strong sense that a movie has one.

[7] Haig Khatchadourian, "Space and Time in Film", p. 176. Italics in original.
[8] Bernard Williams, "Imagination and the Self", in *Problems of the Self: Philosophical Papers, 1956–72*, p. 35.
[9] Walton, *Mimesis as Make-Believe*, p. 294. See also Wollheim, *Painting as an Art*, chapter 2.

mode of fiction of which the novel is the best example, and a consequent elaboration of the showing–telling distinction. With visual fictions, we have a showing: we imagine that our act of looking at the film, stage or picture is an act of looking at the fictional events there portrayed. With poetry and its literary successors we have not a showing but a telling: we imagine that the events of the fiction occur, but not that our reading the text is an act of witnessing those events. That way we have two kinds of media, divided according to the kinds of representations they employ, and two kinds of imagining; the proposal is that they pair off neatly: pictorial fictions with imagining seeing, which is a species of personal imagining, and (predominantly) linguistic fictions with impersonal imagining. All this, I say, is false.

6.3 AGAINST IMAGINING SEEING

I don't say moviegoers *never* imagine themselves to be seeing the characters and events of the fictions portrayed in the movie. Perhaps there are times when viewers, or some of them, imagine this, just as readers of novels sometimes imagine they see the characters and events they read about. People can imagine just about anything, and the viewer may occasionally imagine that he sees the characters and events of the fiction. But that need not be the kind of imagining made appropriate by the film. What I shall argue is that this kind of imagining is not – except in a few extraordinary cases – appropriate for, or required by, the fictions that movies present. In a good many cases this kind of imagining would be confusing because of its tendency to undermine the structure of the fiction so presented. Further, we don't need to invoke the idea of imagining seeing to explain what is distinctive about cinematic fictions.

I said that imagining seeing is not appropriate cinematic imagining – except in a few extraordinary cases. Here is one.[10] In Hitchcock's *Vertigo* there is a shot down a stairwell that employs a dolly–zoom combination to give the effect of a vertiginous experience. To the extent that it is effective, I think this

---

[10] David Hills reminded me of this one.

shot encourages us to imagine that we are *having* the vertiginous experience. Is this a significant concession to the Imagined Observer Hypothesis? I think not. The Imagined Observer Hypothesis is a general thesis about the normal mode of cinematic engagement; all I am conceding here is that it may be true of some very exceptional shots. The thesis that we are all crazy is not supported by the craziness of the few – on the contrary, the salience of their craziness tells against their condition being the norm. Things are like that with imagining seeing.

For me, perhaps the most striking thing about the view of Balázs, Panofsky and the others is that it seems to misdescribe the *experience* of movie watching. Do I really identify my visual system, in imagination, with the camera, and imagine myself to be placed where the camera is? Do I imagine myself on the battlefield, mysteriously immune to the violence around me, lying next to the lovers, somehow invisible to them, viewing Earth from deep space one minute, watching the dinner guests from the ceiling the next? None of this corresponds to my own experience of movie watching. George Wilson, whom I have already quoted in support of the Imagined Observer Hypothesis, is explicit about the sort of imaginative picture the viewer has of herself in relation to the film viewed:

> Thus, the film viewer's impression of his or her epistemic situation is something such as this. The cinematic time machine is a ghostly one in that it is both invisible and massless in relation to anything it does not contain. The spectator sits in the closed capsule before its large and magnifying window and observes a slice of the secondary world in which the machine is situated. Directed by a prescient intelligence that operates the machine for the passive viewer, the capsule has the capacity to change its position and spatial orientation instantaneously so that its window opens onto a series of wider and narrower prospects, which jointly delineate the action outside. Being massless, the capsule can even occupy the position of a person who is in the world outside and thereby present the precise visual perspective of that person at that time.[11]

[11] Wilson, *Narration in Light*, p. 55.

Alone among writers on film, Wilson seems to have grasped the implications of the Imagined Observer Hypothesis, and has, in this quotation, carefully described what that thesis requires us to suppose the viewer imagines. But in so carefully drawing out its consequences, I believe Wilson has effectively sunk the Imagined Observer Hypothesis, because there simply is no evidence that film viewers imagine their situations to be as Wilson describes. And a viewer who did imagine all this would be so mentally occupied as to be scarcely able to attend to the film. Further, such imaginings would very often be prohibited by the film itself. In most films, the fictional world described is not supposed to be accessible by such magical modes of observation and inquiry; in most cinematic fictions the world of the film is pretty much like the real world, where assuredly no such magical access is possible. Such films implicitly prohibit our imagining anyone watching the characters from within an invisible, massless time machine capable of discontinuous movement.

Many familiar cinematic devices also seem problematic when taken in conjunction with the Imagined Observer Hypothesis. Sometimes a long shot of two people in a crowd is accompanied by a very selective sound track, which highlights their own conversation and filters out the irrelevant chatter of other crowd members. One could never in fact see people from such a distance and hear their conversation with such clarity. By what means are we supposed to imagine ourselves having this peculiar combination of visual and auditory access to the events of the fiction? By magic, or by a kind of causality alien to this world? Again, the film may be one which in other ways seems to adopt this-worldly causality and to reject magical interventions. We seem to be discovering hitherto unknown sources of tension within familiar fictions! But the suspicion must be that these tensions are not the product of the fictions themselves but of a false theory about their mode of presentation.

If we are to imagine ourselves seeing fictional things and events when we watch a film, we shall have to imagine that our visual powers are strangely restricted, and that what we see depends in no way on our own decisions. The camera is often placed to restrict our view of the action for dramatic purposes, and in these cases one would often like to see more or see differently. But if we are imagining ourselves to be seeing the fiction itself, what are we to imagine concerning the source of this restriction? Putting aside Wilson's invisible-time-machine hypothesis, the only candidate seems to be this: that we imagine someone to be filming the action as a documentary, and that we are seeing the visually restricted result.[12] But to imagine this (something I have in fact never been aware of imagining) would be to imagine that the fiction contains as a part the assumption that the action is being filmed by a camera crew and that we are watching the result. Occasionally, as with *Culloden* (Peter Weir, 1964) this would be an appropriate piece of imagining, but it certainly would not be for most fiction films.[13]

In other ways, the assumption of my presence within the fiction would seriously distort the content or genre of the movie. Suppose I am watching a movie in which the murderer enters unseen. That the murderer enters unseen is part of the content of the movie. Do I imagine that I see the unseen murderer? There are two ways we can take the claim that I do, according to how much scope we give to the expression "imagine". The narrow-scope reading is: "There is exactly one thing which is an unseen murderer and I imagine that I see that thing." There is nothing intrinsically problematic about a claim of this kind. I can imagine, of something that is seen, that it is not seen. But the narrow-scope reading does not properly express my situation as a movie watcher. For one thing, it commits me to the existence of an unseen murderer, which is false in the relevant context since I do not believe there really is any murderer visible on the screen. For another, it misrepresents the content of my

---

[12] Kendall Walton takes this view: when a fictional killing is shown on the screen, it seems "to the viewer that he is seeing an actual killing via a photographic film of it" ("Transparent Pictures", p. 258).

[13] For further comments on the idea that the filming process arises from within the diegesis itself, see Chapter 9, Section 9.2.

imagining; it ought to be part of my imagining that the murderer is, exactly, unseen. This reading gives "imagine" insufficient scope. The other, wide, reading is: "I imagine that there is an unseen murderer which I see." This does not have either of the two deficiencies noted of the first formulation, but it does make the content of my imagining explicitly contradictory. Perhaps it is possible to perform the feat of imagining something explicitly contradictory. But it is implausible to suppose that the audience on such an occasion as I have just described is called on to do that.

One other response to my scepticism about imagining seeing is that while the fiction precludes the imagined presence of a witness "in the world of the fiction", it does not preclude the possibility that the viewer, who stands outside that world, is a witness.[14] But most films which can be thought of as excluding "internal" observers can, with equal or greater plausibility, be thought of as excluding external ones as well. Naturalistic fictions do not leave open as to whether someone is watching the scene *from another world*: such an idea would be wildly at variance with their conventions.

The intrinsic point of view possessed by a movie raises another difficulty. Occasionally that point of view is one we are required to imagine occupied by a character: then we have a subjective shot. In Hitchcock's *Spellbound* there is a shot, the intrinsic perspective of which is defined by the position occupied by the character John Ballantine, as he raises a glass of milk to his lips, eyeing the psychologist Dr Bruloff suspiciously as he does so. How is the viewer to integrate his supposed imaginative occupation of the camera's point of view with imagining that this point of view is that of a character? Presumably, by *identifying* himself with that character. I had better say something about the idea of identification.

For some writers, identification is the central concept of their theory of cinema; it is what makes the understanding of cinematic narrative possible, and it is to be explained in psychoan-

[14] See, e.g., Jerrold Levinson, "Seeing, Imaginarily, at the Movies".

alytic terms.[15] I wish to take a somewhat different path. I shall concentrate on how identification might take its place in a cognitive theory of imagining of the kind I have outlined. On this view, identification with a character would be a matter of imagining that you are that character. Consider, then, the hypothesis that the viewer, when he views a subjective shot, imagines that he is the character whose subjective view is represented there. What is required in order to engage in that kind of imaginative identification? At a minimum, the viewer must imagine that what is (fictionally) happening to that character is happening to him or her, and that he or she has the most obvious and dramatically salient attributes of that character at that time. But once this is seen to be required as a condition for identification, it becomes very hard to square the claim of identification with the experience of watching a subjective shot. In the shot from *Spellbound*, salient features of Ballantine are that he is drinking milk and that his mental state is one of turmoil. Watching this shot does not incline me in the least to imagine myself doing or being either of these things. Nor, when watching a celebrated subjective shot later in the film, in which the murderer points a gun towards himself and fires, do I imagine that I am killing myself. Further, identification, if it is a notion with any content at all, would seem to require the one who identifies to have, or to imagine having, some concern with and sympathy for the values and projects of the one with whom she identifies. But, as Nick Browne has noted in his study of an important scene from *Stagecoach*, one of the peculiarities of the setup there is that, while we see Dallas the prostitute from Lucy's point of view, we do not, and are not intended to, feel solidarity with Lucy's attempt to exclude Dallas.[16] That the camera occupies Lucy's

[15] "... [the viewer] certainly has to identify ... if he did not the film would become incomprehensible." Christian Metz, *Psychoanalysis and Cinema*, p. 46.

[16] Nick Browne, *The Rhetoric of Filmic Narration*, chapter 1. So far as I can see, Browne does not appreciate that identification is the source of the trouble. He says that we are "asked to see Dallas through Lucy's eyes"; also that we "identify" with Dallas. Things are made more confusing by Browne's moving easily between point of view as a literal place of physical observation to point

point of view has no implications, or only negative ones, for identification. Nor do subjective shots from the point of view of a stalking creature or a homicidal maniac make us identify with the stalker; they typically have the effect of heightening our concern for the potential victim. In all these ways the supposition of imaginative identification does not square with the experience of film.

Some of these objections can be made more vivid if we consider an actual film sequence. I have chosen a short scene from Hitchcock's *The Birds*, during which Melanie Daniels (Tipi Hedron) crosses Bodega Bay in a hired boat. Compositionally, the sequence is of some interest, but it does not seem to be an especially disorienting scene to watch. One can find the repertoire of shots out of which it is constructed repeated in a great many scenes in this and other films. The sequence I have in mind consists of fourteen shots, beginning with three long shots of the boat: one from behind as it leaves the quay, one from the side, with the boat travelling across the screen left to right, and one from more or less front-on. Shot 4 is close in to the boat, and travels alongside. Shots 5 to 14 constitute a sequence of pairs of shots, the first of each pair being a point-of-view shot from Melanie's position, and the second a reverse shot to Melanie herself, with the last shot reversed on her as she ties up the boat and gets out.

As I say, there is nothing especially remarkable about the experience of watching this scene. But if the viewer is to imagine herself seeing the events represented in the sequence from the position of the camera, the experience of watching it would be a very peculiar one indeed. The transitions between the first

---

of view as, in effect, "taking someone's part". This leads to unresolved oxymorons like "identification asks us as spectators to be [sic] two places at once, where the camera is and "with" the depicted person.... This passage [from Stagecoach] shows that identification necessarily has a double structure in the way it implicates the spectator in both the position of the one seeing and the one seen" (p. 8). Simultaneous identification with distinct and indeed antagonistic characters is hardly to be credited. But Browne's analysis is more sophisticated than the inflexible "system of the suture" against which he is to some extent reacting.

three shots would require her to imagine her position shifted instantly through ninety degrees twice, around the edge of the bay. Shot 4 requires her to imagine herself suddenly in the water by the boat, somehow travelling alongside it at the same (considerable) speed. The transitions between 5 and 14 would then have her imagine herself shifting back and forth nine times between Melanie's own position (identifying with Melanie, perhaps?) and different points on the shore, all within the space of a minute or two. You have only to describe the sequence in these terms to realize how clumsy and implausible is the Imagined Observer Hypothesis: the effort of imagining all this during the brief scene I have described would be both disorienting and distracting, and quite unlike the normal experience of watching the scene. Advocates of the Imagined Observer Hypothesis never describe "the phenomenology of cinema" in quite these crass terms. But this is certainly how it ought to be described if we are to take that thesis literally.

One response to these criticisms would be to say that, while we do imagine ourselves to be seeing the fictional characters and events presented onscreen, we do not, and are not expected to, incorporate into our imagining many of the consequences – some of them rather awkward from the point of view of the fiction concerned – of our seeing those things. The argument for this is that we do not, in general, observe any injunction to imagine all the consequences of what we do imagine (we don't, after all, believe all the consequences of our beliefs). Indeed, we couldn't imagine all the consequences of what we do imagine, because everything nontautological has infinitely many consequences.[17]

This response might be elaborated by saying that our imagining seeing is a kind of *purely* visual imagining, unconnected with any imaginings about where we are seeing from or how it is that we are able to see. While we are to imagine ourselves seeing, we are not to imagine ourselves placed anywhere in the scene, or as undergoing any changes of position. This proposal is already a step back from the classical view of cinematic imag-

---

[17] This objection I owe to Kendall Walton.

ining as expressed by Balázs and Panofsky, which requires us not merely to imagine that we are seeing the fictional events, but also to imagine that we are placed where the camera is. It is more like the view outlined by Bernard Williams when discussing the theatrical case: we imagine seeing the castle, but do not imagine seeing it from any position.

Even though this position is weaker than the classical theory I have been examining so far, it is still objectionable on two grounds. First, the new proposal does not solve all the difficulties I have described. For example, it does not solve the unseen-murderer problem. There we are required to imagine that we are seeing something *and* to imagine that no one is seeing it, so in this case contradictory imagining cannot be avoided by being selective about consequences. Second, I believe that the concept of seeing and that of occupying a point of view are closer than this weakening of the classical theory allows. The weakening is based on the idea that the connection between the two concepts is, at most, the relation of entailment; the proposition that I am seeing something entails the proposition that I am placed somewhere in relation to what I see. The defender of The Imagined Observer Hypothesis simply refuses to have the entailment be reflected in the act of imagining; I imagine something, but not what it entails.

Against this I say that the concepts of seeing and of point of view are linked more intimately than by entailment alone. To see *is* to see from a point of view; there is no such thing as nonperspectival seeing. You cannot imagine, of a certain scene represented to you onscreen, that you are seeing it, but not that you are seeing it from any point of view. To imagine seeing it is to imagine seeing it from the point of view defined by the perspectival structure of the picture. You can, of course, imagine seeing it in such a way that your spatial relation to what you see is rendered unclear – imagining that you see the scene with the aid of a complex system of mirrors or perhaps even through the medium of film. But it is not very plausible to suppose that we imagine either of those things when we are confronted with cinematic images.

One final response: you might be tempted to adopt a mixed strategy, asserting the Imagined Observer Hypothesis for a restricted domain of cinematic experience: those situations to which it could apply without gratuitous paradox, or (and this might be a more restricted thesis still) those where the style of filming seems, in one way or other, especially to invite participation. But I'm sceptical of this ecumenical proposal. It seems to me that there is an enormous psychological difference between merely imagining something happening, and imagining yourself there watching it happen. Viewing a movie that constantly took us from one of these kinds of imaginings to the other and back again would be a roller-coaster experience of shifting phenomenology. That's just not the sort of experience – vertiginous shots aside – I have while watching a movie.

6.4 IMPERSONAL IMAGINING AND FILM

By now we have reason enough to abandon the Imagined Observer Hypothesis – reason, at least, to look for a more plausible alternative. The alternative I suggest is simple. What I imagine while watching a movie concerns the events of the fiction it presents, not any perceptual relations between myself and those events. My imagining is not that I see the characters and the events of the movie; it is simply that there are these characters and that these events *occur* – the same sort of impersonal imagining I engage in when I read a novel.

When we substitute impersonal imagining for imagining seeing, our problems start to dissolve. I see displayed on the screen a man with a knife, and I imagine that there is a murderer, perhaps even an unseen one. I do not imagine that I see this unseen murderer. In this case the difference between imagining seeing and impersonal imagining is captured as a difference of scope: it's the difference between, respectively, "I imagine that I see something which is a murderer," and "I see something which I imagine is a murderer."

What does a subjective point-of-view shot, like the milk-drinking one in *Spellbound*, ask us to imagine? We see the shot and recognize that its perspective is defined by a certain position. We imagine, concerning that position, that it is occupied by a character (in this case Ballantine). We imagine that he sees Dr Bruloff as he drains the milk.[18] We imagine that, as he does so, things look pretty much to him as they look to us on the screen – or, more plausibly, that what we see onscreen is a rough guide to what we should imagine his experience is like. That way, the subjective content of the shot is referred to the character's experience, not to our own. We are not required to imagine that we see Dr Bruloff from Ballantine's perspective or any other. In general, subjective shots function to help us imagine what a character's experience is like, not to imagine ourselves being that character and having that experience.[19]

In the same way, the problems of selective sound and restricted view disappear once we abandon the Imagined Observer Hypothesis. They just become effects of an inevitably selective narration, and they appear no stranger in film than they would in literature, which is, of course, selective at every point in what it presents to the reader.

The proposal that cinema typically encourages impersonal rather than personal imaginings is simple enough. What needs to be shown is that it makes the right distinctions between cinematic and other kinds of fictions, including distinctions which concern our *experience* of cinematic and other fiction. But something else needs explaining: if the Imagined Observer Hypothesis is false, how is it that many people believe it? The alternative I propose needs to explain the success of its rival. I hope to make a start at showing that my alternative can do both these things.

---

[18] This shot, like most shots of its kind, is quite unrealistic because it fails to capture the binocular nature of ordinary vision. Ballantine would have to have one eye shut to see anything like what is presented on the screen.

[19] The shot may encourage secondary imagining. That is, in order to imagine appropriately concerning the character's experience, we may have to imagine having that experience ourselves, thereby engaging in a simulation of the character's experience (see Section 5.2 on the distinction between primary and secondary imagining). But this secondary imagining is not a matter of identifying ourselves with the character.

6.5 PERCEPTUAL IMAGINING

Section 6.2 raised the possibility of distinguishing between the experience of fiction in a visual mode like film or theatre on the one hand, and written literature on the other. The suggestion was that the first kind of case involves imagining seeing and the second, literary, kind does not. Given my rejection of the Imagined Observer Hypothesis, that suggestion is not available to me, and I must find another way to draw the distinction.

I might try this: the experience of cinema is an essentially visual one in the sense that what it is appropriate for us to imagine depends on what we see (on what we actually see, that is, not on anything we imagine we see). Watching *Citizen Kane* it is appropriate for me to imagine that a snow globe falls from the hands of a dying man, because I really see onscreen a sick-looking man from whose hand a snow globe (apparently) falls.

But will this suffice to put film in the class of visual media without, unwantedly, including novels as well? I see the words on the page, and thereby engage in a bit of appropriate imagining. But we do not want to say that the novel is a visual medium. There seems to be an obvious response: it is just a contingent fact that we normally read with our eyes; novels can be "read" by using Braille or Morse code symbols, so there is nothing essentially visual about reading. The cinema, so the response goes, is essentially visual, since there is no nonvisual way to communicate a movie's content. A Braille version of *Citizen Kane* would be a different work than the movie, in just the way that the movie *Great Expectations* is a different work than the novel. But this explanation really just begs the question: why count the novel as a work in *one* medium (i.e., written language), whether read by sight, Braille or Morse code? Why not count the novel-as-read-by-sight a work in a visual medium and the novel-as-read-by-Braille a work in a tactile medium, with a comparable category reserved for, say, Morse code? What then would be the difference from the experiential point of view between film and the novel-as-read-by-sight? Surely there is a difference, but the present proposal makes it hard to see what it is.

I start with a distinction, which I introduce through the case of belief. Then I shall apply that distinction to imagination. In light of the hypothesis that imagining is off-line simulation, that seems appropriate; distinctions between kinds of imaginings ought then to have their basis in distinctions between kinds of beliefs.

What is the difference between seeing a thing and reading a description of it, both considered as ways to reach beliefs about its visible properties? In both cases we have belief caused by perception, but only in the first case do we have what might be called a genuinely perceptual belief. What makes the first a case of perceptual belief? First, in the genuinely perceptual case we have a certain kind of *counterfactual dependence* between belief and visible properties of the object; if the thing seen had been a little bit more red, or larger, or had more closely approximated squareness, my belief would correspondingly have been that it was more red, larger or more square.[20] Second, perceptual beliefs tend to have certain characteristic features of structure and content. They bunch together in so far as perception tends to give us beliefs about colour, size and shape as an indissoluble package with a high degree of specificity. When you see someone's eyes you get beliefs about their shape as well as about their colour, and the belief you get about their colour is that they are exactly *that* shade of blue. And perception gives us, as a free bonus, information about the temporal duration of processes; they take as long as it takes us to watch them occur.[21]

This is all in contrast to reading a description. There, your beliefs don't have that counterfactual dependence on the visible properties of symbols; differences in the shapes of the letters

---

[20] Recall the discussion of what is distinctive about pictorial representation in Chapter 1.

[21] It was Frank Jackson, in conversation, who drew my attention to the importance for my argument of characterizing perceptual beliefs in this way. Jackson discusses some of the features I have mentioned in his *Perception: A Representative Theory*, p. 43, but in the context of arguing against those, like George Pitcher, who would define perception itself as, or as the acquisition of, a certain kind of belief. Note that Pitcher's definition of perceptual belief in *A Theory of Perception*, p. 90, is quite different from mine.

would not have induced in you different beliefs about the shape of the thing described.[22] Nor, with descriptions, do your beliefs have the kind of bunched, content-specific character we associate with perceptual beliefs. You can learn about shape from a description, and learn nothing about colour. And what you can learn from a description of colour will lack the specificity that it would have in the case of a perceptual belief. Descriptions rarely authorize us to believe the eyes of the person described are exactly *that* shade of blue. The beliefs we get from descriptions I'll call *symbolic* beliefs. They contrast, obviously, with perceptual beliefs, but I am not claiming that between them these two kinds exhaust the field.

This characterization of the difference between perceptual and symbolic beliefs applies at the level of tokens rather than at that of types. One cannot, in general, say that a certain belief type – for example, that this object is round – is perceptual rather than symbolic. One token of that belief might be perceptual and another symbolic. What makes the token perceptual is the form of its tokening – its tokening within a system of representation that gives to the tokens so represented the features of structure and content I just mentioned. It should, for instance, be a system in which size, shape and colour come together as a single unit of representation. Pictures in the head would serve well in this regard, but I assume we have independent reason not to believe in them. No matter; other things may do as well, including connectionist networks with the right kinds of excitatory links. But for purposes of this argument, I am neutral about what kinds of representations are at work here.

Note that it would not do to characterize perceptual beliefs by saying that they are the ones you get when you see the thing itself rather than a description of it. For you can get genuinely perceptual beliefs, in my sense, by looking at likenesses of things; likenesses stand in the same or similar relations of counterfactual dependence with your beliefs as do the things of which they are likenesses, and the beliefs they induce have the

---

[22] Except in so far as a change of shape would constitute a change in the letter's identity.

characteristics of content and structure I just noted. This has some importance for what follows.

Imagining, on my hypothesis, involves running your belief–desire system off-line. In that case, the distinction between perceptual and symbolic beliefs ought to carry over into a distinction between perceptual and symbolic imaginings. And so it does. Perceptual imagining exhibits the characteristics of counterfactual dependence and structure characteristic of perceptual belief; when we see the screen we imagine that the character's eyes are exactly *that* shape, *that* colour and *that* size in relation to the rest of the character's features. If what we saw on the screen were shaped or coloured in a slightly different way, what we would then have imagined about the character's features would have been correspondingly different. If we had been reading a novel we might, at a certain point, have read something that prompted us to image that the character's eyes were blue. We would be in no position to imagine anything about their shape, because we are told nothing about shape; nor would we be in a position to imagine that the eyes are some specific shade of blue. It would be a matter of indifference to our imaginings, moreover, whether the text was composed in this type face (or size, or colour) or that one.

So what makes the experience of cinema, painting and the other pictorial media an essentially visual one is that it gives rise to perceptual imaginings. Poetry and the novel, on the other hand, give rise to symbolic imaginings, whether the poem is read by sight, Braille or Morse code.

The relation of counterfactual dependence I am pointing to here does not hold between your imaginings about the characters of the fiction and the visual properties of the characters themselves: recall that fictional characters don't exist, so we certainly don't see them in cinemas or anywhere else. The counterfactual dependence holds between your imaginings and the visible properties of *representations*. Does this undermine the parallel I have claimed exists between perceptual beliefs and perceptual imaginings? There certainly is a difference between belief and imagining: our beliefs about Fred, if he is a real person, often derive from perceptual encounters with Fred himself.

But if he is a fictional character, our imaginings about him cannot derive from seeing him. At most they derive, as with film, from seeing representations of him. But beliefs *can* be derived that way also: I may get a belief about Fred's hair colour from seeing a photograph or painting of him, and the belief I get is a perceptual belief.

Now we can understand why we so commonly make the mistake of saying that we see, or that we imagine that we see, the characters and events in the film. The imaginings that movies give rise to are based on the experience of seeing things, or pictorial representations of them; they are structured very much as are the beliefs we get from seeing things. It's natural, then, to say that we *see*, or imagine ourselves to see, the fictional events presented on film. But the imaginings that novel-reading licenses are very unlike what results from seeing things or their likenesses, and there's little temptation to describe them in terms of seeing.

I have made two distinctions: one between personal and impersonal imagining, and the other between perceptual and symbolic imagining. We can now identify the basic confusion which leads people to assert the Imagined Observer Hypothesis. Supposing, rightly, that there is something distinctly visual about cinematic fictions, people then suppose that this peculiarly visual element consists in the fact that cinematic fictions encourage us to imagine that we see fictional things. In fact, what is peculiarly visual about cinema is that it encourages perceptual imagining. Our two distinctions cut across each other, and while some perceptual imaginings are personal imaginings, some are not. In general, film encourages perceptual but impersonal imaginings.

6.6 CLARIFICATIONS AND REBUTTALS

In this section I want to make two clarifications to my thesis and to confront five objections to it.

In making a case for the perceptual nature of cinematic make-believe, I emphasized the correspondence between the visual display on the screen, and what we imagine as a result. It's time to recognize that the correspondence is patchy. The information given in perception needs to be interpreted, an issue I shall take up more fully in Chapter 8. Sometimes the viewer blocks the inference from perception to imagination by tagging the perceptual information, or some part of it, as extradiegetic: when a shot fades out in the movie we don't imagine that objects slowly and mysteriously disappear; with slow motion, we don't imagine that physical processes are taking longer. Sometimes we are required to extend, revise or discount information from vision so as to arrive at something that meets overall constraints of coherence. We try to construct a narrative, the events of which do not always correspond directly to what is seen, as with episodes of fabrication, dreaming and hallucinatory experience. And if the film presents the hero in Chicago one day and in London the next, we are usually required to imagine that he travelled by plane, though no journey by plane was shown. Further, when what we see onscreen warrants a bit of perceptual imagining, it rarely warrants *only* perceptual imagining; our imagining is usually to be supplemented by, and interpreted in the light of, imaginings of a nonperceptual kind. When we see a man onscreen we are usually supposed to have a perceptual imagining to the effect that there is, exactly, a man with that appearance doing such and such. But in *Invasion of the Body Snatchers* we are to imagine instead that there is a terrifyingly emotionless alien creature who has taken on the form of a man. While there is certainly a difference between these two imaginings, the difference is not displayed at the level of perceptual imagining. Visual fictions are those that make it appropriate for us to engage in *some* visual imagining; beyond that, visualness is a matter of degree. So the dependence of imagining on what is seen at the movies is partial, and the imaginings that movies make appropriate are not all perceptual imaginings. I claim only that there is *enough* perceptual structuring there to make plausible my explanation of why movies are – and novels are not – works in a visual medium.

A second clarification. I've argued that engagement with cinematic fiction does not require or license us to imagine that we see the fictional events and characters it presents. But there are occasions, I believe, when the film requires us to imagine that we see *something*. Let me illustrate how this can arise.

Movies, like works in other media, have styles; in particular, a movie can have a visual style. Sometimes the viewer, if he is discerning enough, will recognize that the visual style of the movie allows or encourages a kind of make-believe. André Bazin argued that Renoir's use of irregular panning created an atmosphere of spontaneity which pervaded his films.[23] Now the competent viewer will not suppose that Renoir's irregular panning was genuinely the result of spontaneous composition. He will know that Renoir's shots were as carefully planned and unspontaneous as anyone else's. The spontaneity of Renoir's shots is make-believe; the way those shots are composed makes it appropriate for the viewer to *imagine* that those shots were spontaneous. Does that mean that the viewer imagines himself to be seeing spontaneously composed shots? I think it does. This stylistic feature, like other features of visual style, works on us in the way it does because we imagine ourselves to be seeing something done in a certain way. The viewer imagines himself to be seeing the result of spontaneous composition, but that make-believe isn't part of the make-believe appropriate to the fictional stories that Renoir's films portray. It's not part of the story of a film like *Rules of the Game* that there is a cameraman following the characters around and recording, in a spontaneous way, their actions. Watching a movie involves different levels of imagining, not all of them concerned with the fictional story the movie presents. My scepticism about the claim that we imagine ourselves to see things in the movies is confined to the base level of make-believe, that concerning the characters and events of the fictional story.

Now the objections:

1. Our thought, and sometimes our talk, sometimes seems best explained on the Imagined Observer Hypothesis. "Who is the murderer?" I whisper to my partner at the movie. "That one" (said while pointing at the screen). Only an imagining that

[23] See André Bazin, *Jean Renoir*; see also Noël Carroll, *Philosophical Problems of Classical Film Theory*, chapter 3.

we are right there could underlie such an explanation. I answer: we are notorious transferrers of properties from things represented to representations. I'm told that oscilloscope watchers say things like "That's a loud one" (pointing at the wave on the screen). They mean, "That represents a loud noise." That plausibly is what is going on in our imagined conversation at the cinema.

2. Consider the perceptual imaginings that cinema promotes. These are in a certain sense *perspectival* imaginings. I have said that with perceptual imagining, what we are to imagine depends on what we see; we see a cinematic image of a man with a certain appearance, and we are to imagine that the character played by the man has that appearance. But what we see is seen from a certain perspective: that of the camera. If we imagine that the character looks like that, we must be imagining him looking like that *from that perspective*. There is no such thing as the way a person looks from no perspective. That is the sense in which perceptual imagining is essentially perspectival: a specification of the content of what we imagine must make reference to a certain perspective. But once we admit that we are dealing with perceptual imagining that is perspectival, doesn't this amount to an admission that we are dealing with imagining, the content of which is of the form "I am seeing such and such"?[24]

In order to answer the objection, let us once again compare the case of imagination with that of belief. The general form of the argument just given is this: if the content of an attitude is perspectival, then the content of the attitude is of the form "I Φ that I am seeing (or, more generally, perceiving) that P", where Φ is a variable ranging over attitudes, and P a variable ranging over propositions. But in the case of belief, this is manifestly not so. I see a painting of Uncle Albert and on the basis of seeing it form the belief that his appearance is thus and so.[25] Of course what I believe is that he appears thus and so from a certain perspective. But I do not believe that I am seeing Uncle Albert,

---

[24] Again, this objection was suggested to me, in conversation, by Kendall Walton.

[25] I assume that the pictures in question are nonphotographic, thereby avoiding an argument with the advocates of Transparency.

since I am fully aware that I am seeing a painting. So the argument is wrong as applied to belief; we can assume that it is wrong in the imagining case as well.

3. It may appear that my strategy fails to account for the immediacy of cinema, which is capable of generating feelings of intense concern on our part for the characters. Consider that paradigm of movie suspense, the scene in *North by Northwest* where Roger Thornhill and Eve Kendall (Cary Grant and Eva Marie Saint) cling to the face of Mount Rushmore, trapped by their pursuers. Isn't it because I imagine that I am actually *watching* them that I respond so intensely to their plight? A comparison with novel reading is instructive here. For many of us, the feelings generated by reading are as powerful as those generated by a play or a movie, but these feelings do not arise out of our imagining that we are present at the action described in the novel. Our make-believe is simply that the characters act and suffer as the story says they do. Literary fictions engage our feelings effectively without placing us imaginatively in direct perceptual relation to the events they depict. So intensity of feeling is no argument for the Imagined Observer Hypothesis in the case of cinema.

But let us not go too far. Let us not insist that novels and movies have *equivalent* capacities to generate feeling and concern. I doubt if any novelist could give me quite the experiences Hitchcock gave me in that scene on Mount Rushmore. But the difference in capacities between the two media can be explained without supposing that we imagine ourselves to be seeing the characters in the movie. The difference is due to the structural differences between film and the novel I have described. The perceptual structuring of cinematic make-believe provides us with a wealth of easily assimilated detail. Simply by seeing Cary Grant's hands as he clings to the rock we are put in a position to imagine that the character Thornhill's hands are holding the rock in just that way. A verbal account could hardly provide us with precisely that information, and extended descriptions of visual detail make it difficult to sustain imaginative involvement. If visual fictions more easily engage us when it comes to the presentation of, say, certain kinds of physical danger, that's because of the perceptual structuring of their contents, not because their content involves a perceptual relation between the action and the audience.

4. A central and highly influential tradition of film making has been based on the premise that shooting and editing should produce a result that mimics the experience of an ideally placed observer, and thereby have the audience "see as the attentive observer saw".[26] The devices to which this tradition has given rise, such as eyeline matching and shot–reverse-shot editing, certainly seem very natural. They constitute part of the repertoire of what is called "invisible editing", the kind we easily cease to notice. Why do they seem so natural? If we assume that the spectator's role in cinema is to imagine himself standing before the characters, where the camera is, their naturalness is easily explained: they serve to promote that imagining better than any other choice of orientation would. But if we reject the Imagined Observer Hypothesis, then the set of orientations favoured by invisible editing is just one of an indefinitely large class of orientations that would do equally well. Strange, then, that the film-making tradition has happened to fix on just this class, the class which the Imagined Observer Hypothesis selects as privileged!

Part of an answer to the objection questions its presupposition that standard cinematic orientations mimic perception. Quite a lot of them don't. In order to have a visual experience of a conversation between two people like the experience of watching shot–reverse-shot editing we would continually have to be running between the positions defined by the two cameras. Cutting from long shot to close-up just is not – contra Reisz and Millar – like the process of noticing and focusing on detail.[27] And trains that disappear out of the left visual field rarely reappear from the right. All this suggests that what we find natural in cinematic editing is not what we would find natural in visual experience of the real world. There does seem to be *something* to the objection, however: Shots from the floor or ceiling strike

---

[26] Pudovkin, quoted in David Bordwell, *Narration in the Fiction Film*, p. 9.
[27] See Karel Reisz and Gavin Millar, *The Technique of Film Editing*.

us as less natural than those taken at roughly eye level. But the best explanation for this sense of unnaturalness might not be that we find it unnatural to imagine ourselves in the position from which the shot is taken. A plausible alternative explanation is simply that we are unfamiliar with the views of people that such shots present, together with the fact that facial expressions are usually so important to the narrative that shots which wilfully deny us access to them are very noticeable interventions on the maker's part. And if unnaturalness were a function of the extent to which the camera's position deviated from the norm for a human participant, some shots ought to seem very unnatural which do not seem unnatural at all. Those views of the Earth from deep space that we see so often in science-fiction films do not seem especially unnatural.

5. What, in that case, do we make of the venerable distinction between diegesis and mimesis, between telling and showing? It seems that on my view fictions of all kinds are diegetic; all are experienced as something told. They differ only in the means used for the telling: words in literature, moving images in cinema. This denial of a universally acknowledged distinction looks like a problem for my theory.

I reply that my theory still allows for the making of important distinctions. If all fictions are tellings, there are still fictions which tell by words, spoken and written, and there are fictions which tell by showing, as cinema and other visual fictions do. Also, there are fictions in which the telling is foregrounded, and is therefore a salient part of the audience's unreflective experience of the fiction, and fictions in which the artifice of telling is backgrounded, and easily forgotten. This pair of distinctions will serve us at least as well as the traditional showing/telling distinction.

6.7 THE MYTH OF TOTAL CINEMA

André Bazin argued that the history of cinema is the history of the progressive embodiment of a myth or, better, an ideal, the possibility of "an integral realism, a re-creation of the world in its own image".[28] That way, sound and colour constitute progress towards the cinematic ideal rather than, as some critics have claimed, degeneration from the purity of the original, silent screen.

No doubt Bazin was right about sound and colour being progressive additions to the cinematic repertoire. But if what I have been arguing for in this chapter is correct, we shouldn't base this claim on the idea that progress in cinema is measured by increments of realism. Realism, in Bazin's sense, is the fashioning of more and more "lifelike" re-creations of the world as we experience it through our senses. And the farther we go in this direction the more and more tempting it is for us to participate imaginatively in the fiction the medium presents; to imagine that we really are there, seeing fictional things. I have argued that we do not typically imagine any such thing when we see films, and that it is just as well that we don't, since the attempt to integrate our imagined presence within the film world with the events of the story would produce unnaturalness and even paradox. But we can imagine a cinematic technology so lifelike that it would become difficult for us *not* to imagine ourselves seeing fictional things from within the fictional world; even the crudest 3-D techniques, for example, have a startling tendency to make us imagine ourselves in physical relations to events onscreen. That threatens to undermine the interest of the diegesis, by leaving the viewer absorbed in an attempt to orient himself in an unfamiliar environment. Such technological advances as 3-D might be accretions of realism in Bazin's sense,[29] but in my view they would not be progress in cinema. Any medium that wishes to create rich and rewarding fictions must keep the observer at a distance. Realism and the distancing necessary to discourage imagining seeing are two principles of cinema which are in tension. We might learn a great deal about the

[28] André Bazin, "The Myth of Total Cinema", p. 24.
[29] The failure of 3-D may, of course, have been a consequence of the failure to implement it in a technically adequate way. But it is significant that strenuous efforts were not made within the industry to improve the effect; as ideological critics of the cinema so often tell us, what look like purely technical constraints often have deeper nontechnical explanations.

aesthetics of cinema by examining the various creative attempts there have been to resolve, or to exploit, the tension. But we shall not learn about it here; I am not attempting an aesthetics of film.

6.8 PSYCHOLOGISM

I have argued that the Imagined Observer Hypothesis is wrong. But that thesis is just one example of a fundamentally mistaken way of thinking about the cinema. The most general formulation of the mistake might be that the content of the cinematic image is to be interpreted as the content of *someone's* visual experience. Since the distinctively cinematic mode of presentation is the image, this is, therefore, an assumption by which the cinema as a medium is effectively psychologized – made to be a medium which can be understood, in respect of its content as well as its effect, only in psychological terms.

This psychologism is rather unspecific; it does not give us any indication about whose visual experience the image is supposed to represent. You may say that the image represents the viewer's (imagined) visual experience; that the viewer imagines herself to be viewing the cinematic events from within the space of the movie itself, imagining herself situated where the camera is. On that construal we have what I called the Imagined Observer Hypothesis. But instead of psychologizing the image by way of the viewer, some theorists prefer to go by way of one of the characters within the fiction itself. It is at this point that the idea of the point-of-view shot (POV) becomes an important technical resource for the theory. On this view, each shot is to be interpreted, as far as possible, as a POV shot: a shot which represents what some character within the film's diegetic structure sees. Obviously it is going to be extremely difficult to find a plausible point-of-view interpretation for a great many shots, and one rather predictable strategy employed to overcome the difficulty is an exercise in progressive concept stretching; the concept of point of view is applied to cases where its acceptability is marginal, and then to cases where its application can really only be metaphorical, but concerning which claims are made that de-

pend for their truth on the literal applicability of the concept. In
that way, one gets the impression of a doctrine stoutly defended.
A good example of this technique is given by Edward Branigan,
who begins by asserting that the "glance" which defines the
point of view psychologically must be that of a sentient observer, but not necessarily a human one; he then goes on to
include as examples of POV shots one from the perspective of
a dead man and one from that of a statue, though he calls these
and other examples "metaphorical" POV shots.[30] Here the notion of point of view is being asked to do more work than can
reasonably be expected of it.

Another symptom of the psychologizing of the cinema,
closely associated with the concept of point of view and its
abuse, is the so-called system of the suture, described by one of
its advocates, Dayan, as "to classical cinema what verbal language is to literature".[31] According to Dayan's interpretation of
this model, the typical pattern of cinematic presentation is a pair
of shots, the first of which raises in the viewer's mind the question: what is the source of this image?, and the second of which
gives the answer (a lying and ideologically offensive answer,
according to the advocates of this model) by showing the character whose point of view this was.

Note first that, if the model were correct, the second shot
would not, after all, produce any psychological equilibrium in
the viewer, for it would simply raise the same question as the
first: whose experience is the basis for this image? The answer
to this second question could not be the same as the answer to
the first, because the source of the image of the subject could
not, except in exceptional circumstances, be the subject herself.[32]
But the more important observation about the system of the suture is that it presupposes, without argument, that there is a
strong tendency on the viewer's part to inquire into the psychical ownership of any given shot: a claim for which I have not
seen any convincing evidence and which only a general pre-

[30] Edward Branigan, "The Point-of-View Shot".
[31] Dayan, "Tutor-Code of Classical Cinema", p. 439.
[32] An exceptional circumstance might be where the second shot looks directly
into a mirror.

sumption in favour of psychologism would make plausible. Take away that presumption and the motivation for suture theory collapses.

These and other artificial and sometimes desperate attempts to psychologize the cinema are somewhat ironic in light of what should be a rather obvious fact about the basic cinema apparatus: that it is an impoverished and unconvincing vehicle for subjectivity. Viewing the cinema screen is, I have argued, in important ways rather like viewing the real world; it is not at all like viewing someone's subjective visual experience of the real world (a notion that barely makes sense anyway). It is extremely difficult to make what appears onscreen correspond in a convincing way to the content of anyone's visual experience; the sharply defined boundary of the screen is never effectively overcome by blurring effects, for they never correspond to our own graduated field of vision. The screen cannot mimic the capacity of vision to concentrate on detail, and selective focusing by the camera simply draws attention to the artifice. Nor does deep focus correspond to the visual field. For that reason, episodes of recollection which appear onscreen as visual images rather than as verbal accounts have a tendency to become, unintentionally, episodes of objective recounting. For what appears on the screen always surpasses in detail and clarity the possible content of anyone's memory. Thus it was that Hitchcock was able to confuse the audience in *Stage Fright* by presenting, in visual images, events as recounted from the character's point of view; these events, as it turns out, did not occur but were the fabrication of the character. Why do we take visual images as more authoritative than verbal recountings, which in the context of a mystery are automatically treated with some scepticism? The answer seems to be that the camera's capacity for capturing detail, and its failure to resemble subjective experience, means that it is only for short periods and with considerable effort that we are able or willing to regard what is onscreen as subjective and therefore as representing what someone thinks or claims, rather than what actually is.

The oddness of psychologizing the cinema is evident when we compare it to other media. I should be surprised to learn, for example, that anyone had suggested, with respect to the presentation of fictions on *radio*, that we are required to understand each sound as, or as referred to, the content of some character's auditory experience. Perhaps the reason this has not been suggested is that there is nothing in radio comparable to editing in film, and that it is the editing of shots that enables the viewer to understand the images the screen presents as referred now to this character and now to that. (A sufficiently stereophonic radio might do this, but to my knowledge this suggestion has not been taken up.) But that psychologism has not prevailed with respect to radio is instructive, because it does seem that listeners to radio drama are able to orient themselves and to understand the narrative without psychologizing the auditory information they receive. Why should it be otherwise with the cinema?

It is time, I suggest, to turn the psychologizing paradigm on its head, that is, to take as the default setting an interpretation of the cinematic image as the rendering of events objectively, and to allow a subjective interpretation only when no plausible objective interpretation is available.

6.9 ICONIC SIGNS

I sum up. At the movies, we do not see, nor do we imagine that we see, fictional characters or events. Rather, we see signs: pictorial or "iconic" signs which tell us what it is appropriate to imagine. I say these signs are iconic; they are not linguistic signs, or even signs that bear interesting similarities to linguistic ones, and talk of a language of cinema is very misleading talk, as I argued in Chapter 4. Still, movies and novels have more in common than we might otherwise have thought. As long as we suppose that movies require the spectator to imagine himself seeing fictional things, cinema seems to present fictions of quite a different kind – and present them in different ways – from the fictions of literature. Novels do not *give* us the fictional worlds they create; they describe them for us, they mediate between the fiction and the reader. That is why we speak of literary narration. My argument has been that movies are like that too. They are narrations carried on by other means – by iconic signs. In

Part III we look more closely at cinematic narration and narrative.

There are consequences here that go beyond how we should think about cinema as a fictional medium. One is the idea that we need to rethink the basis of some distinctions within the system of the representational arts and outside it. The showing–telling distinction needs to give way to a distinction between telling by showing and telling by other means, with a consequent rethinking of the ancient distinction between mimesis and diegesis. And we have new grounds for thinking of certain media as belonging to something like a natural kind: painting, sculpture and theatre as well as cinema present visual fictions because they promote perceptual imagining. They do so in various ways: by means of painted surfaces, shaped objects, people distributed on a stage and cinematic images. But these differences among them are less significant than the differences between all of them and those media like the novel which promote symbolic imagining.

Chapter 7
Travels in narrative time

> I had the impression [in *Je t'aime, Je t'aime*] of a sort
> of eternal present. The hero relives his past, but when
> he relives it we are with him, the film always takes
> place in the present. There are absolutely no flash-
> backs or anything like them.
>
> *Alain Resnais*[1]

In Chapter 3 I discussed the representation of temporal properties and relations in film, deciding that film is a distinctively
temporal art in that temporal properties are used to represent
temporal properties. I want now to connect some issues in the
filmic representation of time with the theory of imagining outlined in the previous two chapters.

7.1 TENSE IN FILM

One class of philosophically interesting and controversial temporal properties I did not discuss in Chapter 3 is that of *tense
properties*. This consists of the properties of being past, present
and future. These are properties of events, or so I shall assume
for simplicity's sake.[2] My opening the door is future at one time,
present at a later time and past later still. I have argued that
cinematic representations – moving images – have temporal
properties, and that their temporal properties typically function
to represent temporal properties of the events those images represent. Can we say tensed properties are among those which
function representationally in this way?

For that to be the case, cinematic images would have to have
tense properties, and, in virtue of possessing those tense prop-

---

[1] Quoted in Turim, *Flashbacks in Film*, p. 220.
[2] This is in fact controversial. See, e.g., Hugh Mellor's "Unreality of Tense".

erties, would have to represent fictional events as having tense properties. They would have to represent them, that is, as being past, present or future. So first we need to see whether cinematic images *have* tense properties. A cinematic image, or rather the showing of a cinematic image at a particular place at a particular time, is an event, and the image shown is present when it is shown or projected. So anyone witnessing an image can rightly say, as he or she watches it, that it is now present, was future and will be past. In that sense, cinematic images have tense properties. Does the presentness of that image, on the occasion of its showing, function to represent the presentness of the events that the image represents? For that to be the case, the following would have to hold: that the events of cinematic fictions be typically imagined to be occurring presently for the viewer who would have to imagine those events happening *now*. I shall argue that this is not a feature of cinematic fictions, in which case the tensed properties of cinematic images cannot be thought of as representing anything. This does not abolish time in cinema, for there are temporal relations other than tensed ones, and nontensed temporal relations between cinematic images can and do indicate nontensed temporal relations between fictional events. But the dispensability of tense will require us to rethink our assumptions about what is sometimes called *anachrony* in cinema: the reordering of story time by narrative, of which the flashback is the most common example.[3]

There is a potential confusion here that we have already encountered; the question of tense is raised in connection with the way cinematic images function as representations of the *fictional*. As we have seen, these images function also as representations of the real in virtue of their photographic aetiology. If we consider tense in respect to this second function, we can agree that these images do not represent the events they photographically record – actors performing on sets and locations – as happening now. Perhaps they represent them as past. But that is not rele-

---

[3] "Anachrony" is Gérard Genette's term. See his influential *Narrative Discourse*. Genette's taxonomy is widely applied to cinema: see, e.g., Brian Henderson, "Tense, Mood and Voice in Film (Notes after Genette)".

vant to the question before us, which concerns only the representation of the fiction itself. The question is whether the presentness of the image represents the presentness, to the viewer, of fictional events. There is nothing eccentric about this decision to concentrate attention on the fictional: discussions of tense in cinema normally focus on the relation between the narrative order and the temporal order of the fictional events depicted. We do not count it as anachrony when shot Y, which follows shot X in the intended order of viewing, was filmed before shot X. Rather, we count it as anachrony when shot Y represents a fictional event whose fictional time of occurrence is prior to that of X.

Many film theorists have argued that cinematic images have tense, by which they mean not merely that those images have the property of being present as they occur (which they do) but that those images represent the fictional events themselves as present. Of cinematic and other images, the film theorist Béla Balázs wrote, "They show only the present – they cannot express either a past or a future tense."[4] This view is held by practitioners as well as theoreticians. Alain Robbe-Grillet says that "on the screen verbs are always in the present tense . . . by its very nature what we see on the screen is in the act of happening, we are given the gesture itself, not an account of it."[5] Let us call this the *Claim of Presentness*.

[4] Balázs, *Theory of the Film*, p. 120. See also, e.g., Jurij Lotman, *Semiotics of the Cinema*, p. 77: "In every art which employs vision and iconic signs there is only one possible artistic time – the present." Balázs seems to conflate the view that images have only one tense – the present – with the view that they "have no tenses" (ibid.). See also R. Stephenson and J. R. Debrix, *The Cinema as Art*, p. 115: "Film has no tenses – past, present, or future. When we watch a film, it is just something that is happening – *now*" (emphasis in the original). Some other advocates of the Claim of Presentness are discussed and criticized by Jarvie in *Philosophy of the Film*, pp. 12–19.

[5] Introduction to the screenplay of *Last Year at Marienbad*, p. 12; quoted in Joan Dagle, "Narrative Discourse in Film and Fiction: The Question of the Present Tense". Similar views are occasionally expressed concerning literature: "The reader if he is engrossed in his reading translates all that happens from this moment of [fictional] time onward into an imaginative present of his own

The formulations I have just quoted are somewhat problematic in that they seem to presuppose the reality of what is represented ("what we see on the screen is in the act of happening"), which is false in respect to the fictional. Our earlier discussion suggests a better version: the cinematic image represents something – an embrace, a bank robbery – which does not in fact happen. To say that the image is tensed is to say that it represents that event as happening *now*.[6] Since what it represents is intended as fiction, the viewer is to imagine what is represented. And so the viewer is to imagine not merely the happening, in some abstract sense, of that bank robbery, but its happening now.[7]

The Claim of Presentness is a consequence of the Imagined Observer Hypothesis. If the viewer imagines that she is in the world of the fiction, watching the events of the narrative, she presumably imagines that they are happening as she is watching them (modulo corrections for the finite speed of light!), that they are happening now. So this discussion, directed against the Claim of Presentness, will reinforce the criticisms of the Imagined Observer Hypothesis that were brought forward in Chapter 6.[8]

A problem for the Claim of Presentness is provided by the phenomenon of anachrony: the existence of flashbacks and, less

---

and yields to the illusion that he is himself participating in the action or situation" (A. A. Mendilow, *Time and the Novel*, pp. 96–97); also see Meir Sternberg, *Expositional Modes and Temporal Ordering in Fiction*, pp. 21–22, for criticism.

[6] Gilles Deleuze says, "It is not quite right to say that the cimematographic image is in the present. What is in the present is what the image 'represents' " (*Cinema 2: The Time-Image*, p. xii).

[7] The issue of film tense is sometimes confused by those who hold that the viewer typically comes to believe in the fiction presented by the movie. Thus Victor Perkins holds that the tense of film images is not, strictly speaking, the present, because if it were, "cinema managers would have always to protect their screens against assault by gallant spectators rushing to the aid of embattled heroines" (G. Mast and M. Cohen, *Film Theory and Criticism*, 3d ed., p. 48).

[8] See also Francis Sparshott, "Basic Film Aesthetics"; and Alexander Sesonske, "Time and Tense in Cinema".

commonly, flashforwards, in which the image is to be taken to represent a past or future state of affairs. It is said, by advocates of the claim, that in these cases the assumption of presentness is overridden by contextual cues (dissolve, verbal narration or general considerations of narrative coherence). The default setting is presentness.

In that case cinematic images have two distinct functions for the audience, depending on whether they present fictional events anachronously. Where there is no anachrony, we are to interpret the visual images onscreen by imagining that we actually see before us the fictional events they represent. In the case where they present material out of sequence, we are to interpret them in some other way, for we cannot think of ourselves as seeing past or future events *now*. Perhaps we are to think of those images as signs which provide us with information about what happens in the story at some time earlier or later than the story time we have been involved with up to the point of the time shift. This is implausible. When I watch a film that contains anachronous material, I detect no difference between my experience of the images when they present material in standard order and when they deviate from that order. The theory we are considering postulates a functional discontinuity for which there seems to be no psychological evidence.[9]

Another way to defend the hypothesis that cinematic images are present tensed would be to suppose that, with episodes of anachrony, the viewer imagines herself to be shifted in time along with the image. When the image dissolves to reveal what happened twenty, two hundred or two thousand years before, she imagines herself to be a time traveller, shifted in time by just that amount. This has the advantage of allowing us to say that anachronous and temporally standard images function in the same way for the audience rather than in different ways, as

---

[9] Of course the evidence of my introspection (and that of those to whom I have spoken on this subject) may not be decisive in this matter. But so far as I know, the advocates of the Claim of Presentness have never brought forward evidence to support the idea that there is a functional discontinuity here. Perhaps that is because they do not realize that their theory commits them to the existence of such a discontinuity.

the previous theory would have it. All images, on this view, are experienced as representing present events; it is just that what constitutes the present for the viewer is imagined to change to compensate for temporal shifts in the narrative. But in other ways this theory is just as implausible as the last; I don't think I imagine my own temporal position to shift when I view out-of-sequence images on the screen. It might be claimed that this kind of imagined shift takes place unconsciously. Perhaps. I don't say there never are unconscious imaginings; on the contrary, I have emphasized that my identification of imagination with simulation allows for unconscious imaginings in just the same way that we allow for unconscious beliefs. But we must not allow the category of the unconscious to degenerate into an automatic let-out clause for otherwise falsified psychological hypotheses. When it comes to the hypothesis that the viewer of anachrony imagines himself travelling in time, this is not something that we consciously imagine, nor is it something that prompting naturally brings to mind as part of our previously unconscious imagining. The only evidence for these unconscious imaginings seems to be that they are required in order to save the Claim of Presentness from refutation.

Yet another way to defend the Claim of Presentness would be to argue that flashforwards and flashbacks do not change the presentness of the image: that the content of the image in an anachronous sequence is always the content of a character's present memory of, or premonition concerning, an event located elsewhere in time. In that case there would be no need for us to imagine ourselves moving around in time, and no sense of unease or dislocation on confronting such a sequence would be expected.

I might raise awkward questions here about how it is that we could imagine ourselves to be seeing the subjective mental states of other people, which is what this proposal requires us to imagine. Let us put these awkward questions aside. This view amounts, strictly speaking, to the abolition of anachrony, because it would not allow us to say that any story events are presented out of their strict chronological order. What we normally call a flashback could not be said to present the event itself, but rather to present, "from the inside", a character's current memory or premonition of that event, presenting it in the correct chronological sequence.[10] In that case the view we are considering imposes a very strong and implausible limitation on the kinds of film narrative there can be. It says that there can never be a case where the events of the narrative are presented out of their correct temporal order, and that all apparent cases of anachrony are really cases of memory or premonition. But if a film maker can present scenes which represent a sequence of fictional occurrences in their correct order, why can't she, simply by rearranging the order of showing, present them out of sequence? Further, it seems wrong to claim that every apparently anachronous episode in film is in fact one of memory or premonition. It is true that anachronous episodes in film (of which the majority are flashbacks) are often associated with a character's psychological state; the character begins describing the past event and the image dissolves to the flashback. But at least some cases of the flashback, and especially the flashforward, are *not* associated with any act of memory or premonition on the part of a character. At least, there is in some films no evidence for this association, and to insist that the association is there purely on the grounds that the Claim of Presentness requires it is manifestly ad hoc.

We might, on behalf of the Claim of Presentness, associate the anachrony with the mind of the narrator, an imaginary being who the viewer is to think of as the (veridical) source of the information which the film provides. This being may not appear,

[10] Discussions of anachrony in film seem often to presuppose that current memories and premonitions do constitute the material for anachrony. See, e.g., Stephenson and Debrix, *Cinema as Art*, especially p. 118. David Bordwell goes even farther in this surely mistaken direction. He counts it as a case of the narrative reordering of story time when a character in the story *recounts* a story event, as long as that act of recounting constitutes our source of information about the event. See his *Narration in the Fiction Film*, p. 78. The recounting is itself a story event, presented in the narrative in the conventional temporal order; that it is a recounting of an earlier story event makes for no disruption of story time – otherwise there would be anachrony every time a character gave the date of his birth. (Genette makes the same mistake while analysing a passage from *Jean Santeuil*, in *Narrative Discourse*, p. 38.)

or be referred to, or have any evident connection with the events depicted, and so is not a fictional character in the ordinary sense. The narrator's existence is inferred, if it is to be inferred at all, on grounds of narrative coherence.

It is controversial as to whether every movie, or at least every movie containing anachrony, contains a narrator in this sense; we shall discuss this issue in Chapter 9. Let us assume that it does. The crucial move would then be to establish some image or sequence of images as present from the narrator's perspective at the time of his act of narration, and then to establish the direction of anachrony with respect to this reference point. If X is identified as present for the narrator, and Y follows X in viewing time but preceeds it in story time, we have a flashback. But this proposal requires us to think, not merely that there is a narrator narrating, but that he is narrating the events of the story at the very time that at least some of those events are occurring – those that we are to call present. With most cases of narration this is not so; the narrator, where there is one, is to be thought of as recounting the events of the story at a time later than the time of occurrence of any of those events.

This last proposal draws our attention to a potential ambiguity in the notion of presentness: there is the presentness the fictional events may have for the viewer, and there is the presentness of those events "within the fiction" – their being present for the characters involved in them. We might attempt to explain anachrony by appeal to a disparity between what is present for the viewer and what is present for the characters; in that case a flashback would be a sequence present to the viewer, as all sequences are now assumed to be, but past for the characters. But this intuitively appealing idea is hopeless. For any story event, whether presented in flashback or not, it is fictional that that event is present, at the time it happens, for the characters involved, and past for them at any later time. As we watch the flashback scenes in *Crossfire*, they are present for us (or so the Claim of Presentness says). But the events of those scenes are also present for the characters involved in them at the time they occur, just as every scene in the film is. This proposal fails to distinguish any fictional scene from any other.

None of these proposals I've canvassed helps to reconcile the Claim of Presentness with the phenomenon of anachrony. So it is worthwhile considering whether we can dispense altogether with the idea that cinematic images represent fictional events as present. I believe we can. But there is a counterargument to consider.

7.2 THE PROPER TREATMENT OF ANACHRONY

I have said that the best argument against the Claim of Presentness is the difficulty of explaining anachrony. But it may seem that the argument can be inverted: how can we explain anachrony *without* the Claim of Presentness? Temporal forwardness and backwardness seem to be notions that make sense only in relation to the idea of *temporal presence*, something usually incorporated in definitions of the flashback, as in "a juncture wrought between present and past".[11]

The challenge is to make sense of the concepts of flashback and flashforward without recourse to the (tensed) concepts of presentness, pastness and futurity. It will be helpful at this point to introduce a distinction between two kinds of temporal relations. This distinction was drawn by McTaggart, preparatory to his argument that time is unreal.[12] McTaggart's distinction, which I am going to use, is independent of his larger sceptical purpose, and what I shall say will really be independent of the whole issue of the reality of time. The concepts I shall appeal to in explaining anachrony are, it will turn out, concepts that McTaggart thought were perfectly coherent; they are the untensed temporal concepts. Whether or not these concepts on their own and without the assistance of the notion of tense can

[11] Turim, *Flashbacks in Film*, p. 1. Turim also quotes a similarly tensed account of the flashback from Leslie Halliwell (*The Filmgoer's Companion*, 3d ed.), who calls it "a break in chronological narrative during which we are shown events of past time which bear on the present situation".

[12] See J. M. McTaggart, *The Nature of Existence*, vol. 2, chapter 33. McTaggart argued, roughly, that the A-series involves a contradiction, that without it there is no change, and without change there is no time. So there is no time.

constitute a conception of time is the issue raised by Mc-Taggart's argument, but it is an argument we can avoid here.

McTaggart suggested that there are two ways we can think about the temporality of events. We can, first of all, think of events as past, present or future. McTaggart calls the series of events ordered in this way the A-series, and the relations which order that series are tensed. Alternatively, we can think of events as earlier than, contemporaneous with, or later than other events. These relations are themselves unchanging; the Battle of Hastings always was, is and will be earlier than the Battle of Waterloo. In this schema, no event is privileged as present, and so no event can be called past or future. McTaggart calls this the B-series. Relations in the B-series are untensed.

The point I have been labouring can be put in McTaggart's terms: we cannot explain anachrony in terms of the A-series, because we cannot identify some particular sequence of story events as present without so identifying *all* of them. But in denying ourselves the use of tenses, we have not thereby denied ourselves the use of all temporal notions, as the distinction between the A- and the B-series makes clear. We have at our disposal the B-series relations of earlier than and later than. Of course we may employ other, nontemporal notions as well, and this is what I shall do when I come to explain certain aspects of anachrony. What is important is that we should not make explicit or implicit use of the notion of tense.

I start by observing that there is nothing problematic about saying that story events are related according to the B-series: that, within the time of the story, one event occurs before, co-temporaneously with, or after, another. (Normally, their being so related is represented, automorphically, by their cinematic representations occurring before, cotemporaneously with, or after, one another; the exceptions to this are, precisely, the cases of anachrony.) This does not require the viewer to think of those events as past, present or future.[13] Hoping, then, to define an-

---

[13] As Robin le Poidevin points out, McTaggart himself wondered whether the time of fiction might be a time constructed from the B-series alone, although he seems also to have rejected this view (*Nature of Existence*, vol. 2,

achrony in terms of B-series relations only, I start with this proposal:

> (A) Film F contains anachrony iff F contains representations of fictional events X and Y, where the representation of X in viewing time is after that of Y, but it is fictional that the time of the occurrence of X is before that of Y.

This definition is not quite right. I want to consider a number of problems that it faces. The first, put to me by David Lewis, concerns the relation between anachrony in cinematic fiction and those cinematic narratives which involve time travel. In a time-travel story the narrative might begin in, say, 1982, during which plans are made for a journey into the past; later in the narrative we are presented with events which take place at the time travelled back to, say 1952. Now it is intuitively wrong to assimilate cinematic (or other) narratives involving time travel to anachronous narratives; there seems to be a sense in which, in the time-travel story I described, the events of the story are presented in the chronologically *correct* sequence; after all, the journey back to 1952 takes place *after* the events in 1982, which are presented first – otherwise, how would the events of 1982 constitute a preparation for the journey? But then the objection to my definition (A) is, exactly, that it conflates anachronous narratives and narratives involving time travel.[14] For it is true, concerning the time-travel story just described, that events occurring in 1952 are shown later in viewing time than events occurring in 1982.

Lewis was good enough to suggest a way out of the difficulty for me. The objection shows not that there is an error in defi-

---

p. 16). See Robin le Poidevin, "Time and Truth in Fiction" for an interesting discussion of tense and fiction.

[14] It is possible for there to be a time-travel story that would not count as anachronous according to definition (A). That would be a narrative in which the events "travelled back to" in 1952 are presented first in viewing time and the events leading up to the journey in 1982 are presented later in viewing time. So the objection is not that (A) makes all time-travel stories come out as anachronous, but rather that it makes some of them so appear – and in fact all the time-travel narratives I know about would come out as anachronous on the definition.

nition (A), but rather that there is an ambiguity in its statement. That is, there is an ambiguity in the expression "the time of the occurrence of X". Is this supposed to refer to objective time, or to what is sometimes called personal or subjective time? With time travel, as it occurs in stories and as it might occur in reality if it ever does, there is a disparity between objective and personal time. The traveller travels back to a time earlier in objective time than the time she left; from 1982 to 1952, as it might be. But for her, the events she encounters in 1952 are later (say, an hour later) than the events she previously encountered in 1982. Here the time traveller's journey is thirty years into the objective past, and one hour into her personal future.[15]

Normally, in stories and in reality, objective time and personal time run in the same direction and at the same rate, and there is no need to distinguish between them. Time travel occurs when they come apart. How is that possible? Perhaps in this way: that the direction of time is the direction of causation – the direction from causes to effects. That is why we can remember the past but not the future, and why, more generally, we are familiar with traces of the past in the present, but never encounter traces of the future in the present (unconfirmed reports of premonitions aside). But suppose that not all causal processes move in the same direction – that there is a small minority of causal processes that swim against the tide. In that case we could say that the *predominant* direction of causation is the direction of objective time, and that, given this direction, objects undergoing reversed causation are travelling back in objective time. But for those involved, if they are sentient creatures capable of thought and memory, their journey backwards will end after it began; for them, the reversing of causal processes will mean that objectively later states of consciousness will affect objectively earlier states, and the travellers will remember doing things in 1982 when they get to 1952; if the journey takes a significant amount of time, they may end the journey hungrier than they began it, have fuller beards and longer fingernails.

---

[15] On the distinction between objective and personal time see, e.g., David Lewis, "The Paradoxes of Time Travel".

The journey ends later in their personal time, and earlier in objective time.

With this distinction between objective and personal time, we can solve our problem. In a time-travel story, events that occur earlier in objective time may be recounted after events that occur later in objective time. But according to the model of time travel just proposed, the events occurring earlier in objective time are occurring later in personal time. So if we take "the time of the occurrence of X", as that expression occurs in (A), to refer to a character's personal time, time-travel stories will not count as anachronous according to that definition. Of course it would be awkward to interpret "the time of the occurrence of X" in (A) as sometimes referring to objective time and sometimes to personal time, according to whether the work in question is a time-travel story or not. But we need not do that. We may simply say that "the time of the occurrence of X" always refers to personal time, which, in the case of a story which involves no time travel (whether it involves anachrony or not) will automatically coincide with objective time.

It might be objected to this that what I have said depends upon a complex and highly unobvious metaphysics of time, and that we ought not to appeal to such things when we are explaining the basis of distinctions that ordinary people make, and make in the same way even though they have no knowledge of that metaphysics. But while I grant that the metaphysics is difficult to spell out, I claim that the central distinction it involves – that between objective time and personal time – must in some way be grasped by the viewer if he or she is to make sense of the narrative as one involving time travel rather than anachrony. It is surely part of our understanding of time-travel narratives that "in some sense" the events travelled back to by the characters occur later *for them* than do the events from which they have travelled back; if that were not perceived to be the case, it would be hard to explain how film viewers could ever distinguish between a time-travel narrative and an anachronous narrative – and the whole basis of the objection to (A) above was that we do indeed make such a distinction. So while the metaphysics I briefly outlined may be unobvious, its central distinction I take to be common currency.

The next objection will require some revision of (A), though only a rather minor one; the need for it was pointed out to me, again, by David Lewis. Fictions, including cinematic ones, do frequently give us a good deal of information about the temporal relations between the events they portray. But in this area, as in others, they rarely give us complete information. Sometimes they are unspecific about the temporal relations between events, even when those events are explicitly represented onscreen in a determinate order in viewing time. And sometimes it is not possible to make any reasonable inferences – either from the order in viewing time or from any other source – about the temporal relations between these events. Typical of this phenomenon are those "summarizing" sequences which might concern the arrival of the Martians: Martians are seen landing in Paris, then seen landing in Washington, and so on. But there need not be any implication that the order of showing corresponds to the order of occurrence; we are simply to infer that these events occurred at roughly the same time, and together constitute a sort of collective phenomenon.

In cases such as these we have, as we always do, a determinate order of viewing,[16] but the order of viewing does not correspond to any order of occurrence in the story. I suggest that this phenomenon deserves to be classed as a kind of anachrony – "weak anachrony" we might call it, since it involves a determinate relation in viewing time but no determinate relation in fictional time, rather than the strongly anachronous presentations we have been considering until now, which involve a determinate relation in viewing time and a determinate (but opposite) relation in fictional time. Our definition of anachrony ought to cover weak anachrony as well as strong, and it can be made to do so with a slight alteration:

[16] Devices like the split screen can present material simultaneously, but still the temporal order is determinate – it is co-occurrence.

(A*) Film *F* contains anachrony iff *F* contains representations of fictional events *X* and *Y*, where the representation of *X* in viewing time is after that of *Y*, but it is not fictional that the time of the occurrence of *X* is after that of *Y*.

This differs from (A) in that the final words "it is fictional that the time of the occurrence of *X* is before that of *Y*" are replaced by the words "it is not fictional that the time of the occurrence of *X* is after that of *Y*". Any case of strong anachrony as defined by (A) is also a case of weak anachrony as defined by (A*), but not vice versa.[17]

There may be further objection to (A) on the grounds that it does not provide a necessary condition for anachrony, since it fails to cover the "flashforward ending" exemplified by a film whose temporal structure we might indicate as 1235.[18] Writers on narrative have urged that such a structure should be classified as an *ellipsis* – a mere passing over in viewing time of relevant story events between points 3 and 5 – rather than as an anachrony.[19] If that is right, the (A)/(A*) combination provides a necessary and sufficient condition for anachrony, the only possible cases of which are the flashback and the "returned" flashforward (exemplified in the structure 132), which in my taxonomy is the only flashforward there is. However, I have some doubts about the standard treatment of ellipses which I shall discuss in the appendix to this chapter.

[17] There is an interesting exploitation of the difference between weak and strong anachrony in *Black Widow* (Bob Rafelson, 1986), which begins, apparently, with two episodes of wives murdering their husbands. At first I took this to be weak anachrony: sequential representation of roughly simultaneous events involving distinct pairs of characters. Soon it turns out that it is the same woman in both and that the murder represented second in fact occurred considerably before the first.

[18] Here a number's actual value denotes its position in story time, while its position in the sequence denotes its position in the narrative order.

[19] Describing a flashforward as a leaping ahead "to events subsequent to intermediate events", Seymour Chatman goes on, "These intermediate events must themselves be recounted at some later point, for otherwise the leap would simply constitute an ellipsis" (*Story and Discourse*, p. 64). See also Genette, *Narrative Discourse*, p. 43. But further, see the appendix to this chapter.

But there is a more serious worry concerning the definitions. It can be explained most easily by concentrating on (A): while (A) might be adequate as a condition for the presence of (strong) anachrony, it is inadequate to specify the *direction* of the anachrony in any particular case. Imagine that X and Y are events of the fiction satisfying condition (A). The onscreen representation of Y occurs before the representation of X, but it is fictional that Y occurs after X. Do we have here a flashback or a flashforward? It might seem that we have, unambiguously, a flashback; X occurs before Y in the story, but is represented after Y on screen, so X is represented in a flashback. But this is not necessarily the case. Y might have been represented in a flashforward, and the transition to the representation of X is the return which completes that flashforward. In order to decide whether the transition in question signifies a flashback or a flashforward we shall have to look at the representation of some *other*, suitably related, story event, and decide whether that belongs to a flashback or flashforward. If we are not to start on a regress, we shall have to locate some transition that can be identified as a flashback or flashforward without reference to another such transition. Which one will that be?

We might hope to start with the fictional event presented *first* in the narration, and anchor the rest of the narrative to it by discovering a principle according to which the direction of anachrony can be judged unambiguously from there. But there is no such principle. The event first presented may itself be a flashback or even a flashforward, and which one it is can depend on its relation to *later* representations in the narrative. It is probably true that there is a tendency to give a certain weight to the hypothesis that a scene is temporally standard if that scene is represented first, but that weighting can be overcome. Priority in narration time offers no Archimedean point from which to judge the temporal structure of the rest of the narrative.

It is tempting at this point to say that we need to establish some story event or sequence of events P as *present,* and then to judge the direction of anachrony in relation to P. But that would be to appeal to a notion of tense, which I have said I will not do.

So the problem is this: while B-series concepts enable us to identify an episode of anachrony, they do not enable us to say what is the correct description of it; they do not enable us to say whether it is a flashback or a flashforward. But most of the time we find noncollusive agreement between subjects as to which description is appropriate in particular cases: flashback or flashforward. If B-series notions offer no way of deciding between the two, that agreement cannot be based on our employment of B-series concepts alone. So any explication of the direction of anachrony in terms of the B-series alone must be inadequate.

But I have not claimed that the *direction* of anachrony could be explained in terms of the B-series alone. I have claimed that the concept of anachrony itself could be so explained. It is one thing to decide what constitutes anachrony, another to decide how it is directed in particular cases. Of course I must give an explanation of this direction. I shall do that by describing the sorts of considerations that incline us to say we are dealing with a flashback, or alternatively with a flashforward. These considerations are not themselves temporal, and so they have nothing to do with tense. They have to do with simplicity and the emphasizing of nontemporal connections between events in the story.

Suppose we have an episode that is anachronous. We have to choose between one description of it and another, and our choosing is partly dictated by the principle that we should impose as simple and straightforward a narrative structure as is consistent with the film itself. Of course, the simplest structure we can arrive at may in fact be rather complicated, and the film may so defy our narrative expectations that all efforts to impose on it a consistent structure fail.[20] It is just that we start with the assumption of simplicity and introduce complexity as needed; any other path would make narrative interpretation impossibly difficult. Let us see how, in particular cases, the constraint of simplicity works to dictate, or at least to suggest, one description of anachrony rather than another.

[20] Resnais's *Last Year at Marienbad* and Deren's *Meshes of the Afternoon* are often cited as examples of this.

If the film's narrative structure is represented in B-series terms as 41235, we tend to say that the sequence 123 is a flashback. The alternative, to say that 4 and 5 are separate flashforwards, would ascribe two anachronous episodes to the film instead of one, and the rule of simplicity tells against our adopting that alternative description. If the film's structure is represented in B-series terms as 12356, it looks as if we have a choice between saying that 123 is a flashback or that 56 is a flashforward. Simplicity considerations are not telling here. But the notion of ellipsis will help. We may regard the passage from 3 to 5 as an ellipsis, and so avoid the imputation of anachrony to the film at this point – a victory for simplicity, assuming that ellipsis is not itself a species of anachrony (see the appendix to this chapter).

Simplicity considerations compete for our attention with others. We employ descriptions of anachrony sometimes to reinforce or to cohere with certain aspects of the story or of the "narrative voice" we associate with it. If the structure is 1342, we are bound to admit anachrony, and we could say that 1 and 2 are flashbacks, or that 34 is a flashforward. Simplicity favours the latter, but if 1 and 2 are connected to 34 by some episodes of memory that occurs during 34, we are likely to see 34 as "looking back" to 1 and 2, and so to describe them as flashbacks, even when they present fictional material in an objective way.[21] Indeed, in classical film narration, anachrony is so frequently connected with the inner states of characters that there is something close to a conversational implicature from the anachrony to the existence, within the story, of some relevant state of memory or (less frequently in realistic cinema) premonition.[22] And since premonition is a device hostile to realist assumptions, the implicature works against the flashforward, nudging us towards a description in terms of flashback, even at some cost to simplicity. But the implicature, being conversational, is cancellable, and other aspects of the narrative or the story itself may relieve

---

[21] See the remarks on representation "from the inside", text to note 10 this chapter.

[22] On conversational and other kinds of implicatures see Paul Grice, *Studies in the Way of Words*, part 1, chapter 2.

the anachrony of its psychological associations. The quick cutting between the earlier lovemaking and the later dressing in *Don't Look Now* are not suggestive of premonition, though later anachronies in that narrative can be seen, on reflection, to be so connected.[23] Sometimes in films with a complex or unusual temporal structure, there seem to be distinct but equally good ways of describing that temporal structure; there does not seem to be any uniquely correct answer to the question, "Is this a flashback or a flashforward?" We might call this scene a flashback; but we could arrive at an equally coherent overall structure by calling a later scene a flashforward. That is just what we would expect on my theory, according to which the decision to label a particular shot or scene anachronous depends on weighing a number of factors that may conflict, and which may not point us in one direction rather than another.[24]

A more thorough analysis of our strategies for working out the direction of anachrony I leave to others. I think I have said enough to make it plausible that judging the direction of an anachronous episode is a matter of applying interpretive concepts that are not strictly temporal.[25] In that case it's no objection to my theory that it does not provide for a definition of the direction of anachrony in temporal terms alone.

7.3 IS THIS REVISIONISM?

I have argued in this chapter, as in the preceding one, that some of our common ways of speaking about the cinematic experience

---

[23] Flashforwards unconnected with premonition occur sometimes in credit sequences, for example, in Clayton's *The Innocents* and Wilder's *Double Indemnity*. *The Godfather, Part 2* is notable for its use of objective flashbacks (unless we are meant to view them as flashbacks within flashbacks, filtered through the recollection of Vito Corleone, whose death occurs before the beginning of Part 2; I think there is some evidence for this interpretation).

[24] See, e.g., the discussion of *They Shoot Horses, Don't They?* in Bernard F. Dick, *Anatomy of Film*, p. 178.

[25] Noël Burch, I think, was making a similar point when he asked, "Are not jumps forward and backward in time really identical at the formal organic level of a film?" (*Theory of Film Practice*, p. 8).

are fundamentally wrong. Yet my aim has not really been a revisionary one; I have not been trying to show that we should approach the cinema in a new and unfamiliar way. My aim in this chapter has been largely to rescue our judgements about time and especially about anachrony in film from what I take to be a false theory about the basis of those judgements. I have not tried to argue that people are wrong in any straightforward sense when they describe this or that movement of the film's narration as a movement from the present to the past rather than as one from the present to the future. I say only that we should not take them literally when they employ words like "past", "present" and "future". The Reverend Dr Spooner is said to have ended a puzzling sermon by saying, after a moment of reflection, "Whenever I said 'Aristotle', I meant 'Saint Paul' ". We would do well to believe him. It is sensible to reassign meanings to a speaker's words if in doing so we can interpret him as saying something significantly closer to the truth. At least, it is sensible to do this if we can reasonably credit the speaker with a sensitivity to the concepts that our meaning reassignments introduce, and reasonably explain his utterance as the result of his sensitivity to those concepts. We go along with Dr Spooner's plea for reinterpretation because we believe him to have had a grasp of the concept of Saint Paul, and we find it plausible to think that what he said in the sermon was the outcome, in part, of that grasp. We do not reinterpret the speech of witch finders so as to make them early investigators of epilepsy, because it is not reasonable to credit them with a sensitivity to that concept – they would come out, by our lights, as very poor epilepsy discriminators. But it is perfectly reasonable to assume that competent and alert film watchers have a sensitivity to those concepts in terms of which I explain the phenomenon of cinematic anachrony: temporal but untensed ones, plus the machinery of narrative interpretation. So we should treat them as Dr Spooner would have us treat him.

There is one somewhat surprising consequence of the view I have advanced. It is that the concept of the *direction* of anachrony is on a quite different footing from the concept of anachrony itself. Anachrony is explainable in terms of temporal concepts. The direction of anachrony is not; it is fundamentally a dramatic notion.

In Chapter 3, I asked: in what sense, if any, is cinema a temporal art form? My answer was that it is very centrally a temporal art form because of its capacity for the automorphic representation of temporal relations between events in the fictions it presents. But the argument of this chapter may seem to be in tension with that optimistic conclusion. The argument of this chapter has been that there are certain kinds of temporal relations which the cinema is not apt to represent at all; the tensed temporal properties of pastness, presentness and futurity. Instead, the cinema represents events – fictional events, that is – as standing in tenseless relations of priority and co-occurrence.

But we need to bear in mind here a distinction made earlier, that between presentness for the viewer and presentness for the characters of the fiction itself. The failure of cinema to represent fictional events as tensed is a failure to represent them as tensed *from the perspective of the viewer*, not from that of the characters. When events of the fiction are represented onscreen we are to imagine that those events are present for the characters at the time of their occurrence, future for the characters at earlier times and past for them at later times, just as real events are for us. So the time that cinema represents – the network of temporal relations between fictional events – is not a peculiar time to which no tensed predicates apply. Tense applies only within the fiction itself.[26] Just so with space. While the events of the fiction are not, so I have argued, spatially present for the viewer – the viewer is not to imagine that they are occurring here – they are spatially present for the characters. Characters, if they could be

---

[26] Here I agree with Christian Metz: "The film is able to express space and time relationships of some kind, but only anaphorically, within the film itself . . . and not between the film and someone or something else" ("The Impersonal Enunciation, or the Site of Film", p. 756). But I am puzzled by Metz's talk, here and elsewhere in the article, of anaphora and the related concept of deixis, which I think he misapplies. At least, I have found his point hard to follow.

bothered, could truly and at any time say "I am here now", just as we can. So we can say: the space and time of cinematic fiction is structurally like the space and time of the real world.

APPENDIX: ANACHRONY AND ELLIPSIS

In the body of this chapter I followed the orthodoxy which distinguishes sharply between anachronies and the phenomenon of ellipsis, representable in our simple notation by, for example, 1245. Of course it is true that an ellipsis is not the same thing as either a flashback or a flashforward. But they, in their turn, are different from each other. The question is whether there is some decisive reason for classing the last two together as anachronies and categorizing the first, ellipsis, as something fundamentally different. Or could it be that all three belong together in a general theory of anachrony?

Note first that from the point of view of what we might call "the violation of real time", an ellipsis is in the same boat as a flashforward or flashback. A time traveller, whose activities subvert the order of objective time, might do any of the following: travel into the past, returning (or not) to the present, or accelerate forward into the future, again returning (or not) to the present. If we join ellipses to our flashforwards and flashbacks, we get exactly the class of time-travel possibilities. Ellipsis would be the case of time travel by acceleration forward without return, suggesting that ellipsis is as deserving of the title anachrony as the other candidates. Why should it be treated differently from the others?

Perhaps for this reason. In literary narrative, there is no general correspondence between the time it takes to read the description of a fictional event, and the time which, fictionally, that event took to occur. Since reading speed varies between individuals and occasions, the most carefully embodied intention that the narrative take as long to read as the events it describes could succeed only very approximately. In that sense, *all* literary narrative is in violation of the time of the fiction it describes – or perhaps we should say that its conforming to or violating that time does not arise. In that case, ellipsis, which is a matter of temporal duration rather than temporal order, cannot be seen as a device that works in opposition to any norm that prevails in literature; it is just more of the same. But flashes forward and back (or what are more frequently called prolepses and analepses in literary discussion) are violations of temporal *order*, which can itself be preserved – and typically is preserved – in literature. So when we consider literature, it is natural to think of these two as separated from ellipsis. But in the case of film, that argument does not hold. With film, any continuous shot constitutes the rendition, in a certain space of time – the same for all observers – of events in the fiction that took a certain time to occur, and typically the relation between the time of the shot and the time of the fictional event is identity. So in the filmic case, at least within the confines of a single shot (and frequently across the class of shots that constitute a scene), there is no violation of the time of the film – neither with respect to order nor with respect to duration. So ellipsis, when it occurs, constitutes a violation of a cinematic norm in the same way that flashforwards and flashbacks do. So when we are considering film, there is a case for classing all three – ellipsis, flashforward, flashback – together as anachronies, and for not simply taking over the theoretical divisions inherited from literature.

If, as I am urging, we class ellipsis as an anachrony, we can no longer take definition (A*) as a definition of anachrony; it is instead to be taken as a definition merely of two kinds of anachrony, the flashforward or flashback. To define anachrony fully we need to supplement (A*) with a definition of ellipsis. We can say that ellipsis occurs when there are times of the fiction, x and y, which are represented by viewing times $R(x)$ and $R(y)$, and a time of the fiction, z, lying between x and y, which is not represented by any viewing time. And we can say in general that anachrony is any violation of story time where the kinds of violations possible are just those described in definition (A*) and in the definition just given of ellipsis.

For the filmic case, defining ellipsis is thus relatively straightforward. Not so for the literary case. Because literature is not a time art in the way that film is, we cannot define ellipsis in literature in terms of a relation between times of the story and times of the representation of the story; we have seen that the verbal representations of literature do not, strictly speaking, have times. And the times of, say, a reading of the text of the literary work do not correspond, point for point, to the times of the story, as has been pointed out. Ellipsis in literary fictions seems not to be definable in terms of strict temporal relations between story and representation; that is why ellipsis really does stand apart from the flashforward and the flashback in the literary case. For literature, the closest analogy of the temporally definable concept of cinematic ellipsis is probably the concept of a narrative which omits, or fails to describe, not times but *events* of the story. Thus we might say that an ellipsis in literature occurs whenever the narrative recounts story event A, and story event C, but fails to recount B which (fictionally) happened between A and C.

The problem with this definition is that it is almost entirely unhelpful. The narrative declares, "Albert slept soundly for eight hours." Is there ellipsis here? Certainly there are constituents of this eight-hour sleeping event which are not encompassed by the description: the breaths that Albert took, their order, duration and magnitude, not to mention the events elsewhere in the city as he slept. But this is true of just about any description, however minute its detailing of events; rarely can a description convey everything that happened in a finite time, however brief. The definition forces us to say that every part of every literary narrative involves ellipsis. We need a more demanding characterization of ellipsis; one that does not confuse ellipsis with mere incompleteness.

We might seek instead to define literary ellipsis in terms of the amount of time passed over; ellipses proper involve the passing over of a substantial amount of time. What counts as substantial might be highly sensitive to context: in a narrative given over to the minutia of a brief experience, a gap of a few seconds might count as an ellipsis, while in a novel with pretensions to an historical vision, only a gap of years might count. The problem here is not the context dependence of substantiality, but that a gap that is small even by the standards of the relevant context can induce an ellipsis if it leaves out a *significant* event. We then depend on a notion of narrative significance that is so far undefined – though its application might be relatively clear in practice.[27] But if we define ellipsis in terms of significance – itself suitably defined – then we cannot say, as writers like Chatman have said, that a leap forward in time that is not "returned" is always an ellipsis rather than a flashforward, for now its being an ellipsis would depend on its being a case where some narratively significant event is passed over. We could say that in these cases – narratives that end with a temporal leap forward – what makes them ellipses is their extent, thus returning to the first definition. It looks as if extent explains some of our judgements that we confront an ellipsis, whereas significance explains some others; it might even be that between them, these two criteria exhaust the field, and that we could say that ellipsis is to be disjunctively defined as grounded either in extent or in significance. But the trouble here is that the two grounding concepts – extent and significance – don't seem to have much to do with each other, and it is not likely that an intuitively unified concept like that of the ellipsis is actually the union of two unconnected ones. The true definition must, it seems, be found at some deeper level. I am unsure where. Since our primary concern in this case is with cinematic rather than with literary narrative, we may leave this difficult problem here.

[27] But see the remarks on narrative unreliability and significant questions in Chapter 9, Section 9.4.

Part III

Interpretation

I N Part I argued that the depictive content of film is given
to us courtesy of our capacities for recognizing the objects
depicted. The process of recognizing depictive content
hardly counts as interpretive. But there is more to understanding a film than merely recognizing its depictive content.
That is where interpretation starts. In Chapter 8, I develop a
theory of interpretation for literary and filmic narratives. But
there are important differences between the kinds of narratives available to film and to literature. In Chapter 9, I illustrate this diversity through the example of narrative unreliability.

Chapter 8

The interpretive problem

> Even if we reject the thesis that creative interpretation
> aims to discover some actual historical intention, the
> concept of intention nevertheless provides the *formal*
> structure for all interpretive claims. I mean that an
> interpretation is by nature a report of a purpose.
>
> *Ronald Dworkin*

The subject of this chapter is a problem and how we solve it.
The problem I shall call the *interpretive problem,* and it is this: an
interpreter starts with something and ends with something else.
The interpreter of a novel starts with a text – a sequence of
words and sentences – and ends with a story: the story which,
as the reader/interpreter sees it, is told by that text. The interpreter of a film starts with a sequence of cinematic images and
their auditory accompaniments, and ends with a story: the story
which, as the viewer/interpreter sees it, is told by those images
and sounds. The interpretive problem is how to get from the
one to the other. The philosopher's problem is to give an abstract
characterization of the principles and methodological rules in
accordance with which interpreters solve the interpretive problem. In solving the philosopher's problem, we give a theory of
interpretation.

The interpretive problem looks so forbiddingly difficult it can
seem astonishing it ever gets solved at all. In the filmic case,
images succeed one another quickly, the film cutting across large
chunks of space and time. Sometimes the narrative is reshuffled,
as with flashback. Usually this goes on without any explicit commentary or other onscreen direction to indicate the relation between successive images. With literature such commentary is
more common, but it never makes fully explicit more than a
fraction of what the reader is intended to imagine. Yet somehow,
and frequently with little or no conscious thought or effort,

viewers construct a story from it all. "Interpreter" suggests someone with specialized skills and a reflective, self-conscious approach. But I shall use that term for anyone who gets, or attempts to get, a coherent story out of the bewildering array of sights and sounds: for anyone, that is, who attempts to solve an interpretive problem.

Briefly stated, my theory of interpretation is this: to interpret is to hypothesize about the intentional causes of whatever it is that is being interpreted – a temple, a text, a practice, a picture, the sequence of moving pictures and accompanying sounds that constitute a movie. Interpretation is intentional explanation, and it proceeds according to the methodological canons that govern explanation in general: we count one interpretation as better than another when it is simpler, more plausible, better supported by the evidence and in general more explanatory than the other. In this, textual and filmic interpretation do not differ; where they differ is in respect of what interpretation is to be an explanation of – a text in the one case and cinematic images in the other.

Until late in this chapter, and with the exception of a few asides, I shall concentrate on the literary case as I build up a theory of how we solve the interpretive problem. Towards the end I shall say something about what we need if the model is to apply to film.

8.1 INTERSUBJECTIVE AGREEMENT AND INTERPRETIVE PRINCIPLES

The idea that there might be generally valid principles of interpretation applicable across media, genres, times and communities is not likely to receive much support from literary and cinema theorists. The most that is generally allowed is that there are certain principles that have a local, community-based validity, or which are promoted and fostered by certain powerful, historically specific interests, and that the functioning of these principles to guide interpretation is susceptible to a sociological explanation, but not in any sense to a philosophical justification. Closely related to this is the view that different genres or styles of film making are characterized by their own local interpretive principles, and that successful interpretation is largely a matter of correctly identifying the genre of the work so as to be able to apply to it the appropriate interpretive principles.

An argument for supposing that the rules of interpretation are not universal is that people for whom our culture is alien would interpret works, ours and theirs, in ways different from our own, and would come up with different interpretive hypotheses. I agree; in fact I shall make quite a lot of this point later on. But this does not show that there are no universal principles of interpretation. That Martians might – and humans from other cultures occasionally do – interpret works in ways different from ours need not be because they operate with different interpretive principles. For the principles are and must be employed always in the light of culturally specific assumptions; interpretive divergence may result not from the application of different principles, but from the application of the same principles against different, culturally determined backgrounds. Two scientists may come to entirely different conclusions about the likely outcome of a certain experiment, but this need not show that they disagree about what laws of nature (the analogue of our principles) are operating, though of course this is one possible source of their disagreement. It is possible instead that their conflict is the product of a disagreement about the initial conditions of the experiment. If one of them thinks that the sample of uranium has a mass of one gram, and the other thinks it has a mass of one ton, they are likely to predict very different outcomes, even though they both reason in the same way from the same general theory of matter.

So it is, I believe, with the case of interpretation. We may be able to accommodate interpretive differences between groups, or between the same group at different times, or even between subgroups and individuals within the same community, while holding interpretive principles constant across groups, subgroups, times and individuals. We may all operate on the principle that the work is to be interpreted by figuring out the intentions behind its production, but come up with different interpretations because we operate with different assumptions about what sort of intentions the maker is likely to have. An intention that it would be natural for us to attribute to a maker might be for others highly unnatural, because of its deployment of concepts that are alien to their culture, that lack salience in any reasonable schedule of their concerns, or that are judged by them to be forbidden or shocking. And some of the intentions we naturally attribute to makers get their salience for us from their appearance in other, related works of art that belong to our culture. Our background of exposure to works which conform to certain generic norms means that the maker will have to work hard to get certain nonstandard intentions recognized, while others that conform to the expectations generated by those other works will be recognized easily and without explicit signalling. People without exposure to that same body of work will arrive at the interpretive task with a system for weighting the evidence quite different from ours. All these differences can be assumed to lead to different interpretive results, even where everyone follows the same general interpretive method.

But this talk of disagreement should not obscure an important fact: that there is usually a good deal of agreement between readers and film viewers about how works are to be interpreted, if we confine ourselves, as I do here, to interpretation of the story, or what I am going to call *narrative interpretation*. Narrative interpretation is the kind of interpretation that even the least ambitious of us engage in when we read: working out what is going on in the story. Some of what is going on in the story that a fictional work has to tell may be obvious and uncontroversial. That Mr Dombey is the owner of a shipping firm, that Carkar dies under a railway train, that Florence leaves her father – these things are generally agreed to be true in *Dombey and Son*. In coming to such conclusions about the work we do not think of ourselves as identifying the fictional events by any process that deserves the name "interpretation". But the obvious is merely that which is given by a kind of interpretation of zero degree; interpretation under default assumptions of literal speech, narrative reliability, rationality and evidential relevance. When we fail, under those assumptions, to generate a narrative that is fully coherent we look for nonliteral readings and evidence of narrative idiosyncrasy. At that point we are happy to say we are interpreting; in fact, we are just moving up an interpretive gear.

Narrative interpreting is not, of course, all the interpreting there is, even when we limit the act of interpretation to the fictional. We may agree on what happens in Dickens's novel but disagree on whether the opening chapter maintains a tension between comedy and tragedy, whether the railway serves as a symbol of social change, whether the novel bears the marks of the onerous constraints of serial production under which it was written. All these may fairly be called interpretive questions, but they are not the kinds of questions I have anything to say about here. Similarly, viewers often disagree about things connected with the film outside the realm of narrative interpretation: what kind of mood was conveyed by a particular shot, what moral, if any, the story was supposed to drive home, how successful overall the film's project was. These sorts of disagreements are not, in my sense, about what story the film presented. A disagreement of that kind would be, for example, about who committed the crime, whether the couple who married at the end are going to live happily thereafter, or what the bride's motivation in marrying was. Disagreements over matters like that do occur, but against a background of overwhelming agreement about other matters concerning the story. It is only infrequently, and only in the case of very eccentric narratives, that there is fundamental disagreement about what happened in the story. And in the cases of those eccentric narratives, there is more likely to be a shared bewilderment about what happened than a clash of definite opinion. Seen in this light, it is agreement that is central, and dispute that is marginal.[1]

While narrative interpreting is a small part of what we normally call interpreting, I make no apology for concentrating attention on it. It is, after all, absolutely fundamental to interpretation more broadly conceived. If we cannot agree about what is going on in the story, we shall hardly agree about the

---

[1] Disagreement and its implications I discuss in "Interpretation and Objectivity".

story's significance, message, or relation to other stories. Conversely, an argument about symbols or genres that is not reflected in the least disagreement at the level of what is fictional seems an excellent candidate for being a spurious or at least unresolvable dispute.

You might hope to explain agreement at the level of narrative interpretation without appeal to universal principles of interpretation by arguing that genre-specific principles would be sufficient to generate agreement. This cannot be right. Deciding what genre a work belongs to is itself an interpretive matter,[2] one of deciding to give certain elements in the work a significance that depends on their relations to all the other elements of the work. There is no checklist of features that determines whether the work is a screwball comedy or a film noire. But as with other interpretive judgements, we do find a broad measure of agreement between agents concerning what genre this or that work belongs to, and so the argument for their being interpretive principles applies as much here as elsewhere. It sometimes happens that the viewer knows what genre the work belongs to by some independent route; it might be advertised in such a way as to make its genre clear. But this is not how it always is, and we usually are capable of deciding, in an unprompted way, on the genre of a work by seeing it.

I am not claiming that there are no local principles to be deployed in a media-, genre-, or style-dependent way. There may well be such principles, but they are not the only ones. Nor am I claiming that the interpretive method which I regard as universal always or even usually enables us to arrive at one single and uncontroversially correct interpretation of the story. Interpretive principles are never mechanical rules that can be applied as algorithms, and there is often room for rational disagreement as to whether the rule has been correctly applied in this case; such disagreement is one source of the plurality of interpretations. Another is the fact that the rules, even when there is no disagreement concerning their application, can sometimes lead

---

[2] Interpretive in a broad sense, not in the narrow sense I shall be concerned with here – narrative interpretation.

to a tie between competing interpretations: we shall see that the rules do not guarantee that one interpretation will always be preferable to the rest.

Before I develop the theory of interpretation I shall need some distinctions, and some theses about the relations between the things thus distinguished. That will occupy the next two sections.

8.2 TERMS AND CONDITIONS

"Interpretation" and "narration", like "assertion" and "utterance", are subject to an ambiguity. Do we mean to refer to the act of interpreting/narrating/asserting/uttering, or to the *results* of doing those things, where the result of interpreting is an interpretation, as the result of asserting is an assertion? My concern with interpretation and narration is with both: with actions performed and with their results. In some cases we can say the same things about both – the activity of interpreting is objectively evaluable just in so far as its result is. But in general the act of interpreting has features rather different from its results: the act takes time, it is done by someone and it is (or may be) a rule-governed activity. Similar features distinguish narrating and its results, and we had better not confuse them. We can clarify talk of narration by speaking of a *narrative* when we mean the result, reserving "narration" for the act. But we cannot (at least, I will not) speak in the same way of an "interpretive", so in this case context or explicit disclaimer will have to distinguish the action and its results.

I have said that my talk of narrative and of interpretation will be a good deal more restrictive than much current usage would allow. What I shall say here about narrative interpretation certainly invites generalization, not all of it desirable. For example, the interpretive problem as I have described it is somewhat like that induced by the "poverty of the stimulus" argument concerning perception – an argument sometimes taken to show that perception is itself an interpretive process. The perceiving agent has a rich visual experience of the world around her, yet the input to the eyes consists of mere patterns of retinal stimulation.

Some people have concluded that perception itself – the process by which the relatively impoverished stimulus is converted into our visual experience of the world – must be a richly cognitive one, that visual experience is the joint product of the low-level stimulation and high-level "hypotheses". On this view, to have visual experience of the world is already to interpret the world, to bring to it assumptions and expectations which materially alter the quality of experience. If these assumptions and expectations were different we would experience the world in different ways. In the same way, narrative interpretation starts with a relatively impoverished stimulus – a literary text or cinematic image sequence – and gives rise to a vastly richer experience of a story, many elements of which are simply not available, or even hinted at, in the text or image sequence itself.

We certainly can use the term "interpretation" in so broad a sense as to cover both perception and narrative interpretation, and indeed to cover any process whereby we get more from less. But this is a very undiscriminating sense of interpretation. I put my money on the following hypothesis: while both perception and narrative interpretation are processes by which we get more from less, the first process gets its enrichment from biology, and the second from culture. The first process is relatively impervious to belief, the second richly informed by it. Perception builds up a picture of the external world richer than the perceptual input, and it does so by applying to the retinal stimulation rules which have been selected by evolution, given the sort of physical world in which we live. Human beings, pretty much independently of their cultural background, will have largely the same visual experience on the basis of the same retinal input. They will see edges, volumes and depth relations in very much the same way. But what story they derive from a text depends crucially on assumptions and expectations which are culturally determined. We, or some of us, read *The Turn of the Screw* as ambiguous between a psychological and a supernatural tale; for people whose culture makes no such distinction such a reading is not available. If their culture is uncritical of supernatural explanations, they will not see the governess's narrative as unreliable. We read Ring Lardner's

"Haircut" as unreliable, in the sense that that narrator's moral vision is, and is clearly intended to be seen as, deficient. For people with a moral outlook sufficiently different from ours, no such unreliability would be suggested.

This is not a "their reading is as good as ours" argument. It may be that the correct way to interpret is to do so in light of assumptions from the work's home culture, which might be different from your own, and that to fail to see ambiguity and unreliability in the works just mentioned is to interpret them wrongly.[3] My claim is just that narrative interpretation depends, as a matter of fact, on cultural assumptions in a way that perception does not.

Ambiguity and unreliability in narrative are topics I shall take up in more detail in the final chapter. But the brief remarks already made about them suggest something important about the relation between three concepts: text, narrative and story – concepts which are often not sufficiently distinguished. A text is a sequence of words and sentences, something which can be uttered by someone – an author perhaps – on a particular occasion.[4] A story is a set of propositions to the effect that this happened, and then that happened, that this happening caused that to happen, that character A was involved in such and such a way in initiating the causation, that character B was affected thus and so. Sentences in the text may, and usually do, express certain propositions, but the poverty of the stimulus argument shows that the correspondence between propositions thus expressed and propositions in the story is very unsystematic. Certainly, text and story are not the same thing. What, then, of narrative? I offer the following slogan to encapsulate the relation between text, narrative and story. *A text is narrative in virtue of the story it tells.* That is, a text is a narrative, in the same sense in which a person – Elizabeth Windsor, say – is a monarch. She is queen in virtue of her relations to other people and institutions (to previous monarchs, to the Constitution), and her being

---

[3] The rightness or wrongness of an interpretation is a difficult issue I take up in "Interpretation and Objectivity".

[4] For more on the individuation of texts and their relation to authorship see my "Work and Text".

queen is a contingent fact about her. Someone else might have had those relations and thereby have been queen in her stead. Yet there are not two things here, E.W. and the queen; E.W. *is* the queen. Similarly, those words and sentences authored by Henry James constitute a narrative by virtue of the story they tell. The text itself is not essentially a narrative; it tells that story only by virtue of contingent facts about James's activities and the culture in which he acted. But by virtue of those contingent facts, the text is a narrative, and of a certain kind. Perhaps it is an unreliable narrative. If that is so, it is because the story it tells is different in crucial ways from the story it appears to tell. (Just assume for present purposes and in line with certain interpretive views, that the text appears to tell a ghost story, but actually tells a story of delusion.) Change your assumptions about what story it tells, and the unreliability goes away.

So the concepts of a text and of a narrative are different, just as the concepts of E.W. and of the queen are different. But still, it is the text which is the narrative, just as E.W. is the queen. Text and story, on the other hand, are *substantially* different; no text is a story, and no story is a text. For a text is composed of sentences and a story is not.

I said that the task of narrative interpretation is to find out what is going on in the story. But that is not quite right. I individuate stories by what is going on in them: different events, different stories. Speaking more carefully, I say: the task of interpretation is to discover what story this work has to tell. Interpretive disputes can be large or small, but where there is even a minute difference of opinion as to what the story is, I say we have different narrative interpretations. Not all interpretive disagreements about narrative are significant. Some are.

We now know what an interpretation is: it is an hypothesis about what is true in the story. Recalling an ambiguity earlier noted, I say that an interpretation in this sense is what results from the act of interpretation; an act of interpretation results in your acquiring an interpretive hypothesis. Is *any* act which results in the acquisition of such a hypothesis an act of interpretation? No. To interpret is to acquire a certain kind of understanding of the work, and to acquire it in a certain way.

Not every way of acquiring understanding of the story counts as interpreting. Someone else who has interpreted the work can save you trouble by telling you what she knows. That way you acquire an interpretation, but you do so without interpreting. To interpret is to acquire this understanding by a certain kind of engagement with the work. So far I have merely been offering definitions; saying what kind of engagement I have in mind here – what acts we have to perform if we are to count as interpreting – will take us to the more interesting level of theory.

I have spoken about our knowledge of an interpretation; and knowledge requires, at a minimum, truth, and belief in the truth. Should we say, then, that interpretations are things which are true or false, and that when there is a clash of interpretations at least one of the rivals is false? Not always, in my view. But that is an issue I try to sort out later in this chapter. Prior to that refinement, it will do no great harm to speak of knowledge of interpretations in an unqualified way.

Now I pass to the question: how does interpreting proceed?

8.3 INTERPRETING BEHAVIOUR AND INTERPRETING WORKS

I begin with an apparently unrelated issue: how do we interpret a person's behaviour? We interpret behaviour when we offer an hypothesis about the mental states that caused it. Forming such an hypothesis requires us to attribute beliefs and desires to the agent. It is an hypothesis which says that the subject believed so and so, and desired so and so, and that his so believing and desiring was the cause of the behaviour we wish to explain.

The relation between behaviour and mental states is reciprocal: while mental states explain behaviour, behaviour is the evidence for an hypothesis about mental states, and the mental states explain the behaviour just to the extent that the behaviour is evidence for the mental states. When we ascribe beliefs to people, we do so on the evidence of their behaviour, including their verbal behaviour. But only an extreme and indefensible behaviourism would tell us that beliefs can be read from behaviour in a determinate way. Behaviour is evidence for belief; it is not constitutive of it in any way that would allow us to pair individual items of behaviour with individual beliefs.[5] Here, as with most other explanatory projects, we have a choice between competing hypotheses: there are a variety of combinations of beliefs and desires that would probably have resulted in that behaviour; which one actually did?

We can rule out quite a lot of competing hypotheses by attending to the theoretical virtues of simplicity, coherence, predictive power and rationality. Those virtues might be expressed in the following injunctions. Choose, where you can, explanations that make the connection between mental states and behaviour as direct as possible; avoid, where you can, explanations that attribute mental states without direct behavioural correlates (assume the subject uttered the words "Please pass the salt" because he wanted to salt his food rather than because he believes in the power of salt to magically transform his surroundings). Choose, where you can, explanations that enable you to predict the subject's future behaviour (assume the subject has a relatively stable desire for salt in certain circumstances rather than that this is a one-off choice). Choose, where you can, explanations that make present behaviour cohere with past behaviour (consider what a previously salt-avoiding agent might hope to get from his utterance *other* than that you pass him the salt). Choose, where you can, explanations that attribute to the agent beliefs and desires roughly in line with those you would expect to have in his situation (be sceptical of the hypothesis that he wants to salt his dessert). As the examples show, these injunctions can pull in different directions. You may have to trade off some against the others, and some kinds of behaviour may find their best explanation in an hypothesis that sacrifices all three to some extent; suddenly acquired, hidden, or strange beliefs are not an impossibility. It is just that deviation from any of the injunctions is an explanatory sacrifice, and should never be undertaken without motivation.

---

[5] Complex dispositions to behave may be constitutive of belief, but that is another matter.

When we explain behaviour by attributing beliefs and desires we have to assume an enabling background of *other* beliefs and desires. Explaining the utterance in our example by postulating a desire for salt makes sense only if we assume the agent believes that salt will be of some benefit, that there is salt in the shaker, that "salt" refers to salt, and so on. So in constructing an explanation of any particular behaviour we have to beware of postulating a background that conflicts with the explanation of other behaviour. That way, we end up ascribing a system of beliefs to the subject, and the reasonableness of ascribing one of the beliefs in the system will depend partly on its place in that very system. For part of what makes it reasonable to attribute a belief to someone is that the belief coheres well with other beliefs we attribute to that person, perhaps on the basis of more direct behavioural evidence.

Explanatory purpose, the search for coherent pattern, the holism of confirmation: these features of the interpretation of behaviour are mirrored within the project of literary interpretation. An interpretation is an attempt to explain the text, as the attribution of belief is an attempt to explain behaviour. As with belief attribution, textual interpretation may serve a predictive role, in a somewhat extended sense of prediction. An interpretative hypothesis formed on the basis of a reading of an initial segment of the text may suggest ways in which the text is likely to develop; we may find its confirmation or disconfirmation later in the text. But because interpretation is explanatory, there are constraints on interpretation that go well beyond mere consistency with the text. It may be possible to interpret the Sherlock Holmes stories as the deluded ramblings of Doctor Watson, who never in fact met any detective called "Holmes". Such an interpretation would, let us suppose, be consistent with the evidence of the text taken as a whole, but it would not be explanatory of it any more than if I tried to explain the behaviour of an apparently rational person by supposing her to be in the grip of massive delusions that compensate for one another so as to produce rational-seeming behaviour. We sometimes accept unreliable narrator interpretations, but only, as with the likes of

Nabokov's *Pale Fire*, when they make plausible and economical sense of the text.[6]

We decide what is true in the story according to how well our interpretation explains the text, but we do not proceed cumulatively, pairing off sentences of text with propositions true in the story. As I have noted, some of what is written in a story ought not to be taken literally. Fictional descriptions may contain metaphor, irony or some other nonliteral device, or we may be in the presence of an unreliable narrator. What we take literally and what we don't depends on the overall impression the text makes on us. And much that is true in the story may not be stated at all, forming a kind of implicit background. What's to be taken as background and what not depends, once again, on the overall character of the text.[7]

As with claims about belief, claims about what is part of the story are not to be thought of as corroborated individually by the text, but only in so far as they belong to a *system* of such claims. The reasonableness of one assumption about what is part of the story depends on its place in a system of such assumptions which make good overall sense of the text. A single claim might be poorly corroborated within a given set of interpretative hypotheses, yet well corroborated within another. Consider the claim that it's true in *The Turn of the Screw* that the governess is mad. Whether we regard this as well corroborated depends very much on what other interpretative assumptions we are prepared to make – that there are no ghosts, that the children are innocent, and so forth. Some interpretative claims will not be well corroborated whatever other assumptions we make: that the governess is a figment of Mrs Gross's imagination might be an example. Others will form part of any acceptable interpretation – that Miles and Flora are children rather than adult dwarves, for example.

I summarize: literary interpretation aims to figure out what is true in the story – a project not unlike, from both an evidential and a constitutive point of view, that of figuring out the mental

---

[6] For more on unreliable narrators see Chapter 9.
[7] For more on this point see my *Nature of Fiction*, chapters 2 and 3.

states responsible for a person's behaviour. The next section brings these two projects more closely together.

8.4 INTERPRETING WORKS AS INTERPRETING BEHAVIOUR

I've argued that interpreting behaviour is a matter of explaining it by intentional causes, and that interpreting works is constrained and guided by considerations similar to those that constrain and guide the interpretation of behaviour. But that merely sets the scene for the central claim of this chapter: that *interpreting literary works is a species of the interpretation of behaviour*. Put these ideas together and we get: interpreting literary works is a matter of explaining them in causal and intentional terms.

How can that be, given that behaviour is one thing and text definitely another? Start by observing that a text is always the *outcome* of behaviour; it is a trace left on the world by an agent. Another such trace might be a room full of broken-up furniture. Why is the furniture broken up? Because Smith, angered at the actions of its owner, broke it up. Explain Smith's behaviour (in terms of his desire for revenge, his belief that the loss of the furniture would be grievous) and we explain the outcome as well. Just so with the text; we explain it when we explain the behaviour of which it is the outcome. We interpret it when we formulate a certain kind of hypothesis about its cause.

There are hypotheses we could formulate about the text's cause that would not count as interpreting. We might, if we had the knowledge, causally explain a text by citing the detailed pattern of microphysical events in the author's brain, body and near environment that resulted in the formation of marks on a surface which constitute the original inscription of that text. But at that level of analysis we could not hope to recover intentions in a systematic way. My claim is not that interpreting is the only kind of causal explaining of texts there is, but that it is one kind.

We need to exclude more than just brute physical causality. There are hypotheses we could formulate about the text's *intentional* causes that would not count as interpreting the text. The behaviour that generates the text might be the product of various causes, some of them overdetermining. The text might have been produced with the intention of paying the rent or acquiring a literary reputation. Those intentions, causally efficacious though they might be, won't help us to our interpretive goal, which is to know what story the text has to tell. We as interpreters are concerned with story-telling intentions; the author intends to tell a story in which such and such happens. So intending, he chooses words to implement that intention: words which, so he believes, will suggest that story to the reader. So interpretation is explanation by reference to causally efficacious, story-telling intentions.[8]

Earlier I remarked that there are certain things which we are relatively sure are part of the story of James's *The Turn of the Screw*, for example, that Miles and Flora are children. We can now say *why* we are as sure of this as we are. Not, I take it, because the text says they are children; it might turn out that an examination of the text does not reveal any such explicit statement, and even if it does I doubt whether our assurance on this point is due to the fact that we have noticed such a statement. Anyway, an explicit statement would not by itself clinch the matter. Lots of things explicitly said in novels need to be taken nonliterally, or are to be ascribed to an unreliable narrator. The reason we are relatively sure about the status of Miles and Flora is that what James does say, taking the story as a whole, overwhelmingly suggests that his intention was to tell a story part of which is that Miles and Flora are children. Conversely, an interpretation according to which the governess is a figment of Mrs Gross's imagination would not have much plausibility, because the text as a whole makes this a very unlikely hypothesis about how the author intended his story to be taken. And

---

[8] This argument is a little too quick, at least for those of us who think that mental events are actually causally inert; we think that they mimic relations of causal dependence by supervening on causally efficacious states of the brain. But information about mental states can count as causally relevant information even when those mental states are causally inefficacious. See Frank Jackson and Philip Pettit, "Functionalism and Broad Content".

where there is room for doubt, concerning, say, the reliability of the governess's account of the ghosts, there is corresponding doubt about how the author would have us take his story at this point.

I have said that, in coming to a view about interpretation, no single piece of text, considered on its own, can be decisive one way or another. But this should not be taken to imply that the text is in any sense unimportant for interpretation, that it can be selectively ignored or impressionistically treated. The point is, rather, that it is always the *whole* text that functions as evidence for an interpretive hypothesis. And what would, if taken in isolation, seem to be evidence for one interpretive hypothesis might turn out to be evidence for a contrary hypothesis when seen in context.

The text as a whole is our evidential basis for an interpretation, and it is the text *as meaningful linguistic item* that is in question here – the text as a sequence of words and sentences with certain literal meanings. Our question is not "Why did the author produce this sequence of marks on paper?" but "Why did the author produce this sequence of words and sentences with these meanings?" If we began by asking the first question, we could never hope to arrive at an interpretive hypothesis – unless we went for a two-stage interpretation that interpolated literal meanings between marks and story-telling intentions. But then we might as well start with the literal meanings as part of the evidence itself. And we saw in Chapter 4 that literal meanings are things we may ascribe to the words and sentences that speakers utter at a stage prior to that of interpreting their utterances.

So interpretation is explanation, and the thing to be explained is the text, a meaningful sequence of words. The text is a trace left on the world by an intending agent in the act of telling a story, the story we are trying to reconstruct. We explain that text – we say something about its causal history – when we say something about the author's story-telling intentions, for those intentions were among the causes of its coming into being. The hypothesis we arrive at, if it is correct, specifies the content of the author's intention, and the content of his intention is the content of the story.[9]

On this view, narrative interpretation turns out to be just a special case of ordinary, conversational interpretation, the interpretation of the casual remarks of speakers we encounter every day. We figure out the meaning of a speaker's utterance when we figure out what the speaker meant by uttering it – when we figure out, in other words, what intentions the speaker had that caused him to make that utterance. The difference between the conversational and the literary case is just a matter of the length and complexity of the text concerned; of its having, in the literary case, generally a written rather than a spoken form; and of the consequent leisure that the relative permanence of writing affords us for reflection in our interpretive efforts.

In Part II I argued that fictions are things we typically respond to by engaging in simulations; fictions provide the inputs, or some of them, for off-line simulations. But in order to know what inputs are appropriate – should I give myself the pretend belief that the governess sees ghosts, or the pretend belief that she is mad? – I need to do some interpreting. A decision about what the story *is* determines the contents of my pretend inputs. But this suggests that fictions may encourage simulation in another way: I need to know what the story is, and to do that I need to know what story-telling intentions the author most probably had. The best way to carry out the latter task may be to do some simulating; I put myself in the author's position, thinking of myself as the person who produced the text, and ask myself, "What story-telling intentions would have led me to write that text?" If I can run a simulation in which having *those* story-telling intentions leads to the (off-line) decision to write this very text, then I can say that it is at least initially plausible that the author did have those intentions. That will not be the end of the matter; reflection on the historical and cultural differences between the author and myself may convince me that my simulation did not do enough to correct for differences

---

[9] This, of course, is the interpretive ideal, which acts of interpretation never more than approximate.

in our perspectives. But still, simulation is a way – and in some cases it may be the best way – to generate an interpretive hypothesis. In that case, fictions encourage different kinds of simulations: a simulation in which I try to put myself in the position of the author, and one in which I put myself in the position of one who is learning facts from a reliable source, rather than one who is reading or viewing a fictional work. Add to this another kind of simulation I said was often required by fiction: simulation of a character's state of mind. Fictions can be vehicles for complex, multilayered simulations, and parallels and tensions between the layers might be an interesting source of aesthetic experience.

8.5 REAL AUTHORS, IMPLIED AUTHORS

Let us call the idea that the interpreter's task is to discover the author's intended meaning for the text "Real Author Intentionalism", or RAI. It will soon be apparent why I choose this name. RAI is scarcely a popular option among theorists of criticism, and some of the arguments against it are good ones. For one thing, RAI denies the gap between aspiration and performance, making it impossible for the author to fail to tell the story he intends to tell. The story he does tell is, according to RAI, just the one he intended to tell, and it is consequently the job of the interpreter to discover what his intentions were. But authors can, and sometimes do, fail to tell the stories they intend to tell. The author can think that enough has been said to indicate a certain development of plot or character, and be mistaken, because readers cannot reasonably be expected to grasp that development on the basis of the text he gives them. In that case the story he intends to tell is not, in at least some respect, the story he tells.

Defenders of RAI sometimes claim that the author's intentions to which we may legitimately appeal are not merely private mental occurrences, but *embodied* intentions: intentions which could be understood by a suitably receptive reader on the basis of a reading of the text, and without access to information concerning the author's private opinions.[10] So readings privately intended but not embodied will not count, for interpretive purposes, as intended at all. But the problem is not merely how to exclude interpretations that might have been in the author's mind but never got into the work – the problem the embodiment condition is supposed to solve – but how to allow, on realist grounds, for interpretations which never were in the author's mind at all. For example, some readers of *The Possessed* have found Stepan Trofimovich to be a redeemed character, but Dostoyevsky's notebooks do not indicate that he intended him to be seen in this light. Yet there are some intuitive grounds for saying that readers who interpret the story that way are onto something.[11] How could the intention for us to see Stepan as redeemed get embodied in the work if it was never in Dostoyevsky's mind? If you say, as enthusiasts for RAI sometimes do, that intention is not a matter of what is in the mind, and that the test of what is really intended is whether it can be found in the work itself, then you have given up RAI in all but name. Intentions no longer drive the system; they are now constructed, and not merely inferred, entities that play no role in figuring out the right interpretation. Rather, we arrive, somehow, at the right interpretation, and announce that it is the intended – because embodied – one.

But while I insist on the psychological reality of intentions, I do not insist on their being conscious states of mind. The best current philosophical thinking about intentions emphasizes their being states capable of causing, and thereby explaining, behaviour, but is far from insisting that these states always be transparent to the agent. So it is a distracting side issue that supporters of RAI raise when they sometimes point out that the relevant intentions need not be conscious. The problem for RAI is not that we sometimes endorse an interpretation of which the author was not consciously aware at the time of writing, but rather that we sometimes endorse interpretations which may

---

[10] See, e.g., Hirsch, *Validity in Interpretation*, especially p. 31, the definition of "verbal meaning".

[11] See Seymour Chatman, *Coming to Terms*, pp. 97–99, for an instructive discussion of this example.

very well not have been intended at all, as with Dostoyevsky and Stepan the redeemed. To insist that these interpretations were unconsciously intended merely because they seem in other ways right is once again to operate a mechanism with the wheel marked "intention" running idle.[12]

If we abandon RAI, as I think we should, need we abandon the idea that interpretation aims at an hypothesis about the intentions behind the text? No. It need not matter, from the point of view of explanatory adequacy, that the intentions in terms of which we explain the text were not those of its author. We may explain the text, and explain it adequately, by reference to a personality that *seems* to have produced it, as Dostoyevsky's story seems, in my example, to have been the product of someone with intentions different from Dostoyevsky's own. This personality corresponds to what some critics have called the "implied", "apparent" or "postulated" author.[13] Thus I replace RAI with *Implied Author Intentionalism*, or IAI.

So our interpretation records our decisions about what story-telling intentions can reasonably be supposed to be among the causes of the text. These intentions we attribute to the implied author. But the implied author is not some shadowy entity with a grade of existence somehow lower than that of the real author. The implied author is a heuristic device that no one need believe in, and reference to him is easily eliminated; that the implied author intends P to be fictional means just that the text can reasonably be thought of as produced by someone intending the reader to recognize that P is fictional.[14]

Notice that RAI faces a problem about the relation of the text

---

[12] For a defence of realism by appeal to unconscious intentions see P. D. Juhl, *Interpretation*, section 6.2.

[13] See Booth, *Rhetoric of Fiction*. For applications see Alexander Nehamas, "The Postulated Author: Critical Monism as a Regulative Ideal"; Jenefer Robinson, "Style and Personality in the Literary Work"; and Bruce Vermazen, "Expression as Expression".

[14] Seymour Chatman (*Coming to Terms*, p. 81) says that "the text is itself the implied author". Taken literally, this claim is incomprehensible. But I do not know in what nonliteral way to take it, and Chatman does not tell us. Perhaps the account in the passage above this note is one such way, in which case I can agree with Chatman.

to the story. If we take our goal to be finding the real author's narrative intentions, we have to acknowledge that authorial error can make the text not the best guide to what those intentions are, and interest may shift from the text to psychobiography. But no amount of deconstructive rhetoric should make us forget the centrality of the text. In interpretation, we make inferences to narrative intentions so as to illuminate and render coherent the text we have before us, not some other text the author might have written, one perhaps more in tune with her actual intentions. It is possible for an author to be moved by certain narrative intentions, but fail to give proper effect to them in her text-tokening activity: she can be wrong in thinking that enough has been said to indicate a development of plot or character, and a reading made most plausible by her text can be one she fails to comprehend. When that happens (as in small ways it commonly does) the path recommended by RAI – to infer, from her diaries and acquaintances, the narrative intentions the author actually had – will not, by assumption of authorial error, illuminate and make coherent the text we have. The interpreter who takes that path has ceased to be an interpreter of the work, and his intentional hypothesizing serves rather to interpret another, hypothetical work – the one that would have been written had the author's narrative intentions gone well. By contrast, IAI can guarantee the centrality of the text, irrespective of authorial error. According to IAI, the task is to hypothesize narrative intentions which make as good sense of the text we have as can be made of it, irrespective of whether they were the real author's intentions or not.[15] Since IAI has us look for the interpretation which makes best sense of the given text regardless of the psychological facts, it gives the text a properly constitutive as well as an evidential role.

---

[15] "As can be made of it" because it is not always possible to avoid imputing some degree of authorial incompetence and textual incoherence. The discrepant reporting of Natasha's age in *War and Peace* could be reconciled by assuming Tolstoy intended us to infer that she is a time traveller, but that would clash with the conclusion, well-supported by other aspects of the work, that no fantasy or science-fiction elements are intended in this story. IAI demands only that we maximize coherence.

8.6 WHY WE STILL NEED INTENTION

Having admitted that the real author's intentions are not decisive for interpretation, why insist that the interpreter's task is to construct another, this time hypothetical, author? Why not say instead that the interpretive problem is simply to go from what is explicit in the text to what is implicit, where what is implicit might not correspond to anything anyone intended? But there can be no meaning implicit in the words and sentences of the text itself; the meaning that there is in the text itself is all explicit, literal meaning. What we call implicit in the text is what we think of as intended (perhaps, indeed, unconsciously intended) by an agent who hopes to convey by his words more than the words themselves literally mean. A text can encourage in the reader's mind beliefs about what those intentions were even when, as a matter of fact, the real author had no such intentions. IAI says that it is what the text makes it reasonable to believe was intended, and not what actually was intended, that determines the content of the story.

There is another reason we can't ignore intention. Narratives obstruct, mislead and manipulate us by their selective presentation of events. But no text, no sequence of visual images, can do those things; such things require agency. Most of the ways we describe narrative make no sense if we cut narrative off from the agency which produced it. Writers on narrative sometimes ignore this. Thus David Bordwell, speaking of film:

> As for the implied author, this construct adds nothing to our understanding of filmic narration. No trait we could assign to an implied author of a film could not more simply be ascribed to the narration itself: it sometimes suppresses information, it often restricts our knowledge, it generates curiosity, it creates a tone, and so on. To give every film a narrator or implied author is to indulge in an anthropomorphic fiction.... [Filmic] narration is better understood as the organization of a set of cues for the construction of a story. This presupposes a perceiver, but not any sender, of a message.[16]

[16] Bordwell, *Narration in the Fiction Film*, p. 62

Bordwell speaks of a narration which "suppresses information". There is no literal sense in the idea of an unnarrated narration which suppresses information. Without recourse to the idea of intention you can speak of a system that fails to deliver all the information you want, but not of a system that *suppresses* information. And the idea of suppression (rather than just of informational incompleteness) is essential to Bordwell's description of filmic narration and our reaction to it; we feel, in some cases, that we are being deliberately deprived of information (as when we see only the hands of the murderer), that we are being deprived of it for some dramatic or emotional purpose, that our expectations are being played with. None of this would make sense unless we understood the story as *told*.

If Bordwell's claim has any plausibility for the filmic case, I believe it derives ultimately from what I have called the Imagined Observer Hypothesis. If we think of the viewer's imaginative involvement in the movie as requiring him to imagine that he is viewing the action from within the space of the film, then of course it would be out of place for him to suppose that the images he receives are being presented to him by a controlling intelligence that presents them in a certain way and in a certain order to tell a certain story by their means. But if we reject this view and think of the viewer's imaginative engagement with the film as characterized by perceptual imagining rather than by imagining seeing, there is no such objection to the idea that cinematic fictions are experienced as mediated; in fact we are then *obliged* to think of them in that way.

Those who announced an intentional fallacy were not so far wrong. They were right to think that it is not authorial intention that determines the meaning of the work. They were wrong to think that interpretation could dispense entirely with the concept of intention.[17] All interpretation is intentionalistic; the issue

[17] Some writers on the psychology of narrative have emphasized the importance of so-called schemata for interpretation: knowledge structures which encapsulate a set of standard conditions pertaining to a given situation (air travel, restaurant dining, etc.) and which we use to fill in the details of the story from the sketchy outline of the text (see, e.g., J. M. Mandler, *Stories*,

is whether we should concern ourselves with the real intentions behind the work, or with the intentions which seem to have been productive of the work.[18] I say our concern is with the latter.

8.7 INTERPRETIVE DEADLOCK AND TRUTH

An interpretation of the text is a hypothesis about the intentions which seem to have been productive of the text. So the best hypothesis about what those intentions are is the best interpretation of the work. But two or more hypotheses may be equally good, and none better (they are, as I shall say, *maximal*, rather than best, explanations; there can be only one best explanation). That gives us a plurality of interpretations which can, with equal plausibility, be thought of as intended, and nothing else more plausible. If that happens we have interpretive indeterminacy – rival interpretations with nothing to help us choose between them. To suppose that we can choose between them on the grounds that evidence from the author's diary or letters suggests that one of these hypotheses corresponds to his intentions and the other doesn't is once again to embrace RAI, which I have rejected.

Will such indeterminacy actually occur? We are familiar, of course, with interpretive disputes. But it is always hard to say of any such dispute that it really is a case of indeterminacy; an unresolved dispute is not automatically an unresolvable one. I think there *can be* conflicting maximal interpretations of a text – interpretations which can with equal plausibility be thought of as intended. A single brief remark can be genuinely ambiguous; without further interrogation, we can't choose between two or

Scripts and Scenes: Aspects of Schema Theory). Such schemata are important for interpretation, but their importance is primarily in providing us with evidence about how the author would probably have intended the story to be filled out.

[18] A point made by Ronald Dworkin in *Law's Empire.* Some of my conclusions in this essay have been influenced by Dworkin's work on interpretation (see also his *Matter of Principle*).

more hypotheses about what the utterer meant by it.[19] You might argue that such cases would be the product of textual brevity, that plausible alternatives would be eliminated as the text in question gets larger (and we rarely want to engage in narrative interpretation on a one-line text). But textual increase does not generally correlate with a reduction in interpretive uncertainty. Ambiguity can be removed, or reduced, if the textual additions simply tell us more about the subject of the original remark. But where text functions to convey narrative, that is not in general the case. More text, more story to be interpreted and a textual addition that's narratively significant may close an interpretive option at one end, but will very likely open one at the other.

So I claim that IAI allows for unresolvable hard cases of interpretation. It does not say anything about how frequent they are in theory or in practice. It does not identify any of the celebrated interpretive disputes there have been as examples of interpretive indeterminacy; perhaps these disputes are all the product of confusion, ill will or, less culpably, the uncertainty that attends any judgement of a large body of evidence. Still, it does caution us against writing off all interpretive deadlock in those ways.

Earlier I drew attention to the fact that I was speaking of interpretations as capable of being true or false. But if there are to be clashes, unresolvable in principle, between interpretations, we can hardly say that one or other of the rivals is true and the other false. This is not to say that interpretive claims *never* have truth value. Interpretations consist of large numbers of interpretive claims about what this character did and when, what that character thought about it, and so on, and not all of them are equally controversial. In that case a truth-valueless interpretation may have some truth-valuable constituents. Fred and Freida are deadlocked about how to interpret *The Turn of the Screw*; having exhaustively examined the evidence that both regard as

[19] This can be true even when the remark is semantically unambiguous; context can make the hypothesis that the literal meaning of the sentence was the intended one equiprobable with some hypothesis that the intended meaning was something else.

relevant to deciding the issue, they can find nothing that tips the balance either way. But still, Fred and Freida should not be represented as disagreeing about everything in the interpretation of that story. Their rival interpretations may, and probably will, have a significant common part. Things in that common part, or some of them, may be uncontroversial; they will belong to any interpretation of the story which hopes to withstand critical scrutiny. Thus they agree that Flora and Miles are children, that Mrs Gross is real and not a figment of the governess's imagination. (Or rather, they agree that all these things are fictional.) And perhaps every well-informed and reflective critic will agree with them. Those things which constitute the common core of any acceptable interpretation ought to count as true if anything does. In that case it will be straightforwardly true that it is fictional that Miles and Flora are children. Similarly, claims which no well-informed, reflective interpreter would offer – that Mrs Gross is imaginary – will count as false. In general, an interpretive claim is true if it belongs to *every* maximal interpretation of the text, and false if it belongs to no such interpretation. That way the uncontroversial and the hopeless interpretive claims (Hamlet was human, Hamlet was Venusian) come out true and false respectively, while the controversial claims lack truth value, for they belong to some maximal interpretations and not to others.[20] And where there is – if there ever is – one maximal (and therefore best) interpretation, it comes out true, since all its constituents come out true.

8.8 THE EVIDENCE FOR A CINEMATIC INTERPRETATION

Interpreting the literary work begins with the text – a sequence of meaningful words and sentences. The interpreter's task is to work out what story the text has to tell. That is to be accomplished by discovering what story-telling intentions can most plausibly be thought of as productive of the text. Text is, therefore, the basis of, and the evidence for, a literary interpretation.

[20] For more detail see my "Interpreting Fiction".

Interpretation starts with the text and succeeds to the extent that it explains the text as the outcome of story-telling intentions. It seems, then, that the model here proposed fails for cinema which, as I have argued, lacks a language.

But the nonexistence of a language of film should not lead us to abandon our basic model of interpretation as causal–intentional explanation. Conventional, textual meaning is where we start in interpreting the literary work, not where we end. We end with a system of inferred intentions. Intentions can be inferred from artefacts of all kinds, not just from linguistic ones. Anthropologists infer intentions from the artefacts they discover; that is, they infer the uses intended for them by their makers. A film is an artefact, consisting of cinematic images and their verbal and other accompaniments – a highly complex, structured artefact. Usually, its context of production is familiar to us; we live in, or near, the culture that produces the films. So making a stab at the relevant intentions based on a viewing of the artefactual material itself ought not to be so very difficult. In fact, I claim, we do it all the time. We may do it in ways rather different from the ways we interpret literary works, but the basic strategy is the same; to work out the story the film presents by inferring story-telling intentions from the images or other clues that the film gives us.

What we need is something that will play the same, or a similar, role for the interpretation of film that the literal meanings of words and sentences play for literary interpretation. That thing, whatever it turns out to be, will be the thing which needs explaining in causal–intentional terms if we are to interpret the film. It will be our evidential base, as the text is our evidential base for literary interpretation. Of course we want, if possible, for our base to be richly structured and have fine gradations of texture. After all, our task is to infer a large and complex set of very precisely specified intentions; the more complex the evidential base, the more likely it is that we shall be successful in this. Ideally, we should like to be able to say that our evidential base consists of elements which have meaning, or content, of some kind: if we start with meaning we shall be more likely to end up with meaning. With texts, we start with literal meaning and end up, via our process of causal–intentional explanation, with utterance meaning. Since there is no language for cinema, we cannot, in the cinematic case, begin with linguistic meaning. But perhaps there is something we can identify as the cinematic equivalent of linguistic meaning: equivalent, that is, from the point of view of an evidential role. Let us call this kind of meaning, whatever it is, *evidential meaning*. The task before us is to say what that kind of meaning is. To simplify matters I shall ignore sound and concentrate on the evidential meaning provided by the film image; what I shall say about meaning in connection with images can be generalized to the sound case without much difficulty.

What is the best candidate for the evidential meaning of the cinematic image? One natural proposal is that it is just what the image records. What the image records is actors performing actions among props on a set, or on location. If this "photographic" meaning is what we are to call the evidential meaning of cinematic images, how much like the literal meanings of words and sentences in natural language is it? (Recall the characterization of literal meaning in Chapter 4.) It is like literal meaning at least in this: it is acontextual. The photographic meaning of a cinematic image does not depend on its relation to other images, because that meaning is entirely determined by what was in front of the camera at the time of the take. And by juxtaposing images one simply gets an accretion of meaning: if the meaning of image A is $M(A)$ and that of image B is $M(B)$, then image A followed by image B just means $M(A)$ & $M(B)$, where the order of juxtaposition is irrelevant to meaning; showing B after A does not mean, in the sense of meaning at issue here, that the events that A records occurred before the events that B records. The meaning, in this sense, of a complex of images is just the sum of the meanings of its constituent images. And that's how it is with linguistically formulated assertions; saying A and saying B just commits you to the truth of A and B, irrespective of the order of saying.[21]

---

[21] In both cases – the filmic and the linguistic – the order of production can have consequences for what is *implicated*, in Grice's sense.

This promising beginning notwithstanding, I want to argue that photographic meaning cannot play the same kind of evidential role in cinema that the literal meanings of words and sentences can play in interpreting literary fictions. There are two reasons for this.

The first is that photographic meaning does not bear on the story in cinema in the same way that linguistic meaning does in literature. In literature the text consists of words and sentences which describe events within the fictional world; they can be thought of as doing that in virtue, partly, of the literal meanings they have. Thus if the text says, "Holmes and Watson spent the evening at Baker Street", we may decide to take that sentence as a literal description of the activities of the characters on a particular occasion. We might decide instead to take that statement nonliterally, as metaphor or irony, or even as the words of an unreliable speaker. In that case we would not take the literal meaning of the sentence as a reliable guide to what happened in the fiction. But the literal meaning of the text can be, and sometimes is, a reliable guide, and we always need to know what the literal meaning is.

But with cinema it is different. We cannot ever take the photographic meaning of an image to coincide with what happens in the story at that point. For the photographic meaning is always something to do with real people (actors, mostly) performing real actions in the real world. There cannot be a photograph of something that does not exist, or of an act no one ever performed. But the characters of the fictional film are, at least typically, characters that do not exist, and the events of the fictional story are, at least typically, events that do not occur. There is always a disparity between photographic meaning and what is true in the fictional story.

The second reason photographic meaning cannot be regarded as the evidential analogue of linguistic meaning is that viewers are sometimes unaware of, or mistaken about, the photographic meaning of a cinematic image. But their being unaware of it or mistaken about it does not automatically count as evidence that they lack some piece of knowledge vital to working out what is going on in the story. A shot may be a trick shot; it may seem to show a man falling a distance that no man involved in the filming ever did fall. It may seem to show a fantastical creature, or a man walking on water. Or it may be a shot that seems to be a distant or blurred view of the main actor but is actually a cinematic image of a stand-in. In such cases the members of the audience will sometimes know that there is some trick involved, but they will seldom have any idea what the trick is; they will have little idea, that is, about what the camera actually records. They will, in those cases, therefore have little or no idea about the photographic meaning of the shot in question. But if there is a doubt in the minds of the audience about what is happening in the story – or a disagreement about it – it is implausible to suppose that it will be resolved by teaching them more about the cinematographer's tricks of the trade. By learning those tricks they might learn something about cinema in general, but they would not be put in a better position to work out what is happening in the story. In the case of literary interpretation, on the other hand, it is always true that a reader who lacks knowledge of the literal meaning of a passage in the text will be helped in forming a reasoned opinion about what is going on in the story by learning what that literal meaning is. To have the text and not to know its literal meaning is to be like a monolingual Chinese reader trying to make sense of a novel in English. So what I have called the photographic meaning of cinematic images cannot play the role of evidence for an interpretation in the way that the literal meaning of words and sentences can.

However, while the photographic meaning of the image may be unclear to the viewer, it is at least usually possible for the viewer, given the right background of cultural knowledge, to say that this image *appears* to represent a man falling off a building, or a creature of fantastical appearance, or a man walking on water; you can make a decision about what the image appears to represent without knowing a great deal about the context of surrounding images that occur in the film. It may be that a certain image functions within the diegesis to represent a dream, a lie or an hallucination, and that it does so can be discovered only by seeing and interpreting the whole film. Still, one can say of the image, pretty much on the basis of viewing it alone, that it *seems* to represent a woman running down a corridor while arms protrude from the walls on either side, or whatever. It would be possible, if anyone could be bothered to do it, to establish meaning at this level of "seeming" or appearance for any particular shot by finding a viewer who (i) had no knowledge of the rest of the film, and (ii) could not identify the actors in the film and generally knew nothing about its construction, and then getting this person to describe what the image represents. The answer given, assuming the viewer is alert and cooperative, would correspond roughly to what I shall here call "appearance meaning". There would no doubt be some variation in the detail of each individual's description, reflecting different levels of attention and visual acuity, but there would in general be a large measure of agreement between viewers about what the image appears to represent. It is this possibility of intersubjective agreement that justifies our saying that here we have another kind of meaning for the image – appearance meaning.

It is appearance meaning, and not photographic meaning, which plays the role in the interpretation of film that literal meaning plays in the interpretation of literature. It is the data to be explained. Appearance meaning is evidence meaning. The shot shows what appears to be children being attacked by a flock of birds (though in fact it may be a trick shot that does not record any such event). The question the interpreter needs to ask, then, is: why is that shot, with just that appearance, inserted in the film just at this point, between these other shots? The answer will be: because the insertion of that shot was intended to tell us something about what is happening in the story, and how that event stands in relation to others in the story. But while appearance meaning is, for film, the analogue of literary, textual meaning, it should be evident from what was said in Chapter 4 that appearance meaning is not understood in anything like the way that linguistic meaning is. There are no atoms of appearance meaning out of which are built more complex units of meaning, for every visible part of the image is meaningful. Yet we are able to understand what is represented in images we have not seen before. Appearance meaning displays the natural generativity possessed by all pictorial kinds of meaning.

When we see films we are generally not conscious of what I have called appearance meaning, but this is not grounds for thinking it plays no role in our interpretive strategies. We are rarely conscious, after all, of the literal meaning of the text we read. If we could not identify each shot, as we see it, at least roughly at the level of appearance meaning, we would find it impossible to interpret the film: we would not be able to reidentify characters and locations from one shot to another; we would not be able to say what kind of action was being undertaken or what kind of event was happening; and we would have no expectations about what would follow, and so no sense of the rightness or disparity of succeeding images. To see a film and not be able to specify its meaning at the level of appearance would be like looking at the pages of a book written in an unknown language; in neither case would it be possible to interpret the work.

Sometimes appearance meaning is unclear. If the scene is very dark, or if the location or action undertaken is very unfamiliar, we may not be able to judge the appearance meaning of the shot as we see it, or we may be heavily dependent on the context of surrounding shots and the interpretation of them we have so far built up in order to judge it. For example, the novice viewer of *The Searchers* will not immediately understand that the uniformly dark screen at the beginning has any appearance meaning at all; it is only when the door opens to reveal an exterior scene that she will realize that the featureless screen represented a darkened interior. But the same can happen with a text. We do not understand every sentence we read, and some texts contain sentences that deliberately challenge or defy understanding. But this has no tendency to show that textual meaning is irrelevant to understanding. If the text entirely lacked meaning, or belonged to a language you didn't understand, you wouldn't be able to interpret it. If no image in the film had any appearance meaning, you wouldn't be able to interpret that either.

So filmic interpretation is like literary interpretation in this: it takes as input certain data, and gives as output a hypothesis concerning what story a rational agent would most probably have intended to communicate by means of that data. Filmic interpretation is subject to the same vaguenesses, ambiguities and indeterminacies that attend literary interpretations because in both cases the relation between data, hypotheses and the principles that govern inferences to intention are in various ways vague, ambiguous and indeterminate. But in neither the literary nor the filmic case is every interpretation as good as every other one. It is just that there is not always an interpretation which is uniquely best.

Filmic interpretation differs from literary interpretation both in the nature of its data inputs and the competencies required for processing them. In the literary case the data is linguistic meaning and the required competence is with the syntax and semantics of the language. In the filmic case the inputs are cinematic images correctly juxtaposed; the required competence is the ability to understand the appearance meaning of those images, a competence based on the possession of visual capacities to recognize objects, their properties and relations.

8.9 IMPLIED AUTHOR AND AUTEUR

On this model of interpretation, the idea that the cinematic work is created by an intelligence is central; interpretation is the assignment of intentions to the implied author. There are writers on film who are fond of telling us that films are the product of many people with different roles and skills, that the resulting product rarely if ever reflects the artistic or narrative conception of one person, that the constraints of budget, technology, studio control and prevailing ideology all play their part in determining what the product is like. Usually this is said in response to the so-called auteur theory, according to which we should judge films by the extent that they reflect the individual vision of their directors.

What I have argued in this chapter is in no sense a version of the auteur theory. It is possible to accept what I have said here about interpretation and also to think that the most useful groupings among films for purposes of classification, analysis and criticism are groupings by genre, period or place of origin.

It does not follow from the view I have been advocating that we should look for, still less that we should expect to find, a common implied author for all of Hitchcock's films, another for all of Douglas Sirk's. (Also, it doesn't follow that we shouldn't; my point is that these issues are independent.) It does not even follow that we should expect to find, for every film, an interpretive hypothesis that attributes story-telling intentions to a single implied maker; a film, and indeed a fictional work of any kind, can be such that it seems to be the product of more than one agent, in which case we must speak of "implied makers". The film may be such that these implied makers seem to have shared or even communal intentions,[22] or it may be that they seem to have intentions that to some extent diverge and even conflict. Intentionalism, as long as it is Implied Author Intentionalism, is neutral on issues raised by the auteur theory.

8.10 STRUCTURE AND FUNCTION

In Chapter 4 I argued that cinematic and other images, and their modes of combination, are quite unlike a language. In this chapter I have argued that film images play the same role for us in our interpretation of film that the linguistic text plays in our interpretation of literature. Is there a tension between these two claims? I say no. We need something like a structure/function distinction here. Text and image are unlike in structure; images lack the articulated, convention-based structure of complex linguistic units. Text and image are alike in function – or rather there is one common function they have, along with many functional differences. They both constitute the evidence for the interpretation of a work in their respective mediums. And the existence of structurally distinct but functionally similar entities is, I take it, uncontroversial: the current Tay Bridge has the same function as its collapsed predecessor but – I trust – a different structure.

[22] An intention is communal rather than merely shared when it is shared and when its being so is common knowledge between those who share it.

Chapter 9
Narrative and narrators

> For films as for novels, we would do well to distin-
> guish between a *presenter* of the story, the narrator
> (who is a component of the discourse), and the *creator*
> of both the story and the discourse (including the nar-
> rator): that is, the implied author.
>
> *Seymour Chatman*

I have been arguing that our basic interpretive strategy, for film as for literature, is to look for an intentional explanation of what is put before us – image or text. I have said nothing yet about the role of a narrator in all this. Here we shall find some important differences between the roles of narrators in literature and in film; film offers much less scope for the narrator than does literature. Also, film requires us to acknowledge that there can be unreliable narration without there being any narrator to whom we can ascribe the unreliability. This will require a substantial revision of accepted theory. This chapter will also lend weight to the claims of Chapter 8 concerning the implied author; it will specify in some detail how appeal to the implied author helps us make sense of the text or image. It will also show how the concept of the implied author is more significant for understanding narrative than is that of the narrator.

There is one other issue of general significance on which this chapter will bear. Recent writing on the theory of literature and film has tended to focus on ways in which the act of interpretation resembles or exemplifies pathological behaviour. There have been attempts to characterize the reader's, and sometimes the writer's, relation to the work as having an obsessive, possessive, violent and quasi-sexual nature. No doubt these things find their place in any human activity. But they are very far from being the whole story when it comes to interpretation. In opposition to this tendency I hold that interpretation is a largely rational enterprise governed by the standards of evidence and probability that apply in other areas. One thing I hope to do here is to show how this approach can help us understand why certain kinds of narrative effects are common while others are not.

Briefly, my argument will be this: standard accounts of narrative unreliability require there to be a narrator – a fictional being who belongs within the world of the story and who claims, falsely, to be recounting events of which he or she has knowledge. But I shall argue that there are narratives which are unreliable even when there is no narrator. In these cases, unreliability is not the product of a disparity between two conflicting viewpoints, one internal (the narrator's) and one external. Rather it is the product of a single, external viewpoint which has, as we shall see, a rather complex structure. This, I say, enables us to make sense of unreliability in film, without committing us to implausible claims about the kinds of narrators which films embody. Finally I shall show how unreliability in film and other media connects with another narrative trope – that of ambiguity. Ambiguity, I shall argue, facilitates unreliability in ways that tell us something about the scope and limits of narrative itself.

9.1 IMPLIED AUTHORS AND NARRATORS

Texts are unreliable when there is a certain kind of discrepancy between the fictional story told and the text itself. The problem is to say exactly what that discrepancy is. The mark of textual unreliability is not that the story cannot be deduced from the text; no fictional stories of any interest or complexity can be straightforwardly deduced from their texts alone, for texts need to be taken in conjunction with relevant background information. And even in a reliable text, what is literally said and what is supposed to be part of the story can be in conflict. That is how it is when the text contains irony, metaphor or other non-literal devices. And a text containing irony is not necessarily an unreliable text.

The standard characterization of unreliability appeals to the idea of a narrator. *The Turn of the Screw* is an unreliable narrative, or so we may suppose for the sake of the argument. How so? Simplifying a little, we can say that the story is told to us by a narrator, the governess. She tells of events of which she has knowledge and in which she was deeply involved. But in fiction, as in real life, people may tell what is not true, either through error or through the desire to deceive. And so it is with the governess, who is mistaken – radically mistaken – about the events she recounts. But since the governess is our source of information and we have no independent access to the facts of the case, how do we *know* that she is mistaken? The standard account says that narrative unreliability is the product of a discrepancy between two perspectives. One of these perspectives is that of the implied author, a figure who may in a sense be fictional or imagined, because his or her mental economy does not necessarily correspond to that of the actual author, but who is not to be thought of as occupying a position within the work itself. Rather he is conceptualized as the agent responsible for the story qua fiction.[1] The implied author's perspective is always external to the story.

The other perspective is that of the narrator. Narrators, according to the standard view, come in two kinds: internal and external. An internal or (in the favoured lingo) *intradiegetic* narrator belongs within the world of the story, telling of what he or she knows or believes to be true, or trying to mislead us about what has happened (as in an unreliable narrative). An external or *extradiegetic* narrator is outside that world telling us a fictional story. Watson is the internal narrator of the Sherlock Holmes stories, while the narrator of *Tom Jones* is external.[2]

---

[1] So the implied author, as I use that notion, is always "extradiegetic" in Genette's sense (*Narrative Discourse*).

[2] Here I shall ignore a tendency which some writers on narrative have of using the terms "narrator" and "author" to refer to things which could not literally be narrators or authors because they are not persons. Thus, Christian Metz speaks of the viewer's perception that the film images are organized by a "grand image-maker", which Metz then goes on to describe as "the film itself as linguistic object" (*Film Language: A Semiotics of the Cinema*, pp. 20–21). See also remarks on Seymour Chatman in note 14 to Chapter 8, this volume.

In my view, the category of external narrators is redundant; there is no need to distinguish between the external narrator and the implied author. Advocates of the external narrator point to works in which the narrative voice represents an outlook which the reader seems to be intended to reject; it is natural to say that there is in such cases a tension between narrator and implied author and consequently that we must conceptualize the work by invoking two distinct personalities. But cases of this kind can be handled without appeal to the external narrator by assuming that the implied author is speaking ironically; it is the implied author who speaks, but what is said is intended by that same speaker to be ridiculed or rejected. I shall simply assume that we can dispense with the idea of an external narrator in favour of the implied author. This will have the advantage of greatly simplifying the discussion, and will not prejudice the case in my favour; most of the arguments about unreliable narrators concern narrators agreed to be internal.

From now on, I shall use the term "narrator" exclusively to refer to the possessor of this internal perspective. The governess in *The Turn of the Screw* is an internal narrator in this sense. She is a narrator who stands in a particularly intimate relation to the events she relates, for she was a participant in them, and much of what she tells us concerns herself, even if she is deluded about her role in it all. Not all narrators are like that; some of them tell of events of which they were passive witnesses, or about which they have come to know via the testimony of others. But as long as the narrator is narrating about that of which she purports to have knowledge or at least belief, I count her internal.[3] For it must then be part of the story that the narrator

---

[3] A distinction is sometimes made between intradiegetic narrators who are characters and narrators who are not (cf. Genette's distinction between homo-diegetic and heterodiegetic narrators in his *Narrative Discourse*, pp. 244–245). But this is a distinction without a difference. The narrator is someone who, within the scope of the story itself, knows of certain events and recounts them to us (reliably or unreliably). His knowing requires that he belongs to the world of the fiction, and so he is a character in it, if an unnamed one. Whether he knows because he took part in the action or because he was told about it

belongs within the world of the story, just as Julius Caesar and I belong to the same world (the actual world), even though what I tell you about him I know only through hearsay.

The reader trying to figure out what happens in this story now has two voices to attend to: the (implied) author's and the narrator's. The authorial voice may not be explicitly signalled, but readers are aware of its presence if they know that what they are reading is fiction, because fictions have to be thought of as works produced with certain intentions. Sensitive readers may be able to spot a tension between these two voices, the authorial and the narratorial. The narrator insists that there are ghosts. But why has the author made this a story in which no one else, apparently, sees or has knowledge of them? These and like clues suggest that, perhaps, the author's intentions concerning the story conflict with the narrator's certainties. But in such a conflict the author always wins. Author and narrator do not speak with the same authority. The narrator, within the world of the story, is a mere reporter of events, and a fallible one like all such reporters. The author, standing outside the story, is not conveying to the audience a set of possibly erroneous beliefs about the story world; the author makes things be true in that story world (makes things "be fictional", as I say) simply by decree or stipulation. If we as readers find it reasonable to infer that the author intended that there not be any ghosts in the story, then we must conclude that there simply aren't any. So narrators are unreliable when their claims contradict the inferred intentions of the author. This view of narrative unreliability, or something broadly like it, is widely accepted. It is expressed in a summarizing remark of Wayne Booth's: "I have called a narrator *reliable* when he speaks for or acts in accordance with the norms of the work (which is to say, the implied author's norms), *unreliable* when he does not."[4] That, roughly, is how it is in

---

later (or because of the operation of magic, if that's how things are in the story) is of no moment to his being a character. There is a distinction here, but it is best understood as that based on epistemic proximity to the action, and it admits of degrees. It is of no special relevance to our present concerns.

[4] Booth, *Rhetoric of Fiction*, pp. 158–159, emphasis in the original. One misleading feature of this remark is the implication that narrative unreliability is

Ford's *The Good Soldier*, in Camus's *The Fall*, in Ishiguro's *The Remains of the Day*, and in many other literary narratives we commonly describe as unreliable.[5]

But what of those narratives which are intuitively unreliable, but where the unreliability is not, or at least not obviously, attributable to a narrator? In the literary case you might insist that there is always a narrator to blame for the unreliability, however unobvious her presence may be.[6] This seems rather ad hoc; it is worth asking whether there is some more elegant solution to the difficulty. And with film, the idea of a narrator such as would be postulated in order to save the Boothian definition of unreliability strains the bounds of coherence. It will take a moment to see why.

9.2 THE ASYMMETRY BETWEEN LITERATURE AND FILM

I want to introduce a distinction between kinds of narrators. The distinction is one between *controlling* and *embedded* narrators. Narrators as I have defined them are characters within the world of the fiction who are to be thought of as telling us facts, lies or deluded ravings.[7] Narrators tell by making utterances, and we can speak of the text of that utterance. Now that text – the text of which it is fictional that it is uttered by the narrator – may coincide with the text we are reading when we read the work. In that case, we imagine the narrator to be controlling; it is fic-

---

always and exclusively a matter of value (Booth's "norms"), which is certainly not the case, as many of Booth's examples attest. Booth's definition is taken over, more or less, by Chatman, *Story and Discourse*, p. 233, and is repeated in Gerald Prince, *A Dictionary of Narratology*, p. 101.

[5] The film version of *The Remains of the Day* is not an unreliable narrative.

[6] "Some important narrators are only *implicit* in the text, that is, their 'presence' must be inferred and constructed by the spectator" (Branigan, *Narrative Comprehension and Film*, p. 75).

[7] This, of course, is a simplification, since there are stories within stories where a narrator internal at one level is external at another; in these stories it is fictional that the narrator is telling us that it is fictional that . . . etc. Inclusion of such cases into our present taxonomy would further complicate an already complex structure, and ignoring them will not affect the argument.

tional that he or she is the source of the text before us. We know, of course, that the text is fictional and we probably know the identity of its real author, but we may think that it is part of the fiction itself that the narrator is the source of this text, and accept the fiction's implicit or explicit invitation to imagine exactly that. In this sense, Watson is a controlling narrator of the Holmes stories, and to some extent an unreliable one in the sense of Booth.[8] But some narrators are *embedded* rather than controlling. Where there is an embedded narrator, the text we read tells us of someone's telling, but that teller is not, fictionally, responsible for the text we read. Rather, it is fictional that the text we read *reports* that person's telling.[9] Embedded narrators are common in film: think of all those conflicting accounts in *Rashomon*, the bits of Charles Kane's life told by various folk in *Citizen Kane* and Walter Neff's disillusioned narrative in *Double Indemnity*.

Now this distinction between controlling and embedded narrators is very important for understanding narration in film. There are embedded narrators in film: I've just mentioned some examples of them. But there is something awkward – indeed, something close to incoherence – about the idea of a *controlling* narrator in film. With literature it is often natural to imagine that what one is reading is a true account of certain events witnessed or otherwise known about by someone, who then went to the trouble of setting it all down for us in writing; some of John Buchan's adventure stories, we are to imagine, are the product of a careful editor who has heard from the parties concerned and has created a judicious account on paper from their

---

[8] F. K. Stanzel supposes that all "first-person" narrators (in my terms: internal narrators) are necessarily unreliable, because of the limitations on their knowledge (*A Theory of Narrative*, p. 89). But failure to be omniscient is one thing and failure to be reliable another. Perhaps the thought here is that a non-omniscient narrator could not be certain of the truth of any of his beliefs. But it is an error of the Cartesian tradition to suppose that lack of certainty translates into unreliability.

[9] The term "embedded narrator" is sometimes used to refer to any character-narrator. This strikes me as misleading usage; a character-narrator who is controlling in my sense is not necessarily embedded in the story. He tells the story, but he does not tell of his own telling. See, e.g., Wallace Martin, *Recent Theories of Narrative*, p. 135.

reports. It is that report we imagine ourselves to be reading, and its imagined author counts as a controlling narrator. But what are we to imagine that would be analogous to this in the filmic case – that the person in the know has gone to the trouble of recreating it all for us on camera, spending millions of dollars, employing famous actors and a vast army of technicians? That seems implausible, especially in cases where the narrator, if there is one, would most naturally be thought of as living in the precinematic age.

Yet writers on film have, unfortunately, spoken of narrators in film as controlling, or at least as if they have partial control. Take the example of Hitchcock's *Stage Fright*, a filmic narrative which tells, in part, of a character named Johnny, who relates how he discovered the body but has been mistakenly identified as the murderer. And the film tells of Johnny's telling, not by reproducing for us his verbal account, but by translating that verbal account into images which constitute a flashback. We initially assume the flashback is correct. But at the end we learn that it is not, that Johnny was really the murderer, that his story of having found the body was a lie. The images we saw at the beginning, of Johnny discovering the body, turn out to be unreliable. In one sense Johnny is the source of this unreliability: it is his (fictional) act of false telling which causes us to be misled. But is Johnny also to be regarded as the source of the unreliable images we see? Seymour Chatman says yes: Johnny, he says, "is 'responsible' for the lying images and sounds that we see and hear".[10] That cannot be right. Johnny, like the other characters, exists within the story, and it is not part of that story that he produced and edited cinematic images in order to convince his fictional fellows (and us?) of his innocence – a transparently self-defeating enterprise. There are films in which some of the images we see onscreen are the product of a character, and it is fictional, of that character, that what we see onscreen is produced by him or her – *Peeping Tom* is perhaps the most famous

---

[10] Chatman, *Coming to Terms*, p. 132. Chatman also says, of Alain Resnais's *Providence*, that "Langham's voice-over, we eventually surmise, is somehow constructing the images filling the screen" (p. 133). Compare this with the discussion in his *Story and Discourse*, p. 237.

example of this. So there is nothing incoherent in the idea of an embedded narrator who tells, partly or wholly, by means of cinematic images of which he or she is the source. But that is manifestly not the situation in *Stage Fright*, and an analysis like Chatman's, which puts *Stage Fright* and *Peeping Tom* in the same category, must be wrong.

If controlling narrators in film are ruled out, how can we have unreliability in film? One way would be by ascribing unreliability to an embedded narrator:[11] we have a filmic narrative in which it is fictional that one of the characters speaks falsely, and that narrative may tell us what is falsely spoken in a number of ways – by voice-over, or, more commonly, by transforming the character's words into images without at the same time making it clear that what is spoken is false. In these cases we needn't suppose it fictional that what we see onscreen proceeds from the character. The filmic source of the images lies outside the diegesis. That, it seems, is how it must be for any unreliable filmic narrative that aspires to coherence: unreliability, where it occurs, must be the product of an embedded narrator, because that's the only narrator which comfortably fits the constraints of filmic presentation.

It certainly is that way with many filmic narratives which aspire to a kind of unreliability, as with *Stage Fright*. The question is, is all filmic unreliability of this kind? George Wilson claims to have found a case which is not: Fritz Lang's *You Only Live Once*.[12] The film tells, apparently, of the problems of a young man who has been in trouble with the law and who is subsequently and falsely accused of a murder-robbery. Wilson argues that this natural interpretation of the film is, on closer examination, not supported by, and is in fact at certain crucial points undermined by, the film's narration and its studiedly selective presentation of events. On Wilson's view, a right interpretation of the film would have us withhold judgement as to Eddie's guilt or innocence. But that is certainly not what most viewers

[11] I agree with Christian Metz that "the explicit enunciators in the film are always embedded" (Metz, "The Impersonal Enunciation", p. 768).
[12] Wilson, *Narration in Light*.

of the film have done; generations of critics and lay viewers have accepted the view that Eddie is an innocent victim. But there does not seem to be any embedded narrator in the film to whom unreliability might be described. And, given the film's dramatic structure, it is not easy to come up with a *covert* embedded narrator of any plausibility.[13]

I am not entirely convinced by Wilson's interpretation, but it does mesh well with parts of the film which are otherwise hard to understand. And if Wilson's interpretation does not apply in all detail to Lang's film, it is not difficult to imagine a film, different from Lang's in minor ways, to which it does. So we may conclude that it is *possible* for there to be unreliable narration in film where no embedded narrator is present – and when it comes to definitions, possible counterexamples are as telling as actual ones. In that case we really will have to look for another definition of narrative unreliability if we are to accommodate *You Only Live Once* and like cases. Anyway, I shall assume, for the sake of the argument, that Wilson is right about the film.

So *You Only Live Once* is an unreliable narrative without an unreliable narrator.[14] What, then, is the source of its unreliability, if not the tension between author and embedded narrator? Unreliability can have its source, I claim, in a certain kind of *complex intention* on the part of the implied author. Let me explain.

An agent can do something with an intention of the following complex kind: she creates or presents something which she intends to be taken as evidence of her intentions, and she intends that a superficial grasp of that evidence will suggest that her intention was Φ, whereas a better, more reflective grasp of the

---

[13] Perhaps you think it analytic that narrative must have a narrator (as does Sarah Kozloff: "Because narrative films are narrative, someone must be narrating"; *Invisible Storytellers*, p. 115, quoted approvingly in Chatman, *Coming to Terms*, p. 133). But then you simply object to my terminology, and I could avoid the objection by using another term to refer to the vehicle of narrator-less story-telling. Consider it done.

[14] As Cary Groner pointed out, *An Occurrence at Owl Creek* (1961) seems to be a case of unreliability without a narrator. But here the unreliability is temporary; that the film's images are largely the imaginings of a character is made evident at the end.

evidence will suggest that her intention was Ψ. An example: Freida compliments Fred on his sophisticated sense of humour. Her flattery seems out of line with what we know of Freida's acerbic personality. But now we see that it was all ironic and intended to be recognized, ultimately, as more of the abuse she usually heaps upon Fred. Freida's performance was unreliable in my sense, and there may be people, Fred among them, who didn't get to the second stage, because that took just a little more calculating than some of us can be relied on to make.

That seems to be what is going on in *You Only Live Once*; we take the images and sounds that make up the film as intended one way. But if we are scrupulous in our examination of those images, we find peculiarities, incongruities and apparently unmotivated elements that start to fall into place when we see that it can be interpreted in another way. Their falling into place consists in their being seen as intended to suggest that second, less obvious interpretation. Narratives which are the product of this kind of two-tier system of intentions constitute a distinctive and especially challenging class, and I do not think that they are very well understood. I hope to change that somewhat in the rest of this chapter.

9.3 KINDS OF UNRELIABILITY

Defining unreliable narrative in terms of complex intentions attributable to an implied author allows us to count a narrative as unreliable when there is no narrator we can identify as the source of unreliability. What are the relations between this kind of unreliability and the cases of narratorial unreliability covered by Booth's definition? Some of the cases that are unreliable on Booth's definition would not be unreliable on mine. In Lardner's "Haircut," for example, we have an internal narrator whose outlook (his "norms", as Booth puts it) is different from, and undermined by, that of the implied author. But this is not a case where we should attribute a complex intention to the implied author. The disparity of outlooks is too obvious in this case for us to conclude that the implied author has intentions which can be grasped only on reflection. Of course, it is possible to imagine someone who is misled by this or by any narrative; someone might think that the speaker in "Haircut" is saying things which, within the framework of the story, represent a correct assessment of the situation. But if the test of the implied author's complexity of intention is the mere possibility that someone will be fooled in this way, we shall end up saying that all narratives are unreliable. We need a criterion of unreliability that is more discriminating. We should say that a narrative is unreliable in my sense only if it has a tendency to mislead an attentive, intelligent reader with some experience of the relevant genre – here the short story. I do not think any such reader will be long misled by Lardner's tale. The warranted conclusion is surely that the implied author intends us to see, straight off, the moral shortsightedness of the narrator. "Haircut" is unreliable in Booth's sense, but not in mine.

That is not to say that the extensions of Booth's definitions and mine are disjoint, for it is possible for a work to satisfy both of them. Such a work would be one where the implied author intends the plot to be understood one way on a superficial reading, another way on a more attentive reading, *and* where there is a lying or deluded narrator. In fact, it is common for an unreliable narrator to be the mechanism whereby unreliability in my sense is achieved. At first we take, and are intended to take, the narrator at her word and so interpret the story one way; on reflection we see her, as we are intended to, as unreliable, and revise our reading.[15] So there is overlap between our definitions, but they are not the same; mine was introduced, after all, to cover cases that Booth's does not cover – and so the definitions characterize different concepts.

But I shall not endorse the comfortably ecumenical position that these definitions are merely different but equal. I believe

---

[15] In that case we have a "seductive" unreliable narrator. The classic case is *The Turn of the Screw*. Where Booth's definition applies and mine does not, we have an unseductive one. See James Phelan, "Narrative Discourse, Literary Character and Ideology", in idem, *Reading People, Reading Plots*, p. 137. Sometimes cases of unobviously unreliable narratives are described as "ambiguous" (e.g., by Shlomith Rimmon-Kenan, *Narrative Fiction*, p. 103), but I wish to use this term for another purpose. See Section 9.4.

that my characterization of unreliability in terms of a complex intention – call it "complex unreliability" – is of greater theoretical and critical interest than the familiar Boothian characterization in terms of a disparity of outlook between the narrator and the author – call it "Booth unreliability". There are of course interesting cases of Booth unreliability, but they tend also to be cases of complex unreliability, that is, cases in which the narrator's unreliability is to some degree intended as unobvious. We are past the point where a narrator's unreliability is *intrinsically* interesting, because we no longer presume that narrators will be reliable. Without that presumption, narratorial unreliability is, of itself, no more significant than the mendacity of a dramatic speaker – no more significant, that is, from the point of view of a theory of narrative. But unreliability that is to some degree hidden is of theoretical interest because its operation depends on delicately balanced inferential strategies that the reader must undertake. To get a good sense of the nature of these inferences will require the introduction of another narrative concept, that of an *ambiguous* narrative.

9.4 AMBIGUOUS AND UNRELIABLE NARRATIVES

An ambiguous narrative is one which does not enable us to answer all the questions which arise concerning the story. In a sense, every narration is ambiguous, since no narration can possibly provide complete information about the characters and events it describes. What did each character have for breakfast that morning? At what exact moment was each character born? You might say that these are not meaningful questions within the context of the fiction, as they would be in the real world, and to suppose that they are is to endorse the fallacy of taking fictional characters for real people concerning whom every question, interesting or not, has an answer. But such questions are not meaningless. Most fictional narratives present stories in which the characters are assumed, except where there is evidence to the contrary, to have the sorts of characteristics that real people have. No one doubts, I think, that Marlowe in *The*

Big Sleep is a man who, like others, was born at a particular time; there is no suggestion, for instance, that he is immortal. So there must, according to the story, be a time of his birth. It is just that the narrative does not elect any particular time as that time. And if it is part of the story that Marlowe was born at a certain time, it can hardly be senseless to ask when.

But it would be a fallacy to assume that there must be an *answer* to that question. That would be to assume that fictional characters are real people. The question of Marlowe's birth date is not meaningless, but it is insignificant, and *The Big Sleep* is not in any interesting sense an ambiguous narrative just because it fails to resolve that question. It is only when a question is significant that the narration's failure to answer it gives grounds for saying that the narration is ambiguous. When is a question significant? One answer is this: when members of the audience are (normally) inclined to ask it concerning that narrative. The friend of this theory can note with satisfaction that the question about the time of Marlowe's birth is not a question that viewers are inclined to ask. But this proposal will not do. Many people are inclined to wonder what will happen to Rhett and Scarlett at the end of *Gone with the Wind* (as the recent and long-awaited sequel indicates), but this would not be grounds for saying that the narrative (either the book or the film) is ambiguous in the sense I am interested in here. Questions about the continuation or noncontinuation of relationships are ones we are almost always inclined to ask – at least they arise fleetingly in our minds – at the end of the work. This proposal is going to make too many narratives ambiguous.

A proposal with a similar defect has it that the narrative is ambiguous if it leads us to expect an answer to a question when in fact it does not provide an answer – though the proposal would at least explain the intuition that *Gone with the Wind* is not ambiguous, since that narrative does not lead us to expect that an answer will be given to the question, "What happens to them after the narrative breaks off?" But this proposal is neither necessary nor sufficient for ambiguity. The narrative might make it clear from the start that a certain question is not going to be answered (in the case of a film that might require a voice-over to be convincing). So we are not led to expect an answer, and indeed the question may not be answered by the narrative. Yet the question might be one such that, in not answering it, the narrative takes on the character of ambiguity. So satisfaction of the proposed criterion is not necessary for ambiguity. And a question may arise to which we expect an answer, but where we put down failure to provide an answer to incompetence in the construction of the narrative. In that case we would be doing the work a favour it does not deserve by calling it ambiguous.

The case of narrative incompetence is the clue to solving our problem. When a question arises which is not answered in the narrative, but where we ascribe the nonanswer to incompetence, we do not think that a question has been deliberately raised by the implied author, and deliberately left unanswered; we think, exactly, that either the raising or the failure to answer was due to some oversight or other failure of execution. So I propose the following as the criterion for determining when a narration is ambiguous: when it raises a question in the reader's/viewer's mind which it fails to answer, and where the raising and the nonanswering seem to have been intentional. This proposal gives the result that *The Big Sleep* is not ambiguous, even though it fails to determine the answer to the question of Marlowe's age: the narrative gives no indication that the maker intended that question to be raised. It does the same for *Gone with the Wind*; while viewers and readers may wonder about the future of Rhett and Scarlett, and the makers may have expected that they would wonder about it, and while all this may be common knowledge between audience and maker, the question does not seem to be intentionally raised and intentionally left unanswered by the narrative.[16]

---

[16] The film narratives used by Bordwell and Thompson to illustrate ambiguity (*Day of Wrath* and *Last Year at Marienbad*) would count as ambiguous on my definition. Bordwell and Thompson associate ambiguity closely with causality (*Film Art*, p. 250). Their idea seems to be that the work is ambiguous to the extent that the causes or effects of narrative elements are unclear. Since most narrative events, like most events in real life, have many distinct partial causes and many distinct effects, we shall need to distinguish the significant

It is easy at the level of theory to see the differences between unreliable and ambiguous narratives. But it is not always easy to say which kind a particular work belongs to. Is *Rashomon* an ambiguous or an unreliable narration? If there figure within it embedded narrators who are unreliable, we may grant that it is unreliable in the narratorial sense of Booth. It would be ambiguous if it left it an open question which of the conflicting accounts is true. But is it unreliable in the sense that I have defined, that it is possible to detect in its making the influence of a complex intention of the kind I have described in connection with *You Only Live Once*? That would be so if we thought of *Rashomon* this way: as intended, first, to suggest to us that the problem is to decide which account is true, and second, to suggest on deeper reflection the relativity of truth and, in consequence, the falsity of our first question's presupposition that there is a right answer. For some of us, the easy relativism of the last option is too banal to be an attractive candidate for interpretation – but this may be just an indication that there is sometimes no neutral perspective from which to choose between ambiguity and unreliability, a situation we sometimes experience with other interpretive choices.[17]

But while ambiguity and unreliability are distinct interpretive options, they are compatible, not merely in the sense that there is sometimes no principled choice between them, but in the stronger sense that a single interpretation of the work may require the application of both. We might, for instance, take *Rashomon* as complex unreliable in that at first glance the options are between the explicit accounts of the various narrators, while on reflection we see that there is another option – the relativistic one – and that the story is ambiguous between those collected at the first round and this one. (I would count that as only marginally less banal than straightforwardly opting for relativism, but it might still be the best thing we can come up with.) On that view, *Rashomon* is both complex unreliable and ambiguous.

from the nonsignificant causes and effects. My proposal can be read as doing that.

[17] See my "Interpretation and Objectivity".

Note that *You Only Live Once* is, on Wilson's account, both ambiguous and unreliable. At first the question "Is Eddie guilty of murder?" seems to be answered by the narrative. But we see, on closer inspection, that it is left open by it. That also seems to me the best case that can be made on behalf of a psychological interpretation of *The Turn of the Screw*: reflection doesn't show that there are no ghosts; at best it shows that another hypothesis does about as well as the supernatural one when it comes to explaining the text.[18] In that case might there be some internal connection between unreliability and ambiguity?

Complex unreliability does not necessitate ambiguity. But complex unreliability is an easier effect to achieve when it involves ambiguity than when it does not. The task of the maker of a complex-unreliable narration is difficult. It is to set clues at two levels: at level 1, where the clues are more obvious but only superficially persuasive; and at level 2, where they are less obvious but more weighty when reflected upon. But the degree of difficulty of the task varies from case to case, and one determinant of it is what we might call the *epistemic distance* between the two levels: increase the distance and you increase the difficulty. By "distance" I mean the disparity between what you want to convey at a first impression and what you want the audience to grasp on further reflection. The greater the distance in this sense, the greater the subtlety and complexity of the reasoning the audience will have to go through to cover the gap, and the less likely it is that they will succeed. Trying to raise the probability of success in such a case by reinforcing the clues at level 2 may simply undermine the whole project by making the inference to level 2 more obvious and natural than that to level 1.

---

[18] Jack Clayton's *The Innocents*, a film version of *The Turn of the Screw*, is interesting in this regard. One difficulty the film makers had to contend with was that a significant proportion of the film's audience would bring with them their knowledge of the unreliability in James's story, which would make it impossible for the film to achieve the same effect; the audience would be primed for the discovery of the higher-level clues from the start. As I understand the film, their solution, intelligently enough, was to forgo any attempt at complex unreliability and to settle for ambiguity.

In this sense of "distance" there will generally be a greater distance between the two levels if at one level we are given, say, a yes answer to a question, and at the other a no answer, than if at one level we are given an answer (yes or no) and at the other we are told that no answer is forthcoming. In the first case you first have to persuade the audience to conclude that the answer to a certain question is, say, yes, and then to revise their opinion and conclude that the answer is no. In the second case you first have to persuade the audience to conclude that the answer to the question is yes (or no), and then simply to withdraw that opinion, remaining thereafter agnostic on the question, thinking of the work now as ambiguous. So the second is an easier thing to do than the first, and we would expect to find the second more commonly than the first in cases of complex unreliability. Indeed, that seems to be how things are with notable cases of complex unreliability like *You Only Live Once* and *The Turn of the Screw*.

When an unreliable narrative is one that seems, superficially, to close a certain issue but reveals on reflection that the question is left open, as in *You Only Live Once*, let us say that we have a "transition to openness". Consider a transition in the opposite direction – a "transition to closure" – where the narrative seems, superficially, to leave a certain issue open but is seen on reflection to answer the question one way or another. Would a transition to closure be easier or more difficult to effect than a transition to openness? Taking into account only what I have called epistemic distance suggests that it would be neither more nor less difficult, since distance is symmetrical; the distance between two things is independent of the order in which they are taken. However, there are grounds for saying that it would, other things being equal, be more difficult to effect a transition to closure than to openness. The task, in creating a complex-unreliable narration, is to suggest one hypothesis by means of more obvious but ultimately less convincing evidence, and to suggest another by means of less obvious but more convincing evidence. The difficulty is to ensure that the more convincing evidence will in fact be less obvious, without having it disappear entirely from view. That difficulty will be greater the stronger is the hypothesis for which it is evidence. After all, it takes more evidence to get us to believe a strong conclusion than a weak one. It's not hard to convince me that either Oswald shot Kennedy or someone else did; it's much harder to convince me that someone else did. So, other things being equal, you will have to provide stronger evidence to support a definite conclusion than to support a mere ambiguity. But then the transition to closure requires stronger evidence at the level of the less obvious, and that kind of transition is going to be more difficult to effect than one to openness. So we would expect to find transitions to openness more frequently in literature and other narrative forms than transitions to closure. And that, I believe, is exactly what we do find.[19]

Perhaps there is a lesson here. The old structuralist project was to find patterns and regularities – even to some degree nomological ones – within the apparent diversity of literature. This is not generally thought to have been a success. But perhaps the project was not entirely doomed. Perhaps there is something like an "order of narrative" to be discovered by appeal not to structure but to reason. If tales, cinematic or literary, are generated by someone for someone, a major determinant in the evolution of tales, and in the patterns of invariance detectable through that evolution, will be what we might call *the constraints of reciprocal reason*. Tellers have to decide what they can expect hearers to pick up by way of clues to their intentions, and hearers have to decide what tellers will think hearers can pick up, and so on. As story-telling evolves, as new narratives piggyback on the communicative breakthroughs of their predecessors and as new and more complex narrative intentions become common knowledge in the community of tellers and hearers, these inferences will become more complex, with the most inventive tellers always operating on the thin boundary between surprising the audience and having the audience completely miss the point.

[19] George Wilson argues that there is what I am calling a "transition to closure" in Ford's *Searchers*: that the narrative appears to be ambiguous on the question of Ethan's motives, but that it can, on reflection, be seen to disclose a motive. See Wilson, *Narration in Light*, pp. 45–50.

But we shouldn't expect a simple linear development of increasingly complicated narratives, for engineering constraints will quickly exhaust the capacity of any given narrative trope. Consider narratives which display what I have called complex unreliability. Tellers cannot move forward, if that's the word, by steadily increasing the epistemic distance between the obvious and the unobvious interpretation; as I have pointed out, epistemic distance and unobviousness pull in different directions, and beyond a certain point increases in epistemic distance become self-defeating. At that point tellers have to look to a different trope or play against the rising expectations of hearers by going into reverse – for example, presenting what hearers will expect to be a complex-unreliable narrative which turns out, surprisingly, to be quite straightforward. With constraints pulling against one another in this way we can expect that narrative will not be a wholly amorphous, infinitely stretchable bag of tricks, but something with identifiable boundaries and perhaps a centre, and with tellers and hearers chasing each other away from and back towards that centre in various directions. The structure here will not be set by the laws of genre, of literary archetypes or by the structure of language, but by the rules for assessing the reasonableness of inferences about people's intentions.

I have suggested that there is a kind of narrative unreliability not covered by the standard account. I have given a general characterization of it, and suggested how it stands in logical relation to the more familiar kind of unreliability. I have also described what I call ambiguous narrative and suggested that there is a close connection between this and the kind of unreliable narrative I defined – a connection forged by the difficulty readers and viewers face in making the inferences to the implied author's intentions that are necessary if unreliability is to be detected. I conclude that unreliability in narrative makes no sense without appeal to the concept of an implied author, but that the concept of a narrator is required by only one kind of unreliability. The implied author, we may say, is an absolute presupposition of unreliability, the narrator a merely conditional one. That is why there can be narratives which are genuinely unreliable – rather than merely ambiguous or misleading – even when there is no narrator in whom we can locate the source of the unreliability.

In conclusion

A fiction film is a visual and a pictorial work. It is visual because our mode of access to it is visual; it is pictorial because its mode of representation is pictorial. Its material is moving pictures – pictures which really move rather than simply create the illusion of movement. Nor is film typically productive of any cognitive illusion to the effect that what it represents is real; our standard mode of engagement with the film is via imagination rather than belief. Imagination is, however, parasitic on belief, for it consists of running our belief (and desire) system off-line, disconnected from standard inputs and outputs. But while the pictures of film are not productive of illusions, they are typically realistic pictures: pictures which are like, in significant ways, the things they represent. And it is partly in virtue of their likeness to these things that we are able to recognize the depictive content of these pictures. For this reason film is not a linguistic medium, nor is it in any interesting sense like a linguistic medium.

There is something distinctive about our imaginings in response to film. It is not, as many theorists have claimed, that we imagine ourselves to be witnesses of the action, placed where the camera is. Rather, it is that our imaginings have a distinctively visual structure. Nor do we imagine that the action represented is occurring in the present as we watch; film is preeminently an art of time, but it does not represent fictional things as co-occurrent with our watching. Despite the fact that film is an essentially nonlinguistic medium, it is possible to develop a general theory of interpretation which accounts for both literature and film. According to this theory, interpretation is explanation – explanation by reference to intentional causes. With a novel or a film, the interpreter's task is to formulate plausible hypotheses about the story-telling intentions productive of the work. Still, literature and film offer rather different kinds of narrative possibilities and, in particular, the role for unreliable narrators is more restricted in film than in literature. Film shows the need for a category of unreliable but narratorless narratives.

Named propositions

(Starred propositions are accepted.)

Illusionism: That film typically causes the viewer to undergo an illusory experience.

There are two versions of this claim:

Cognitive Illusionism: That film creates an illusion of the reality of the fiction it presents.

Perceptual Illusionism: That film typically creates an illusion of movement.

Presentation Thesis: That photographs and cinematic images do not merely represent the things they are of, but rather present those things to us.

As a special case of this:

Transparency: That when we see a photograph or cinematic image of X, we see X.

Perceptual Realism*: That pictures in general, and cinematic images in particular, are in significant respects like the things they represent.

Imagined Observer Hypothesis: That the standard mode of imaginative engagement with film involves the viewer imagining that she is watching the events of the story from the position of the camera.

Claim of Presentness: That fiction films typically represent the fictional events as occurring in the viewer's present.

Implied Author Intentionalism*: That narrative interpretation requires us to discover the narrative intentions of the work's implied author.

Real Author Intentionalism: That narrative interpretation requires us to discover the narrative intentions of the work's real author.

Bibliography

Affron, Charles, *Cinema and Sentiment*, University of Chicago Press, 1982.

Akins, Kathleen A., "What Is It Like to Be Boring and Myopic?" in B. Dahlbom (ed.), *Dennett and His Critics: Demystifying Mind*, Cambridge, Mass.: Basil Blackwell, 1993.

Altman, Rick, *Sound Theory, Sound Practice*, London: Routledge & Kegan Paul, 1992.

Anstis, Stuart, "Motion Perception in the Frontal Plane: Sensory Aspects", in K. Boff, L. Kaufman and J. Thomas (eds.), *Handbook of Perception and Human Performance*, vol. 1, New York: Wiley, 1986.

Arnheim, Rudolf, *Film as Art*, London: Faber & Faber, 1983.

Aumont, J., "The Point of View", trans. Arthur Denner, *Quarterly Review of Film and Video*, 11 (1989): 1–22.

Aumont, J., A. Bergala, M. Marie and M. Vernet, *Aesthetics of Film*, trans. R. Neupert, Austin: University of Texas Press, 1992.

Bach-y-Rita, P., et al., "Vision Substitution by Tactile Image Projection", *Nature*, 221 (1969): 963–964.

Bal, Mieke, "Description as Narration", in *On Story–Telling*, Sonoma, Calif.: Polebridge, 1991.

Balázs, Béla, *Theory of the Film: Character and Growth of a New Art*, New York: Arno, 1972.

Baron-Cohen, S., "The Autistic Child's Theory of Mind: A Case of Specific Developmental Delay", *Journal of Child Psychology and Psychiatry and Allied Disorders*, 30 (1989): 285–297.

Baron-Cohen, S., A. Leslie and U. Frith, "Does the Autistic Child Have a 'Theory of Mind'?" *Cognition*, 21 (1985): 37–46.

Baudry, Jean-Louis, "Ideological Effects of the Basic Cinematic Apparatus", in Bill Nichols (ed.), *Movies and Methods*, vol. 2, Berkeley and Los Angeles: University of California Press, 1985.

Bazin, André, *What Is Cinema?* vol. 1, trans. Hugh Gray, Berkeley and Los Angeles: University of California Press, 1971.

"The Myth of Total Cinema", in Mast and Cohen (eds.), *Film Theory and Criticism*, 3d ed., New York: Oxford University Press, 1985.

Jean Renoir, trans. W. W. Halsey II and W. H. Simon, New York: Da Capo, 1992.

Biederman, Irving, "Visual Object Recognition", in Alvin Goldman (ed.), *Readings in Philosophy and Cognitive Science*, Cambridge, Mass.: MIT Press, 1993.

Boghossian, Paul A., and J. David Velleman, "Colour as a Secondary Quality", *Mind*, 98 (1989): 80–103.

Booth, Wayne, *The Rhetoric of Fiction*, 2d ed., University of Chicago Press, 1983.

Bordwell, David, *Narration in the Fiction Film*, Madison: University of Wisconsin Press, 1985.

Making Meaning: Inference and Rhetoric in the Interpretation of Cinema, Cambridge, Mass.: Harvard University Press, 1989.

Bordwell, David, and K. Thompson, *Film Art: An Introduction*, New York: Random House, 1986.

Branigan, Edward, "The Point-of-View Shot", in Bill Nichols (ed.), *Movies and Methods*, vol. 2, Berkeley and Los Angeles: University of California Press, 1985.

Narrative Comprehension and Film, New York: Routledge, 1992.

Brown, E. L., and K. Deffenbacher, *Perception and the Senses*, New York: Oxford University Press, 1979.

Browne, Nick, *The Rhetoric of Filmic Narration*, Ann Arbor, Mich.: UMI Research Press, 1976.

Bryson, Norman, et al. (eds.), *Visual Theory: Painting and Interpretation*, Cambridge: Polity, 1991.

Burch, Noël, *Theory of Film Practice*, trans. Helen Lane, Princeton, N.J.: Princeton University Press, 1981.

Carroll, Noël, "The Power of Movies", *Daedalus*, 114, no. 4 (1985): 79–103.

Mystifying Movies: Fads and Fallacies in Contemporary Film Theory, New York: Columbia University Press, 1988.

Philosophical Problems of Classical Film Theory, Princeton, N.J.: Princeton University Press, 1988.

The Philosophy of Horror: Paradoxes of the Heart, New York: Routledge & Kegan Paul, 1990.

"Review of Gregory Currie, *The Nature of Fiction*", *Mind*, 103 (1994): 542–545.

Caughie, John (ed.), *Theories of Authorship: A Reader*, London: Routledge & Kegan Paul, 1981.

Cavell, Stanley, *The World Viewed: Reflections on the Ontology of Film*, Cambridge, Mass.: Harvard University Press, 1979.

"Ugly Duckling, Funny Butterfly: Bette Davis and *Now, Voyager*", *Critical Inquiry*, 16, no. 1 (1990): 213–247.

Chatman, Seymour, *Story and Discourse: Narrative Structure in Fiction and Film*, Ithaca, N.Y.: Cornell University Press, 1978.

Coming to Terms: The Rhetoric of Narrative in Fiction and Film, Ithaca, N.Y.: Cornell University Press, 1990.

Churchland, Paul M., *Scientific Realism and the Plasticity of Mind*, Cambridge University Press, 1979.

"Perceptual Plasticity and Theoretical Neutrality: A Reply to Jerry Fodor", *Philosophy of Science*, 55 (1988): 167–187.

Cohen, Ted, "What's Special About Photography?" *Monist*, 71 (1988): 292–305.

Comolli, Jean-Louis, "Machines of the Visible", in Stephen Heath and Teresa de Lauretis (eds.), *The Cinematic Apparatus*, London: Macmillan, 1980.

Corballis, M. C., "On the Evolution of Language and Generativity", *Cognition*, 44 (1992): 197–226.

Currie, Gregory, *The Nature of Fiction*, Cambridge University Press, 1990.

"Work and Text", *Mind*, 100 (1991): 325–340.

"Interpreting Fiction", in R. Freadman and L. Reinhardt (eds.), *Literary Theory and Philosophy*, London: Macmillan, 1991.

"Text without Context: Some Errors of Stanley Fish", *Philosophy and Literature*, 15 (1991): 212–228.

"Interpretation and Objectivity", *Mind*, 102 (1993): 413–428.

"Imagination and Simulation: Aesthetics Meets Cognitive Science", in M. Davies and T. Stone (eds.), *Mental Simulation*, Oxford: Basil Blackwell, 1994.

"Simulation-Theory, Theory-Theory and the Evidence from Autism", in P. Carruthers and P. Smith (eds.), *Theories of Theories of Mind*, Cambridge University Press, 1995.

Dagle, Joan, "Narrative Discourse in Film and Fiction: The Question of the Present Tense", in Syndy M. Conger and Janice R. Welsch (eds.), *Narrative Strategies*, Macomb: Western Illinois University Press, 1980.

Bibliography

Dahlbom, B. (ed.), *Dennett and His Critics: Demystifying Mind*, Cambridge, Mass.: Basil Blackwell, 1993.

Davies, Martin, "Function in Perception", *Australasian Journal of Philosophy*, 61 (1983): 409–426.

Davies, M., and T. Stone (eds.), *Mental Simulation*, Oxford: Basil Blackwell, 1994.

Davies, W. M., *Experience and Content: Consequences of a Continuum Theory*, Ph.D. dissertation, Flinders University, 1993.

Dawkins, Richard, *The Blind Watchmaker*, Harlow: Longman Scientific and Technical, 1986.

Dayan, Daniel, "The Tutor-Code of Classical Cinema", in B. Nichols (ed.), *Movies and Methods*, vol. 1, 1985.

Deleuze, Gilles, *Masochism: An Interpretation of Coldness and Cruelty*, New York: Braziller, 1971.

Cinema 2: The Time-Image, trans. H. Tomlinson and R. Galeta, London: Athlone, 1989.

Dennett, Daniel, *Brainstorms: Philosophical Essays on Mind and Psychology*, Montgomery, Vt.: Bradford, 1978.

"Real Patterns", *Journal of Philosophy*, 88 (1991): 27–51.

Dick, Bernard F., *Anatomy of Film*, 2d ed., New York: St Martin's, 1990.

Durgnat, Raymond, review of Metz's *Psychoanalysis and Cinema*, *Film Quarterly*, 36, no. 2 (1982–3): 58–64.

"Theory of Theory – and Buñuel the Joker", *Film Quarterly*, 44 (1990): 32–44.

Dworkin, R., *A Matter of Principle*, Cambridge, Mass.: Harvard University Press, 1985.

Law's Empire, London: Fontana, 1986.

Eco, Umberto, *A Theory of Semiotics*, Bloomington: Indiana University Press, 1979.

"On the Contribution of Film to Semiotics", in G. Mast and M. Cohen (eds.), *Film Theory and Criticism*, 3d ed., New York: Oxford University Press, 1985.

Ellis, John, *Visible Fictions: Cinema, Television, Video*, London: Routledge & Kegan Paul, 1982.

Fish, Stanley, *Is There a Text in this Class? The Authority of Interpretive Communities*, Cambridge, Mass.: Harvard University Press, 1980.

Doing What Comes Naturally: Change, Rhetoric and the Practice of Theory in Literary and Legal Studies, Durham, N.C.: Duke University Press, 1989.

Flitterman, Sally, "Woman, Desire, and the Look: Feminism and the Enunciative Apparatus in Cinema", *Cine-Tracts*, 2 (1978), reprinted

Bibliography

in Caughie, John (ed.), *Theories of Authorship: A Reader*, London: Routledge & Kegan Paul, 1981.

Fodor, Jerry, *The Language of Thought*, New York: Crowell, 1975.

"Observation Reconsidered", *Philosophy of Science*, 51 (1984): 23–43.

"Précis of *The Modularity of Mind*", *Behavioral and Brain Sciences*, 8 (1985): 1–42.

"Meaning and the World Order", in *Psychosemantics: The Problem of Meaning in the Philosophy of Mind*, Cambridge, Mass.: MIT Press, 1987.

Friedberg, Anne, "*Les Flâneurs du Mal(l)*: Cinema and the Postmodern Condition", *PMLA*, 106, no. 3 (May 1991): 419–431.

Genette, Gérard. *Narrative Discourse: An Essay in Method*, trans. J. E. Lewin, Ithaca, N.Y.: Cornell University Press, 1980.

Gilman, Daniel, "Pictures in Cognition", *Erkenntnis*, 41, no. 1 (July 1994): 87–102.

Glymore, Clark. "Freud's Androids", in Jerome Nue (ed.), *The Cambridge Companion to Freud*, Cambridge University Press, 1991.

Goldman, Alvin, "Interpretation Psychologized", *Mind and Language*, 4, no. 3 (1989): 161–185.

"The Psychology of Folk Psychology", *Behavioral and Brain Sciences*, 16, no.1 (1993): 15–28.

Goldman, Alvin (ed.), *Readings in Philosophy and Cognitive Science*, Cambridge, Mass.: MIT Press, 1993.

Gombrich, E., "Image and Code: Scope and Limits of Conventionalism in Pictorial Representation", in *The Image and the Eye: Further Studies in the Psychology of Pictorial Representation*, Oxford: Phaidon, 1982.

Goodman, Nelson, *Languages of Art: An Approach to a Theory of Symbols*, Indianapolis: Hackett, 1976.

Gopnik, Allison, "What is It if It Isn't a Theory?" in Peter Carruthers and Peter K. Smith (eds.), *Theories of Theories of Mind*, Cambridge University Press, 1995.

Gordon, Robert M., "Folk Psychology as Simulation", *Mind and Language*, 1 (1986): 158–171.

Grice, Paul, "Logic and Conversation", in *Studies in the Way of Words*, Cambridge, Mass.: Harvard University Press, 1989.

Guarniero, G., "Experience of Tactile Vision", *Perception*, 3 (1974): 101–104.

Hacking, Ian, "Do We See Through a Microscope?" in P. M. Churchland and C. Hooker (eds.), *Images of Science: Essays on Realism and Empiricism*, University of Chicago Press, 1985.

289

Bibliography

Halliwell, Leslie, *The Filmgoer's Companion*, 3d ed., New York: Hill & Wang, 1970.

Hardin, C. L., "Color Subjectivism", in A. Goldman (ed.), *Readings in Philosophy and Cognitive Science.*

Harman, Gilbert, "Eco Location", in M. Cohen and G. Mast (eds.), *Film Theory and Criticism*, 2d ed., New York: Oxford University Press, 1979.

"Semiotics and the Cinema: Metz and Wollen", in M. Cohen and G. Mast (eds.), *Film Theory and Criticism*, 2d ed., New York: Oxford University Press, 1979.

Harvey, Nigel, "Wishful Thinking Impairs Belief–Desire Reasoning: A Case of Decoupling Failure in Adults?" *Cognition*, 45 (1992): 141–162.

Haugeland, John, "The Nature and Plausibility of Cognitivism", *Behavioral and Brain Sciences*, 2 (1978): 215–260.

Heal, Jane, "Replication and Functionalism", in J. Butterfield (ed.), *Language, Mind, and Logic*, Cambridge University Press, 1986.

Henderson, B., "Tense, Mood and Voice in Film (Notes after Genette)", *Film Quarterly*, 36, no. 4 (1983): 4–17.

"Two Types of Film Theory", in B. Nichols (ed.), *Movies and Methods: An Anthology*, vol. 1, Berkeley and Los Angeles: University of California Press, 1985.

Hirsch, E. D., *Validity in Interpretation*, New Haven, Conn.: Yale University Press, 1967.

Holton, Richard, "Intentions, Response-Dependence and Immunity from Error", in Peter Menzies (ed.), *Response-Dependent Concepts: Working Papers in Philosophy*, no. 1, Canberra: Research School of Social Sciences, Australian National University, 1991.

Humphreys, Glyn W., and Jane M. Riddoch (eds.), *Visual Object Processing: A Cognitive Neuropsychological Approach*, London: Erlbaum, 1987.

Irwin, Timothy, *Meaning and Convention*, M.A. thesis, Otago University, 1988.

Jackson, Frank, *Perception: A Representative Theory*, Cambridge University Press, 1977.

"Metaphysics by Possible Cases", in Brian Garrett and Peter Menzies (eds.), *1992 ANU Metaphysics Conference, Working Papers in Philosophy*, no. 2, Canberra: Research School of Social Sciences, Australian National University, 1992.

Jackson, Frank and Phillip Pettit, "Functionalism and Broad Content", *Mind*, 97 (1988): 381–400.

Jarvie, Ian, *Philosophy of the Film*, London: Routledge & Kegan Paul, 1987.

Jeannerod, M. "The Representing Brain: Neural Correlates of Motor Intention and Imagery", *Behavioral and Brain Sciences*, 17 (1994): 187–202.

Johnson, C. N., and Paul L. Harris, "Magic: Special but Not Excluded", *British Journal of Developmental Psychology*, 12 (1994): 35–51.

Johnston, Mark, "Dispositional Theories of Value", *Aristotelian Society Supplementary Volume*, 63 (1989): 139–174.

Jones, R. K., and M. A. Hagen, "A Perspective on Cross–Cultural Picture Perception", in M. A. Hagen (ed.), *The Perception of Pictures*, vol. 2, New York: Academic, 1980.

Juhl, P. D., *Interpretation: An Essay in the Philosophy of Literary Criticism*, Princeton, N.J.: Princeton University Press, 1980.

Kanner, L., "Autistic Disturbances of Affective Contact", *Nervous Child*, 2 (1943): 217–250.

Khatchadourian, Haig, "Remarks on the 'Cinematic/Uncinematic Distinction in Film Art' ", in *Music, Film and Art*, New York: Gordon Breach, 1985.

"Space and Time in Film", *British Journal of Aesthetics*, 27 (1987): 169–177.

Kozloff, Sarah, *Invisible Storytellers: Voice–Over Narration in American Fiction Film*, Berkeley and Los Angeles: University of California Press, 1988.

Lapsley, Robert, and Michael Westlake, *Film Theory: An Introduction*, Manchester University Press, 1988.

le Poidevin, Robin, "Time and Truth in Fiction", *British Journal of Aesthetics*, 28 (1988): 248–258.

Leslie, Alan, "Pretence and Representation: The Origins of 'Theory of Mind' ", *Psychological Review*, 94, no. 4 (1987): 412–426.

"Pretending and Believing: Issues in the Theory of ToMM", *Cognition*, 50 (1994): 211–238.

Leslie, Alan., T. German and F. Happé, "Even a Theory-Theory Needs Information Processing: ToMM, an Alternative Theory-Theory of the Child's Theory of Mind", *Behavioral and Brain Sciences*, 16 (1993): 57.

Levinson, Jerrold, "Seeing, Imaginarily, at the Movies", *Philosophical Quarterly*, 43, no. 170 (1993): 70–78.

Levinson, Jerrold, and Philip Alperson, *What Is a Temporal Art?* Vol. 16 of Midwest Studies in Philosophy, French et al., ed. Notre Dame Ind.: Notre Dame University Press, 1991.

Bibliography

Lewis, David K., *Convention*, Cambridge, Mass.: Harvard University Press, 1969.

"Veridical Hallucination and Prosthetic Vision", in *Philosophical Papers*, vol. 2, New York: Oxford University Press, 1986. First published in *Australasian Journal of Philosophy*, 58, no. 3 (1980): 239–249.

Postscript to "Truth in Fiction", *Philosophical Papers*, vol. 1, New York: Oxford University Press, 1983.

"The Paradoxes of Time Travel", *Philosophical Papers*, vol. 2, New York: Oxford University Press, 1986.

"Counterfactual Dependence and Time's Arrow", *Philosophical Papers*, vol. 2, New York: Oxford University Press, 1986.

Lotman, Jurij, *Semiotics of the Cinema*, trans. Mark E. Suino, Michigan Slavic Contributions, no. 5, Ann Arbor: University of Michigan Press, 1976.

Lycan, W. G., "Form, Function, and Feel", *Journal of Philosophy*, 78 (1981): 24–50.

Lyons, John, *Language and Linguistics: An Introduction*, Cambridge University Press, 1981.

Mandler, J. M., *Stories, Scripts and Scenes: Aspects of Schema Theory*, Hillsdale, N.J.: Erlbaum, 1984.

Margolis, Joseph (ed.), *The Worlds of Art and the World*, Amsterdam: Rodopi, 1984.

Marr, David, *Vision: A Computational Investigation into the Human Representation and Processing of Visual Information*, New York: Freeman, 1982.

Martin, Edwin, "On Seeing Walton's Great–Grandfather", *Critical Inquiry*, 12 (1986): 796–800.

Martin, Wallace, *Recent Theories of Narrative*, Ithaca, N.Y.: Cornell University Press, 1986.

Mast, Gerald, *Film/Cinema/Movie: A Theory of Experience*, New York: Harper & Row, 1977.

Mast, G., and M. Cohen (eds.), *Film Theory and Criticism*, 3d ed., New York: Oxford University Press, 1985.

Maynard, Patrick, "Drawing and Shooting: Causality in Depiction", *Journal of Aesthetics and Art Criticism*, 44 (1985–6): 115–129.

McTaggart, J. E., *The Nature of Existence*, vol. 2, chapter 33, Cambridge University Press, 1927.

Mellor, D. H., "The Unreality of Tense", in R. Le Poidevin and M. MacBeath (eds.), *The Philosophy of Time*, New York: Oxford University Press, 1993.

Mendilow, A. A., *Time and the Novel*, New York: Humanities, 1972.

Metz, Christian, *Film Language: A Semiotics of the Cinema*, trans. M. Taylor, New York: Oxford University Press, 1974.

Language and Cinema, trans. Donna J. Umiker-sebeok, The Hague: Mouton, 1974.

"Trucage and the Film", in W. J. T., Mitchell (ed.), *The Language of Images*, University of Chicago Press, 1980.

The Imaginary Signifier: Psychoanalysis and the Cinema, trans. Celia Britton et al., Bloomington: Indiana University Press, 1982.

"Some Points in the Semiotics of Cinema", in G. Mast and M. Cohen (eds.), *Film Theory and Criticism*, 3d ed., New York: Oxford University Press, 1985.

"On the Notion of Cinematographic Language", in B. Nichols (ed.), *Movies and Methods: An Anthology*, vol. 1, Berkeley and Los Angeles: University of California Press, 1985.

"The Impersonal Enunciation, or the Site of Film (in the Margin of Recent Works on Enunciation in Cinema)", *New Literary History*, 22, no. 3 (Summer 1991): 747–772.

Millikan, Ruth Garrett, *Language, Thought, and Other Biological Categories*, Cambridge, Mass.: MIT Press, 1984.

Mitry, Jean, *Esthétique et psychologie du cinéma, I: les structures*, Paris: Editions Universitaires, 1963.

Moreno, Julio, "Subjective Cinema: The Problem of Film in the First Person", *Quarterly Review of Film, Radio and Television*, 7 (1952–3): 341–372.

Mulvey, Laura, "Visual Pleasure and Narrative Cinema" in G. Mast and M. Cohen (eds.), *Film Theory and Criticism*, 3d ed., New York: Oxford University Press, 1985.

Münsterberg, Hugo, "The Means of the Photoplay", in G. Mast and M. Cohen (eds.), *Film Theory and Criticism*, 3d ed., New York: Oxford University Press, 1985.

Nehamas, Alexander, "The Postulated Author: Critical Monism as a Regulative Ideal", *Critical Inquiry*, 8 (1981): 133–149.

Newman, E., and P. Hartline, "The Infrared 'Vision' of Snakes", *Scientific American*, 246 (March 1992): 98–107.

Nichols, Bill (ed.), *Movies and Methods: An Anthology*, vols. 1 and 2, Berkeley and Los Angeles: University of California Press, 1976, 1985.

Ogle, Patrick, "Technological and Aesthetic Influences on the Development of Deep–Focus Cinematography in the United States", in Bill Nichols (ed.), *Movies and Methods*, vol. 2, Berkeley and Los Angeles: University of California Press, 1985.

Panofsky, Erwin, "Style and Medium in the Motion Pictures", in G. Mast and M. Cohen (eds.), *Film Theory and Criticism*, 3d ed., New York: Oxford University Press, 1985.

Peacocke, Christopher, *Sense and Content: Experience, Thought and Their Relations*, Oxford University Press, 1983.

Petitto, L. A., "On the Autonomy of Language and Gesture: Evidence from the Acquisition of Pronouns in American Sign Language", *Cognition*, 27 (1987): 1–52.

Pettersson, Anders, "On Walton's and Currie's Analysis of Literary Fiction", *Philosophy and Literature*, 17 (1993): 84–97.

Pettit, Philip, "Realism and Response-Dependence", *Mind*, 100 (1991): 587–623.

Phelan, James, *Reading People, Reading Plots: Character, Progression and the Interpretation of Narrative*, University of Chicago Press, 1989.

Piattelli-Palmarini, M., "Ever Since Language and Learning: Afterthoughts on the Piaget–Chomsky Debate", *Cognition*, 50 (1994): 315–346.

Pitcher, George, *A Theory of Perception*, Princeton, N.J.: Princeton University Press, 1971.

Premack, D., *Gavagai! Or the Future History of the Animal Language Controversy*, Cambridge, Mass.: MIT Press, 1986.

"Minds with and without Language", in L. Weiskrantz (ed.), *Thought Without Language*, Oxford University Press, 1988.

Premack, D., and G. Woodruff, "Does the Chimpanzee have a Theory of Mind?" *Behavioral and Brain Sciences*, 1 (1978): 515–526.

Prince, G., *A Dictionary of Narratology*, Lincoln: University of Nebraska Press, 1987.

Pylyshyn, Zenon, "Computation and Cognition: Issues in the Foundations of Cognitive Science", *Behavioral and Brain Sciences*, 3 (1980): 111–132.

"Imagery and Artificial Intelligence", in Ned Block (ed.), *Readings in Philosophical Psychology*, vol. 2, Cambridge, Mass.: Harvard University Press, 1981.

Ray, Robert, *A Certain Tendency of the Hollywood Cinema*, Princeton, N.J.: Princeton University Press, 1985.

Reisz, Karel, and Gavin Millar, *The Technique of Film Editing*, London: Focal, 1968.

Rimmon-Kenan, Shlomith, *Narrative Fiction: Contemporary Poetics*, London: Methuen, 1983.

Robinson, Jenefer, "Style and Personality in the Literary Work", *Philosophical Review*, 94 (1985): 227–247.

Roth, D., and A. Leslie, "The Recognition of Attitude Conveyed by Utterance: A Study of Preschool and Autistic Children", *British Journal of Developmental Psychology*, 9 (1991): 315–330.

Sartwell, Crispin, "Natural Generativity and Imitation", *British Journal of Aesthetics*, 31 (1991): 58–67.

Savage-Rumbaugh, S., et al., "Spontaneous Symbol Acquisition and Communicative Use by Pigmy Chimpanzees *Pan paniscus*", *Journal of Experimental Psychology: General*, 115 (1986): 211–235.

Schier, Flint, *Deeper into Pictures: An Essay on Pictorial Representation*, Cambridge University Press, 1986.

Scruton, Roger, "Photography and Representation", in *The Aesthetic Understanding: Essays in the Philosophy of Art and Culture*, London: Methuen, 1983.

Sesonske, Alexander, "Time and Tense in Cinema", *Journal of Aesthetics and Art Criticism*, 38 (1979–80): 419–426.

Silverman, Kaja, *The Subject of Semiotics*, New York: Oxford University Press, 1983.

Skow, John, "Harold Brodkey's New Novel is Erotic – But Not to Everybody", *Time*, May 9, 1994.

Snyder, Joel, "Photography and Ontology", in J. Margolis (ed.), *The Worlds of Art and the World*, Amsterdam: Rodopi, 1984.

Sobchack, Vivian, *The Address of the Eye: A Phenomenology of Film Experience*, Princeton, N. J.: Princeton University Press, 1992.

Sorensen, Roy, "Self–Strengthening Empathy", unpublished manuscript.

Sparshott, Francis, "Basic Film Aesthetics", in G. Mast and M. Cohen (eds.), *Film Theory and Criticism*, 3d ed., New York: Oxford University Press, 1985.

Stalnaker, Robert, *Inquiry*, Cambridge, Mass.: MIT Press, 1984.

Stampe, Dennis, "Toward a Causal Theory of Linguistic Representation", *Midwest Studies in Philosophy*, vol. 2, Morris: University of Minnesota Press, 1977.

Stanzel, F. K., *A Theory of Narrative*, trans. Charlotte Goedsche, Cambridge University Press, 1984.

Stephenson, R., and J. R. Debrix, *The Cinema as Art*, New York: Penguin, 1976.

Sternberg, Meir, *Expositional Modes and Temporal Ordering in Fiction*, Baltimore, Md.: Johns Hopkins University Press, 1978.

Stich, S., and S. Nichols, "Second Thoughts on Simulation", in M. Davies and T. Stone (eds.), *Mental Simulation*, forthcoming.

Studlar, Gaylan, "Masochism and the Perverse Pleasures of the Cinema", in Bill Nichols (ed.), *Movies and Methods: An Anthology*, vol. 2, Berkeley and Los Angeles: University of California Press, 1985.

Todorov, Tzvetan, *The Poetics of Prose*, trans. Richard Howard, Ithaca, N.Y.: Cornell University Press, 1977.

Turim, Maureen, *Flashbacks in Film: Memory and History*, New York: Routledge, 1989.

Vermazen, Bruce, "Expression as Expression", *Pacific Philosophical Quarterly*, 67 (1986): 196–224.

Vygotsky, L. S., "Play and Its Role in the Mental Development of the Child", *Soviet Psychology*, 5 (1967): 6–18.

Walton, Kendall, "Transparent Pictures: On the Nature of Photographic Realism", *Critical Inquiry*, 11 (1984): 246–277.

"Looking Again Through Photographs: A Response to Edwin Martin", *Critical Inquiry*, 12 (1986): 801–808.

Mimesis as Make-Believe: On the Foundations of the Representational Arts, Cambridge, Mass.: Harvard University Press, 1990.

Warburton, Nigel, "Seeing Through 'Seeing Through Photographs'", *Ratio*, new series, 1 (1988): 64–74.

Weiss, Paul, *Cinematics*, Carbondale: Southern Illinois University Press, 1975.

Wellman, H., and K. Bartsch, "Young Children's Reasoning about Beliefs", *Cognition*, 30 (1988): 239–277.

Whyte, Jamie, "The Normal Rewards of Success", *Analysis*, 51 (1991): 65–73.

Wilensky, R., "Story Grammars Revisited", *Journal of Pragmatics*, 6 (1982): 423–432.

Williams, Bernard, "Imagination and the Self", in *Problems of the Self*, Cambridge University Press, 1973.

Wilson, George M., *Narration in Light: Studies in Cinematic Points of View*, Baltimore, Md.: Johns Hopkins University Press, 1986.

Wimmer, Hans, and Josef Perner, "Beliefs about Beliefs: Representation and Constraining Function of Wrong Beliefs in Young Children's Understanding of Deception", *Cognition*, 13 (1983): 103–128.

Wollheim, Richard, "Imagination and Identification", in *On Art and the Mind: Essays and Lectures*, London: Lane, 1973.

Art and Its Objects, 2d ed., Cambridge University Press, 1980.

Painting as an Art, London: Thames & Hudson, 1987.

Woolley, Jacqueline D., and Katrina E. Phelps, "Young Children's Practical Reasoning about Imagination", *British Journal of Developmental Psychology*, 12 (1994): 53–67.

Index

Affron, C., 165n
Akins, K. A., 59n
Alperson, P., 92n, 101n
ambiguous narrative, 272–274; and unreliable narrative, 275–278
anachrony: filmic and ellipsis, 220; and its direction, 213–218; and tense, 199–200, 201–206; and untensed temporal relations, 207–208; weak, 211–212
Anna Karenina (Tolstoy), 152
Anstis, S., 45n
Arnheim, R., 19–20, 57n
Attack of the Fifty Foot Woman (Guest), 103

Bach-y-Rita, P., 59n
Bal, M., 97n
Balázs, B., 23, 166, 171, 178, 200
Baron-Cohen, S., 143n, 157n
Bartsch, K., 145n
Battleship Potemkin (Eisenstein), 104
Baudry, J.-L., 30n
Bazin, A., on transparency and realism, xxiii, 19–21, 50–51, 79, 165–166, 187, 191–192
behaviorism, 25, 235–236
Bergman, I., 23, 48
Berkeley, G., 113
Biederman, I., 123n, 136n
Big Sleep, The (Hawks), 272–274
Bigelow, J., xxi

Birds, The (Hitchcock), 176–7
Black Widow (Rafelson), 212n
Blow Up (Antonioni), 52
Boghossian, P. A., 31n, 39n
Booth, W., 245n; on narrative unreliability, 264–266, 270–272, 275
Bordwell, D., xiiin, xxii, 105n, 107, 190n, 204n; on ambiguity, 274n; on implied author, 247–248
Branigan, E., 20n, 106n, 167n, 265n; on point of view, 193–194
Brennan, A., xxi
Brown, E. L., 46n
Browne, N., 26n, 175–176n
Bryson, N., xvii
Buchan, J., 266
Burch, N., 216

Camus, A., 265
Carroll, N., xiiin, xxii, 27, 80n, 160n, 161n, 187n
Castle, W., 167, 168n
Cavell, S., 1n, 48, 50n
Chatman, S. 14n, 212n, 222, 244n, 245n, 260, 262n, 265n, 267–268, 269n
Chomsky, N., xxiii, 115n
Churchland, P. M., 29n, 64n
cinematic image: the reality of, 32–34; as representation, 2, 9–12 (*see also* pictures); as tensed and anachrony, 198–206

297

cinematic movement: as apparent but nonillusory, 42–46; the reality of, 34–42
Citizen Kane (Welles), 14, 181, 266
Cohen, T., 58n
colour: and cinematic image, 33; and film, 6–7; the reality of, 31–32, 39–40
Comolli, J.-L., 26n, 116n
Constable, J., 52
Cooper, N., xxi
Corballis, M. C., 123n
Couvalis, G., xxi, 21n
Crossfire (Dmytryk), 205
Culloden (Weir), 173

Dagle, J., 200n
Davies, M., xxi–xxii, 53n
Davies, W. M., 29n, 59n, 64n
Dawkins, R., 59
Dayan, D., xixn, 194
Debrix, J. R., 200n
Deffenbacher, K., 46n
Deleuze, G., 141n, 201n; on film and physics, xviii–xix
Dennett, D., 37–38, 84n
Deren, M., 214n
Descartes, R., 83
Dick, B. F., 216n
Dickens, C., 229
Dombey and Son (Dickens), 228
Don't Look Now (Roeg), 216
Dostoyevsky, F., 244–245
Double Indemnity (Wilder), 216n, 266
Durgnat, R., xviin
Dworkin, R., 225, 249n

Eco, U., 117n, 131–133
Eisenstein, S., 104
ellipsis, 212, 215, 220; in literture, 219–222
Ellis, J., 22n

Fall, The (Camus), 265
Feagin, S., 46n
fiction: doing moral damage, 162–163; and imagination, 141, 147–148, 150, 152–155, 158–160; and interpretation, 242; visual, 169–170, 181–185

film, 1–16; and controlling narrator, 266–268; documentary/fiction, 14–16; engendering cognitive illusion, 22–23, 27; engendering perceptual illusion, 29–30, 35, 39; and imagining someone's visual experience, 193–196; and impersonal imagining, 179–180; and personal imagining, 165–179; realism, 19–22, 106–108; and seeing the world, 48, 69; as spatial art, 103–106, 218–219; as temporal art, 96, 99–103, 218–219; unlike language, 114, 117–124, 128–131, 134–135; *see also* photography
Fish, S., 126n
Flitterman, S., 27n
Fodor, J. A., 29n, 81n, 85–86, 87n
Ford, F. M., 265, 278n
Freud, S., xxiv
Friedberg, A., xviiin

Galileo, G., 111n
Genette, G., 94n, 199n, 204n, 212n, 262n, 263n
Gilman, D., 46n, 86n
Glymore, C., xvn
Godfather, The, Part 2 (Coppola), 216n
Goldman, A. I., 143n, 153n
Gombrich, E., xvi
Gone with the Wind (Fleming), 14, 273–274
Good Soldier, The (Ford), 265
Goodman, N., xvi, 12n
Gopnik, A., 143n
Gordon, R. M., 143n, 154n
Gospel According to St. Matthew, The (Passolini), 99
Grant, C., 23, 38, 40–41, 48, 189
Great Expectations (Lean), 181
Gregory, R., xvi
Grice, P., 127n, 215n, 253n
Groner, C., 59n

Hacking, I., 59n
Hagen, M. A., 110n
"Haircut" (Lardner), 232–233, 270–271
Haldane, J., xxi
Halliwell, L., 206n
Hamlet (Shakespeare), 95

Index

Harman, G., 132n
Harris, P. L., 163n
Hartline, P., 64n
Harvey, N., 163n
Haugeland, J., 84n
Heal, J., xxi, 143n
Henderson, B., xviin, 199n
Hills, D., xxi
Hirsch, E. D., 244n
Hitchcock, A., 52, 153, 170, 174, 176, 189, 195, 259, 267
Holton, R., 43n
Hopkins, R., xxi
Hudson, W., 110n
Humphreys, G. W., 89n
Hunt, I., xxii

imagination, 141–142; and belief and desire, 151; perceptual and symbolic, 184; personal and impersonal, 166; as simulation, 144–147, 149–150, 155–161
Incredible Shrinking Man, The (Arnold), 103
Innocents, The (Clayton), 216n, 276n
interpretation: 226, 247–249; and appearance meaning, 255–258; indeterminacy in and truth, 250–251; and interpretive differences, 227–228; literary, 237–242; narrative, 228, 230–235; and real/implied author, 243–246, 258–259; and utterance meaning, 255–258
Invasion of the Body Snatchers, The (Siegel), 186
Irwin, T., 121n
Ishiguro, K., 265

Jackson, F., xxii, 36n, 182n, 240n
James, H., 234, 240
Jarvie, I., 23n, 58n, 200n
Jeannerod, M., 163n
Johnson, C. N., 163n
Jones, R. K., 110n
Juhl, P. D., 245n

Kanner, L., 157n
Khatchadourian, H., 34n, 169
Kitcher, P., xxii

knowledge of other minds, xv, 142–146, 150, 158, 161
Kozloff, S., 269n

Lacan, J., xiv, xvii, xix, 141
Lady from Shanghai, The (Welles), 128–129
Lang, F., 131, 268
Lapsley, R., 111n
Lardner, R., 232–233, 270–271
Last Year at Marienbad (Resnais), 101–102, 214n
Lawrence of Arabia (Lean), 5
le Poidevin, R., 207n
Leslie, A., 142n, 143n, 157n, 161n
Levinson, J., xxii, 37n, 92n, 101n, 174n
Lewis, D. K., xxii, 53n, 55n, 66n; on anachrony and time travel, 208–209; on convention, 121; on flash-stockman problem, 158–159; on time in fiction, 211
Lippi, F., 95–96, 99
Livingston, P., xxii
Lotman, J., 111n, 200n
Lumière Brothers, 24
Lycan, W. G., 84n
Lyons, J., 117n

M (Lang), 131
Malebranche, N., 62–63, 65
Malinas, G., xxii
Mandler, J. M., 248n
Marr, D., 69n, 85n
Martin, E., 55n, 57n
Martin, W., 266n
Mast, G., 3n, 4n, 101n, 201n
Maynard, P., 50n, 76n
McTaggart, J. E., 206–207
Medlin, B., 42n
Mellor, D. H., xxii, 198n
Mendilow, A. A., 201n
Meshes of the Afternoon (Deren), 214n
Metz, C., xvi, xviin, xixn, 24n, 26n, 27n, 110, 116n, 119n, 175n, 218n, 262n, 268n
Millar, G., 190
Millikan, R. G., 53n
Mitry, J., 165–166, 168
Moreno, J., 167n

299

Index

Mulvey, L., xixn
Münsterberg, H., xxiii, 34

Nabokov, V., 238
narrator, 262–263; controlling and embedded, 265–266; reliable, 264; unreliable, 237–238, 240, 264; and unreliable narration, 260–262, 265, 268–270
Nehamas, A., 245n
Nerlich, G., xxii, 38n
Newman, E., 64n
Nichols, S., 143n
North by Northwest (Hitchcock), 189–190

Occurrence at Owl Creek, An (Enrico), 269n
Ogle, P., 108n

painting: as representational medium and art, 49, 51, 53–55, 61, 71, 77–78; and temporality, 95–96, 99
Panofsky, E., 23, 166, 168, 171, 178
Passolini, P. P., 99
Peacocke, C. A. B., 29n, 64n
Peeping Tom (Powell), 267–268
Perkins, V., 164, 201n
Perner, J., 142n 157n
Petitto, L. A., 116n
Petterson, A., 161n
Pettit, P., xxii, 31n, 240n
Phelan, J., 271n
Phelps, K. E., 163n
photography: as representational medium, 12–13, 51, 71, 77; and seeing the world, 48, 50–51, 53–56, 63–64, 66–68, 70
Piaget, J., 115n
Piattelli-Palmarini, M., 115n
pictures: and perceptual imagining, 184–185, 197; and representation, xvii, 80–81, 84–87
Pigden, C., xxii
Pink Flamingos (Waters), 167n
Pitcher, G., 182n
Popper, K., xvi
Poussin, N., 95
Premack, D., 110n, 123n
Price, A., xxii

Prince, G., 265n
Profane Friendship (Brodkey), 154n
psychoanalysis, xii, xiv, xv, xix, 27, 165, 174–175
Pudovkin, V., 190n
Pylyshyn, Z., 29, 87n

Rafelson, R., 212n
Rashomon (Kurosawa), 266, 275
Ray, R. B., 22n
Rear Window (Hitchcock), 52
Reisz, K., 190
Remains of the Day, The (Ishiguro), 265
Renoir, J., 187
representation, 49; automorphic and homomorphic, 97–98; linguistic, xvi–xvii, 7–8, 113–137, 181–185, 189–190, 251–258; visual and pictorial, 7–8; 10–12
Resnais, A., xviii, 198, 214n, 267n
Rey, G., xxii
Riddoch, J. M., 89n
Rimmon-Kenan, S., 271n
Robbe-Grillet, A., xviii, 200
Robinson, J., 245n
Rosen, G., xxii
Roth, D., 157n
Rules of the Game, The (Renoir), 187

Saint, E. M., 189
Sartwell, C., 88n, 131n
Saussure, F., xxiii
Savage-Rumbaugh, S., 123n
Schier, F., 80n, 83n, 88, 131n
Scruton, R., 50n, 72–74, 75n, 130n
Searchers, The (Ford), 257
seeing, 53, 55, 57; egocentric and temporally extended information from, 66–68; and light, 59; and natural dependence, 61–62; paintings and photographs, 53–62; and uninterrupted transmission, 60, 70
semiotics, xvi–xvii, 116–117, 165
Sesonske, A., 201n
Sharp, R., xxii
Silverman, K., xvn
simulation: and belief/desire, 149–151; and fiction, 152–155; and

imagination, 147–148, 151–152; and interpretation, 242–243; and other minds, 144–147
Sirk, D., 259
Skow, J., 154n
Snyder, J., 50n
Sobchack, V., xviii
Sober, E., xxii
Soll, I., xxii
Sorensen, R., 146–147
Sparshott, F., 34, 201n
Spellbound (Hitchcock), 174–175, 179–180
Squires, R., xxii
Stage Fright (Hitchcock), 195, 267–268
Stagecoach (Ford), 175–176
Stalnaker, R., 78n
Stampe, D., 78n
Stanzel, F. K., 266n
Sternberg, M., 200n
Stich, S., 143n
Stokes, J., xxii
structuralism: errors of, 114–116, 122n; and narrative intentions, 278–279
Studlar, G., 141n
Sturgeon, S., xxii

Taylor, K., xxii
They Shoot Horses, Don't They? (Pollack), 216n
Third Man, The (Reed), 10–11
Thompson, K., 274n
Tingler, The (Castle), 168
Todorov, T., 115
Tolstoy, L., 246n
Tom Jones (Fielding), 262
Tooley, M., xxii
Townsend, A., xxii
Turim, M. C., 22n, 198n, 206n
Turn of the Screw, The (James), 232, 238, 240, 250–251, 261–262, 276–277

unreliable narrative, 261–262, 265; Booth, 268–270; in terms of complex

intentions of implied author, 270–272

Velleman, J. D., 31n, 39n, 111n
Vermazen, B., 245n
Vertigo (Hitchcock), 170–171
visual perception, xv; as nonlinguistic, 136–137
Vygotsky, L. S., 161

Walton, K., xxii, 13n, 24n, 147n, 152n, 161n, 169n, 177n, 188n; on transparency, 20, 50–51, 55n, 56n, 57n, 61–63, 75n, 173n
Wages of Fear, The (Clouzot), 100n
War and Peace (Tolstoy), 246n
Warburton, N., 66n
Waters, J., 88, 167
Weir, P., 173
Weiss, P., 23n
Welles, O., 10
Wellman, H. M., 145n
Westlake, M., 111n
Wetherall, P., xxii
White, M., 46n
Whyte, J., xxii, 149n
Wilder, B., 216n
Wilensky, R., 113n
Williams, B., 169, 178
Williamson, T., xxii
Wilson, G., xiiin; on cinematic images as unlike language, 128–130; on imagining seeing, 165n, 166, 171–173, 178; on unreliability, 268–269, 276, 278n
Wimmer, H., 142n, 157n
Wittgenstein, L., 97, 123n, 136
Wollheim, R., 88, 90, 110n, 141, 169n
Woodruff, G., 110n
Woolley, J. D., 163n

Yalowitz, S., xxii
You Only Live Once (Lang), 268–270, 275–277